Talking with Psychopaths and Savages

LETTERS FROM SERIAL KILLERS

Born in 1948 in Winchester, Hampshire, **Christopher Berry- Dee** is descended from Dr John Dee, Court Astrologer to Queen Elizabeth I, and is the founder and former Director of the Criminology Research Institute (CRI), and former publisher and Editor-in-Chief of *The Criminologist*, a highly respected journal on matters concerning all aspects of criminology from law enforcement to forensic psychology.

Christopher has interviewed and interrogated over thirty of the world's most notorious killers – serial, mass and one-off – including Peter Sutcliffe, Ted Bundy, Aileen Wuornos, Dennis Nilsen and Joanne Dennehy. He was co-producer/interviewer for the acclaimed twelve-part TV documentary series *The Serial Killers*, and has appeared on television as a consultant on serial homicide, and, in the series *Born to Kill?*, on the cases of Fred and Rose West, the 'Moors Murderers' and Dr Harold Shipman. He has also assisted in criminal investigations as far afield as Russia and the United States.

Notable book successes include: *Monster* (the basis for the movie of the same title, about Aileen Wuornos); *Dad, Help Me Please*, about the tragic Derek Bentley, hanged for a murder he did not commit (subsequently subject of the film *Let Him Have It*); and *Talking with Serial Killers*, Christopher's international bestseller, now, with its sequel, *Talking with Serial Killers: World's Most Evil*, required reading at the FBI Behavioral Analysis Unit Academy at Quantico, Virginia. His *Talking with Psychopaths and Savages: A Journey Into the Evil Mind*, was the UK's bestselling true-crime title of 2017; its successor volume, *Talking with Psychopaths and Savages: Beyond Evil*, was published in the autumn of 2019. In 2020 a new edition of his *Talking with Serial Killers: Dead Men Talking* appeared, and he has since published *Talking with Serial Killers: Stalkers*, *Talking with Psychopaths and Savages: Mass Murderers and Spree Killers* and, in 2022, *Talking with Serial Killers: Sleeping with Psychopaths*. He is the UK's bestselling true-crime writer.

https://www.christopherberrydee.com//

Christopher Berry-Dee

Talking with Psychopaths and Savages

LETTERS FROM SERIAL KILLERS

A chilling study of murderers' minds

First published in the UK by John Blake Publishing
an imprint of The Zaffre Publishing Group
A Bonnier Books UK company
4th Floor, Victoria House
Bloomsbury Square,
London, WC1B 4DA
England

Owned by Bonnier Books
Sveavägen 56, Stockholm, Sweden

www.facebook.com/johnblakebooks
twitter.com/jblakebooks

First published in paperback in 2023

Paperback ISBN: 978-1-78946-658-4
Trade paperback: 978-1-78946-657-7
Ebook ISBN: 978-1-78946-659-1
Audiobook ISBN: 978-1-78946-660-7

British Library Cataloguing-in-Publication Data:

A catalogue record for this book is available from the British Library.

Design by www.envydesign.co.uk

Printed and bound in Great Britain by Clays Ltd, Elcograf S.p.A

1 3 5 7 9 10 8 6 4 2

John Blake Publishing is an imprint of Bonnier Books UK
www.bonnierbooks.co.uk

Health warning

This book contains extremely disturbing material written by highly dangerous, psychopathic criminals. It is not for the faint of heart, or intended as a snug-as-a-bug bedtime read.

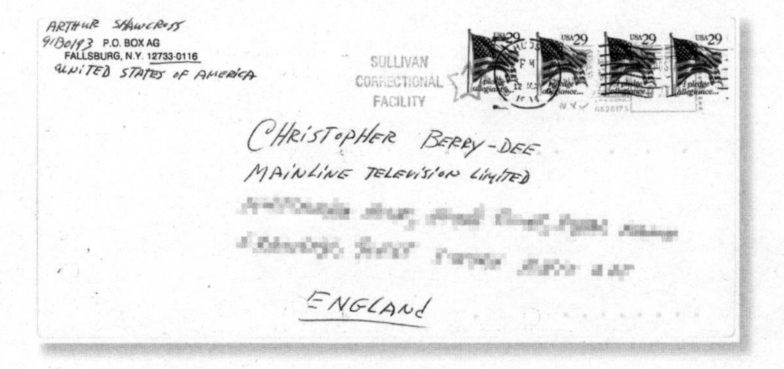

Envelope addressed to the author by Arthur Shawcross, 'the Genesee River Killer', sent from Sullivan Correctional Facility, New York State.

Contents

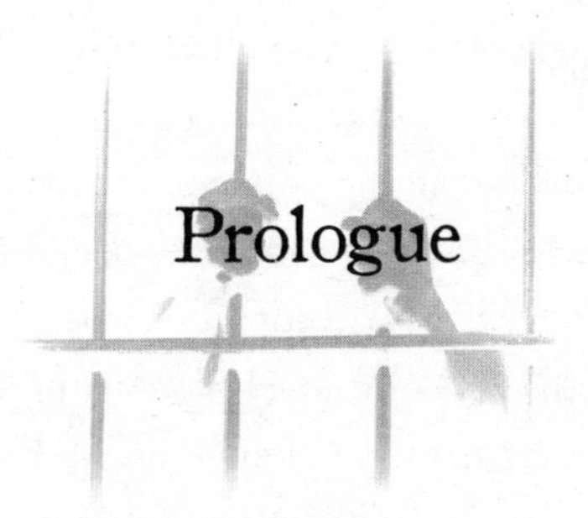

Prologue

There are road trips and then there are road trips. Christopher and I travelled to the four corners of the USA, covering twenty-two states by car, truck, boat and plane filming The Serial Killers, *the ratings-topping thirteen-part TV series. Etched on my mind are many unforgettable experiences from the streets of New York to the 'one-horse' prairie towns of Texas and from the depths of death rows to the boulevards of Hollywood. Deadly serious in parts but also great fun in others. An experience I would undertake again tomorrow if there was a chance. After all, who could resist being one of two English guys driving along the unbelievable long straight mid-western roads singing country music songs out loud. 'Look out – the boys were back in town.'*

The late Frazer Ashford, ARPS (1951–2022)

Way back in the 1970s, television producer Frazer took a brave step into the unknown when he enabled me to interview many of the most notorious serial killers in the United States of America. I say 'a brave step' because although there are countless documentaries broadcast in the same genre today, back then we broke all the rules because this had never been achieved before.

The genesis for this idea came about because I had been corresponding with these criminal psychopaths for a long time; learning their stories, gaining their trust. I had a wealth of unique material to hand. The plan was for Frazer and me to go on some road trips across 'The Land of the Free' doing recces: talking to cops, attorneys, judges and the grieving next of kin of some of the victims; visiting crime scenes or newspaper offices to hoover up articles and documents; eating junk food; bickering; getting on each other's nerves; trying to avoid any mass-murder event (an almost weekly ritual in the US – see my book *Talking with Psychopaths and Savages: Mass Murderers and Spree Killers*). And generally do all the things needs must before hauling in a film crew with all their kit to repeat what we had done in reverse order.

Before we went on our road trip into murder most foul, I'd never met a serial killer in the flesh. But throughout the years of corresponding with them, I now felt comfortable about getting up close and personal with this hellish evil. The TV series would allow the killers to talk on camera about their lives and terrible crimes. It was screened as *The Serial Killers*. One can still buy the DVDs of these programmes online, but it also occurred to me that I should write a book about my experiences. John Blake bravely stepped in as publisher, to spawn the best-selling brand: *Talking with Serial Killers*. Today, its many sequels have been translated into quite a few languages, including Polish, German, Russian and even Japanese. It may strike the reader as rather strange that true-crime fans from across the world are so fascinated with monsters thousands of miles away who have committed abominable crimes. Actually, there is a very good reason for it. Allow me to explain.

It matters not from which country one hails, nor which language one speaks, because heinous acts of serial homicide, mass-murder, rape and spree or rampage killing are committed by offenders with very similar mindsets – mindsets being universal too. A sadosexual serial killer at large in Poland or the sovereign state of the Czech Republic will have very similar motivational drivers as one from North America, the United Kingdom or the Russian Federation.

To clarify: the crimes committed by sadosexual serial murderer Ted Bundy are mirrored by killers in other countries and vice versa. The motives can be almost identical. The methods such killers use to hunt their human prey are often strikingly similar. This is not to suggest that these are 'copycat killings'. It is because when it comes down to committing mass murder (as distinct from serial homicide), the motives are usually religious, political or grudge-driven, and not usually sexual gratification, which is mostly a serial killer's motive. Mass murder and serial homicide are a universal phenomenon, are they not? For that reason, I believe this book may prove an enlightening read, for the letters featured here could have been penned by any offender without conscience from any country at any time past, present, or into the future.

Initially, there was some mild criticism about Frazer and me allowing these disgusting monsters to spew out what they needed to say on camera. However, we consulted some of the victims' next of kin, who often had tears streaming down their cheeks as they talked about their departed loved ones, and they agreed that we should go ahead. They felt that despite the tragedies these wanton beasts had heaped upon their lives, if we allowed these murderers to tell it how it was, then society might learn a few lessons from them.

As my loyal readers will know, I always treat the relatives, close friends and work colleagues of the deceased – not forgetting the police who have to clear up the sickening mess in the aftermath of a murder – with the deepest respect, for they are victims too. I always imagine how I'd feel if it were one of my children or a loved one who had been used, abused, raped, tortured, murdered, then dumped like so much garbage. As you read through this book, you might think about that, too.

This book goes way back to some of the letters these killers wrote to me years ago, alongside some more recent missives. We will analyse them in a way never previously attempted in the history of criminology – something that once again, I would argue, breaks new ground. I write from my heart and, as always in my books, I say it exactly as it should be, with no leftie PC BS thrown in to appease anyone, whatever side of the moral aisle they sit on.

On a lighter note, and in relation to Frazer's observations at the start of this chapter, our road trips took us through big cities, little cities, small towns and one-horse towns, with the rich tapestry of American history seamlessly woven throughout. Our research demanded we visit strip-joints, aka clip-joints, only to leave hastily. We called in at pool rooms, where the cigarette smoke drifted like grey smog two feet below the ceilings and where almost every patron, including the women, seemed to be genetically cloned from everyone from miles around. We did visit some nice locations and several quite nice motels, and some mean old penitentiaries too.

So, as I've done in my previous books, I invite you to come along and join me for the ride. I hope you enjoy it.

And now to the letters, please.

CHRISTOPHER BERRY-DEE

SOUTHSEA, UK, AND EL NIDO, PALAWAN, PHILIPPINES

christopherberrydee.com

Introduction

There is nothing to writing. All you do is sit down at a typewriter and bleed.

ERNEST MILLER HEMINGWAY (POSSIBLY ...)

Now that I've typed this book's first flush of enthusiasm onto my keyboard, the reader will have cottoned on to me having some literary 'fun' with our American cousins. However, allow me to acknowledge that their republic is awash with some of the finest true-crime writers in the world, past and present across the world, and I truly applaud them. That said, I rather doubt that if perchance any of these talented people read the book you have in your hands they will reciprocate. I say this because at the time of writing, the USA is a politically divided place to be. Fifty per cent of the population, including most probably the majority of its writers and TV broadcasters, support the somewhat wishy-washy Democrats, while the rest believe that the storming of the Washington Capitol on 6 January 2021 was simply about a lot of innocent sightseers anxious to visit the place where Americans allege democracy was born, as opposed to a semi-illiterate Trump-incited armed mob of insurrectionists determined to kill police officers then lynch some politicians; to rip up and shit-can one of the greatest documents ever penned in the history of mankind: the Constitution of the United States. I wonder what the Founding Fathers would have made of 'the Donald'?

Still, as this book is all about correspondence, as is par for the literary course I shall start by explaining that the quote at the head of this chapter is not, as many – including me – had previously thought, from Ernest Hemingway. Nope, it is generally attributed to the distinguished American sportswriter Walter 'Red' Smith, of whom Hemingway was an admirer. Paul William Gallico, an American author and sportswriter is in the mix here too, I am told. 'Pedantic maybe, yet I rather think that the quote applies to everyone who wishes to see their work published,' says my editor-in-chief, putting me straight on that point. Well, we learn something new every day!

For several reasons, I very much like Ernest Hemingway: to wit, he sported a beard similar to mine; he had steely blue eyes that twinkled (mine do not). Moreover, he wrote in longhand while standing up, on account of him having damaged his feet while serving as a volunteer in the Great War. That's a strange thing, is it not? One might have thought that having dodgy feet, one would want to sit down as often as possible. Although my feet are in perfectly good order, I type sitting down using a PC, employing a word-processing system that most often seems to have a mind and vocabulary of its own. And, my computer has the damned impertinence of frequently insisting that I am American because my car has 'tires'; the noun crudely misapplied because the 'tyres' on my car are not 'tire[d]' – only when they are flat.

Occasionally, Dutch pops up, my PC reminding me that I am talking 'double Dutch', with even French *un peu* or Swahili *kidogo* thrown in. Then, just about when I think I have things about right, up pops a local undertaker's ad followed in short order by a will-writing service implying that my community and family would be better off without me and who might be lucky enough to cash in when my sell-by date expires. Ernest Hemingway, who honed his signature sparse style as a reporter and often covered crimes, never had any of these problems, even less so after he shot himself in the head. And I almost forgot to add that he was a literary alchemist who turned ink into gold – mucho dollars, to be precise – so on this score, I like him: his writing, bad feet and all.

I can hear you muttering, 'Hey, Christopher, let's get with the programme, shall we? *Letters from Serial Killers* is what we need; it's advertised on the tin.' But as my tens of thousands of loyal readers around the world already know, I do venture into trivia from time to time. Occasionally it's my wont to use it to lighten the load, because we are soon heading off to a dark, terrible place, a foul homicidal literary landscape. I want this book to have some 'fun' in it, simply because real-life murder is a wretched business.

> Handwriting is an electrical impulse originating in the brain. The hand and the pen are its tools, and inky traces.
>
> Margaret Gullan-Whur, *Discover Graphology: A Straightforward and Practical Guide to Handwriting Analysis* (1991)

You are now embarking on a homicidal literary road trip with me and we will find signposts to direct us along our way. The above quote from Margaret Gullan-Whur will be a fundamental guide in helping us to try to understand the mindsets of the monsters we will meet on our journey. As part of the process, we will also be looking at Locard's 'Exchange Principle' in a completely different light. According to that well-established criminological principle 'every contact leaves a trace', and I will apply this not only to what is written on the page, but to what the offender is hiding between the lines, or intentionally neglects to say.

To assist us further: we all know that an offender's modus operandi (MO) – his or her method of operation – can vary over time. Indeed, even you and I have our own particular way of doing different things; we get set in our ways, then we change those ways as we develop better practical and social skills. During the course of this book, I will also develop in detail the theme of a criminal's modus vivendi (MV), in other words the manner in which he or she lives their life. But how can we more accurately define handwriting as 'an electrical impulse originating in the brain'?

Without becoming entangled in the complex psycho-analytical studies of Carl Gustav Jung and Sigmund Freud, and with great impertinence on my part, I think that I have rediscovered the congruent way of thinking or 'modus cogitandi' (MC). Initially, this idea took a bit of tweaking as all of my brain's 120 billion neurons sent chemical and electrical signals whizzing along my neural extensions, sometimes bumping into each other in a confused way, before hooking up with other neurons across tiny junctions called synapses, to form my own thoughts about the phrase 'modus cogitandi' and how to apply this and then permit to travel in fits and starts down to my fingers and onto the typed page. I suggest this is because MO and MV have to originate from our MC.

Phew! That was a bit heavy was it not? Gosh, no doubt I'll soon be receiving thousands of grumpy emails and text messages from psychologists and psychiatrists across the world, all of them using their own cogitandi to inform me that it was Heraclitus 'The Obscure' (or 'The Dark One') of Ephesus, and the later Greek philosopher Parmenides, who came up with this jolly good idea – and a long time before a Mr Morris invented the Morris Minor. Nevertheless, as far as I can tell, neither Jung, Freud nor the ancient thinkers such Heraclitus and Parmenides, nor any forensic shrink since, have studied in depth such reams and reams of letters by fully emerged sexual psychopaths as I have.

We will also examine a killer's behavioural 'trophy-taking' from his victims (and all the killers bar one are male in this book) from a different perspective. These 'trophies' need not just be physical items, such as a lock of hair, jewellery, items of underclothing or crime-scene photographs, they can also be sickening memories that the perpetrator relives, and often masturbates to, long after he has been incarcerated. In *Letters from Serial Killers*, we will witness these mental trophies being transmitted from an evil mind onto paper. And this may not make for nice reading at all.

Grim stuff, you will agree, but as mentioned earlier, I do periodically digress into trivia by way of relief. I prefer to go off the wall rather than up the fucking wall, because getting into the minds of these monsters can be a debilitating process, so trivia is my form of escapism, like it or not.

Finally, for your edification and at no further cost to you, the reader, we will be visiting some fascinating locations en route – at least, I find them so. And I can reassure you that although I will be having a pop at our American cousins across the pond from time to time, I ~~truly love~~, ~~deeply admire~~, okay, okay – I mean I quite like them, if you can read between those lines.

Hershey bar, anyone?

Pens and Ink Can Cause a Stink

How wonderful it is to be able to write someone a letter! To feel like conveying your thoughts to a person, to sit at your desk and pick up a pen, to put your thoughts into words like this is truly marvellous.

Haruki Murakami, *Norwegian Wood* (1987)

Long gone are those times when bleary-eyed writers gazed into glasses of dark porter, candles nearby spluttering to cast eerie shadows on a wall of a Fleet Street pub, and dipped their well-trimmed goose quills into pots filled with iron gall ink to scribble-scratch away. Back then, parchment and ink were more than a trifle expensive. Back then, geese were so scared they suffered incontinence on an hourly basis. Back then, one had to actually 'think' before a single scratch of ink touched the page. No Tipp-Ex, back-spacing key, or spell-checker to make good your mistakes. Allegedly, William Shakespeare said that when starting with a blank sheet of vellum, it 'was God's will what happened next' and confessed 'to be heartily relieved' when he reached the end of a work.

Back then – before, I think, America was properly invented then patented as a republic – most of the British population were illiterate, so writing really was a craft. As Haruki Murakami notes above, it represents an extension of one's creative thinking processes (the modus cogitandi, or 'way of thinking') as transmitted to others in what one sets down. This is what the great wordsmiths, writers, historians, soothsayers, novelists, romanticists, poets, mystery-makers were all about – an extension of one's thoughts, emanating from the wondrous machine that is our mind, travelling down to our fingers via electrical impulses, to dip quill into ink. And most often in the spirit of 'Let the Devil take the hindmost', to quote a popular proverb probably dating back to the sixteenth century, those people had time on their hands because it took a good while to trim a quill – even longer when 'Gerry the Goose' was having none of it. None of this nipping across the street to pick up a biro from a 7-Eleven store malarkey, that's for sure.

So, as this book is all about writing, let us consider this not insignificant fact. Every letter – including the correspondence from serial killers and their ilk discussed here – book, news article, menu, potboiler, magnum opus, magazine piece, script, poem, document, dissertation, indeed every single piece of reading material that has ever been written or chiselled into stone for the benefit of those to follow has involved grey-matter-thinking. The same is true today, of course, when typed or twittered into one's PC, laptop, notebook, or the gadgets we call mobile phones – some of which even try to translate our spoken words into the written word, as in when you tell someone to 'Go and duck off!'

Take the British Library, which holds some 14 million printed books and e-books, as well as millions of periodicals and thousands of rare manuscripts. Within its King's Library alone (works collected by George III), you can, if you have nonillions of hours to play with, read through some 65,000 volumes of printed books. The British Library has a major collection of manuscripts, along with around 19,000 pamphlets, music scores and historical items, some dating back to 2000 BC. This collection is calculated at approximately 150 million bits and pieces in more than 400 languages. As to the latter, I think that they need to pull their socks up because there are roughly 7,000 languages in the world today, so the bibliothecaries are falling a tad short, if you ask me!

> Take away from Genesis the belief that Moses was the author, on which only the strange belief that it is the word of God has stood, and there remains nothing of Genesis but an anonymous book of stories, fables, and traditionary or invented absurdities, or of downright lies.
>
> Thomas Paine, *The Age of Reason*
> (three parts, 1794, 1795, 1807)

Thomas Paine was an English-born philosopher and writer who supported revolutionary causes in America and Europe. In later life, he had to contend both with poverty and ill health (worsened by being continually chemically unbalanced with the drink), but indubitably Thomas was a man of remarkable insight and his cogitandi was very much up to scratch – when it wasn't floating around in ale, that is. Thomas was born in the British market town of Thetford. His father, a corsetier and farmer, had high ambitions for his son, but by the age of twelve the lad had fallen out of school due to his shortcomings, then went on to become such a respected and influential writer. There is a gilded bronze statue of him standing on a stone plinth outside King's House on King Street in Thetford. There is also one of him in New Rochelle, New York, dedicated to the perpetuating legacy of this Founding Father. I would ask the reader to read up on this guy. Okay, he was sozzled for much of his waking time, but what would one expect when there are many breweries close by!

If you can't make it to the British Library in London, amble into any bookstore, wander around any Sunday car-boot sale ('swap meet' in the US) or your local public library, and marvel at how many different pieces of literature there are, all researched and written by someone anxious to see their words passed down for the benefit of generations to come. And according to Exodus, the Ten Commandments were inscribed by the finger of God on two stone tablets. Well I don't like being 'commanded' to do anything, do you? There is far too much of this damned impertinence these days, so had God been a bit more diplomatic he might have titled them the 'Ten Polite Requests', since people would then have been less likely to break them.

Moving on, it should be noted that Fran Lebowitz wrote in *Metropolitan Life* (1978), 'Contrary to what many of you might imagine, a career in letters is not without its drawbacks – chief among them the unpleasant fact that one is frequently called upon to actually sit down and write.' However, as all people of letters know – be they long gone deep in graves with the sides falling in, those at it today, or those to come – the craft can become addictive. It has been said that if one takes away a professional writer's pen, he or she could become so depressed they might kill themselves!

Still, it's hard work, this writing business, I can tell you that much. Between you and me, previously I have become so distraught over it that I started looking for a way out – planting my head inside a gas oven seeming the best option open to me. Then I realised that I only have an electric hob, so I gave up on that idea altogether, a microwave oven being completely out of the question.

It is also to be noted that many writers are prone to sensitivities, are subject to fragile mental states, and there is some substance to this because writing can be a lonely profession; one where occasionally fantastic flights of fantasy reign supreme. So let's get down to some nitty-gritty, some claret and brains splattered over some walls, for in 1961, aged sixty-one, the aforementioned Ernest Hemingway, he with the bad feet, shot himself in the head. The narrative of this remarkable man's life is fascinating, ranging from the highs of his literary success and fame to the lows of the mental anguish that eventually led him to his death.

In 2005, aged sixty-seven, Hunter S. Thompson also shot himself. Aged fifty-nine, Virginia Woolf, who suffered from various mental illnesses for years, committed suicide by drowning in 1941, leaving a note to her husband, Leonard, that read in part: 'Dearest, I feel certain that I am going mad again. I feel we can't go through another of those terrible times. And I shan't recover this time. I begin to hear voices, and I can't concentrate. So I am doing what seems the best thing to do.' It also included this somewhat small compensatory flourish for him: 'You have given me the greatest possible happiness.'

So, a risky occupation, this writing business can be. A few more examples: Author Louis Adamic shot himself in 1951, aged fifty-three. In 1963, thirty-year-old poet Sylvia Plath placed her head in a gas oven to dispatch herself, having sealed off the kitchen with wet towels to stop the fumes drifting into the room where her children were sleeping. Off-kilter humourist Richard Brautigan popped his clogs using a pistol in 1984, aged forty-nine. In 1989, social activist and wordsmith Abbie Hoffman overdosed on barbiturates aged fifty-two. In 2004, forty-four-year-old Drake Sather fired a live round into his literary head, he being best known for his contributions to TV comedy shows such as *Saturday Night Live* and *The Larry Sanders Show*. Troubled, like so many of the above, by years of depression, forty-six-year-old David Foster Wallace – a novelist, essayist and short story writer – hanged himself in 2008. And five years later, twenty-six-year-old tech wizard, Reddit co-founder and writer Aaron Swartz signed himself off in the same way. And one would be remiss if one missed out Oscar Fingal O'Flaherty Wills Wilde (1854–1900): an Irish poet and playwright best known for his epigrams and plays, his criminal conviction for gross indecency for consensual homosexual acts in one of the first celebrity trials – almost monthly events these days – his imprisonment, and early death from meningitis at the age of forty-six.

> Coleridge was a drug addict. Poe was an alcoholic. Marlowe was killed by a man whom he was treacherously attempting to stab. Pope took money to keep a woman's name out of a satire, then wrote the piece so she could

> be recognised anyhow. Chatterton killed himself. Byron was accused of incest. *Do you still want to be a writer – and if so, why?*
>
> Bennett Cerf, *Shake Well before Using* (1948)

So if you are still inclined to take up the idea of writing, you might wish to consider this: the mean terminal age of the wordsmiths above is about fifty years, which is considerably less than blind-as-bat lumberjacks, one-armed steeplejacks and perhaps even all-weather lightning-rod installers. After I wrote my first book, *Dad, Help Me Please*, decades ago, I swore in God's name I'd never go through the same pen-pushing trauma again, but I did. I am still above ground, and not under it with a wooden stake driven through my heart – so far.

> I had considered writing my memoirs old chap, but as you know I made a mess of things and in a bit of a fix right now. They are going to hang me in a few days. Damned inconsiderate it is too.
>
> Neville George Clevely Heath,
> undated letter from the condemned
> cell to an acquaintance, 1946

The killers whose correspondence features in this book had, or have, time on their hands: pitiless chains of days, months and years. And it's not always what they say, or the competency of their handwriting, their literacy skills or their previous education – if they had any schooling worth mentioning – that matters. It is their thinking processes, concealed like invisible ink between the lines they write, that should concern us most.

To Speak or Not to Speak? That is the question.

Billy Fallon, Professor of Communication,
San Diego State University (2007)

I recall interviewing killers who have consciously attempted to present themselves as socially acceptable people. As I have discussed extensively in other books, this presenting of normality is the mask they wear to hide the beast breathing deeply within, and in almost every instance this is *precisely* what we see when reading their writings, for this generally conceals what is 'hidden between the lines'. And, often, what the killers do *not* say in their correspondence (because they do not want to say it, or they conveniently forget to say it) matters much more to us in terms of our understanding their psychopathologies, for they have a cunning knack of knowing when to speak or not to speak.

To add a little literary seasoning here, when examining the killers' letters published in this book, perhaps we might think of them as three-dimensional exercises, combining 'the written word against the true facts' versus 'what is hidden between the lines' versus 'the offenders' modus cogitandi, or actual thinking process'. If we can bring the three together, we might be able to learn more about their mindsets, because we cannot see the whole picture until all three of these components are in place.

When I've interviewed serial killers behind bars, they sometimes come across as conciliatory, remorseful, wearing a hangdog expression, perhaps with watery eyes or rounded shoulders; they present, in short, as lost souls. All of which is designed to elicit a compassionate response. I referred earlier to letter writing as merely the extension of one's thought-processing system transferred via pen to paper. These criminals' letters are more or less echoes of what we would physically see when interviewing one of these beasts in the flesh.

> Look Chris. Letters, letters everywhere. Piles of letters from adoring women. Ya know, I am even learning to write Braille in efforts to help the blind. I've got so many books, to store them they've given me the empty cell next to mine.
>
> Michael Bruce Ross: from his condemned cell to the author, 26 September 1994

I have interviewed serial killers who rant and rave. The highly intelligent, articulate Connecticut-born, Connecticut-executed Michael Bruce Ross came across as a bookish, bespectacled fresh-faced all-American guy. Previously a door-to-door Prudential Insurance salesman, on death row he gloated and boasted to me during a TV interview about his terrible killing of young women and two little schoolgirls, one of whom he anally raped post-mortem. He revelled in it all, often breaking into hysterical fits of giggles. He wrote extensively to me about his crimes too and if one looked carefully enough, one could see Michael's twisted psychopathology writ large across every page. Because he was Cornell University-educated, he had a way with words. He once said to me: 'Chris, I'm not afraid of dying. I just don't want to be around when it happens.' On that score, I am inclined to feel the same way. The reader can find a photo of me chatting to Michael through the bars of his death row cell at christopherberrydee.com.

With my Polish readers in mind, we will meet Phillip Jablonski soon enough. His letters reveal the thought processing of a highly dangerous schizophrenic (and 'highly dangerous' in this case is one of the biggest understatements in criminal history), while the beguiling correspondence from petite former nurse Melanie Lyn McGuire proves just what a cunning and manipulative 'Black Widow' she truly is.

> Gentlemen, you must not mistake me. I admit that the French Emperor is a tyrant. I admit he is a monster. I admit that he is the sworn foe of our nation, and, if you will, of the whole human race. But, gentlemen, we must be just to our great enemy. We must not forget that he once shot a publisher.
>
> Poet Thomas Campbell (1777–1844):
> an apocryphal toast to Napoleon

Regarding penmanship: my publisher's editor-in-chief writes exquisitely, as does my colleague Frank Pearce, and the once upscale 'hot-to-trot' prisoner #584496, Melanie McGuire, whose letters are written behind the walls of the Edna Mahan Correctional Facility (EMCF) in Clinton, New Jersey. Their correspondence is a delight, yet such examples of handwriting perfection are as rare as hens' teeth these days. So as we are talking about correspondence, let's consider the implements involved for a moment. I would be remiss in not doing so, because pens have been used to kill people – prisoners make them into 'shanks' to stab each other – proving that, to paraphrase the well-known saying: 'Sometimes the pen truly is mightier than the sword.' And so on to pens.

While praying that the following trivia doesn't damage what credibility I do possess and while Lewis Waterman (founder of Waterman pens) is said to have invented the fountain pen, he was merely improving on an idea patented by a Romanian inventor called Petrache Poenaru.

> Genius is one percent inspiration and ninety-nine per cent perspiration.
>
> Thomas Edison, American inventor (1847–1931), circa 1900

Edison was a bright spark, but so was Petrache Poenaru (1799–1875) who, when aged twenty-one, came up with an idea that had popped into his cogitandi while studying geodesy and surveying at the École Polytechnique in Paris. Poenaru was so occupied with note-taking and writing that he devised a new kind of pen that utilised a swan's quill, which served as a reservoir of ink. Alas, history fails to inform us from where he got the quill. On 25 May 1827, the Manufacture Department of the French Ministry of the Interior registered Poenaru's invention with the code number '3208' and the somewhat over-hyped description: *'plume sans fin portative . . . qui s'alimente d'encre d'elle-même'* ('never-ending portable pen, which recharges itself with ink'). This was a seminal landmark in the history of writing; a eureka moment, so much so that in 2010 Posta Română issued a 5 lei stamp portraying Poenaru alongside some working drawings for his famous creation. Sadly, this belated recognition all rather passed over Poenaru's grave, for the last time his pen touched paper was when he signed his will with him expiring probably before the ink had dried on the paper.

> My invention consists of an improved reservoir or fountain pen, especially useful, among other purposes, for marking on rough surfaces – such as wood, coarse wrapping-paper, and other articles where an ordinary pen could not be used.
>
> John Jacob Loud 1888

Although the first 'true' ballpoint pen was invented by inventor John Jacob Loud, and patented in 1888, it was not a commercial success for reasons unknown to us even today, and indeed to Mr Loud himself, it seems to me. There were certainly plenty of murders to write about circa this time. One contemporary killer who knew how to read and write perfectly well was Theodore 'Ted' Durrant, aka 'The Demon of the Belfry'. He was a San Francisco Sunday school teacher who raped and strangled two women who rebuffed his advances, then dumped their bodies in the church's library and bell chamber. Somewhat ironically, Theo was to find himself, in 1898, suspended, like a church bell, but at the other end of a rope.

George Chapman, who turned himself into an Englishman when he took the surname of his mistress Annie Chapman (he was born Seweryn Antonowicz Kłosowski in Poland in 1865, moved to London in his early twenties, went to live in the US then returned to London), poisoned *three* of his mistresses with tartar emetic. He was suspected at the time of his hanging in 1903 to be the real Jack the Ripper and it's alleged that he declared 'I am Jack the Rip—' before being cut terminally short as he plunged to his doom. Well, he would have said that to get a stay of the inevitable – wouldn't you? But I hasten to add if one were to ingest tartar emetic, one would certainly experience vomiting, severe chest pains, cardiac abnormalities, renal and hepatic toxicity and some stress (as in: mega stress) – all very similar symptoms to someone who has overdosed on American TV soaps. If you end up in intensive care you will still wish you'd never been born, as you'll find yourself as bald as a goose egg, as white as a mortician's sheet and forced to wear incontinence panties for the remainder of your days.

Not to be outdone by Loud, in 1938 Hungarian-Argentine inventor and journalist László József Bíró invented a 'miraculous pen' – a ballpoint that actually worked. Bíró had noticed that the type of ink used for printing newspapers dried quickly and did not smudge the paper. Making a complete mess of his kitchen and truly upsetting spouse Elsa, he decided to make a pen using the same type of ink. However, printers' ink could not flow through a normal pen, so he tried something else. I could say that 'Bíró had a lot of balls', but my publisher will scold me. Nevertheless, that is how the ballpoint, as we know it today, works: 'the ink inside the pen covers one side of the tiny ball at the pen's nib; this rotates as the writer moves the pen on paper and the ink is transferred to the page' – in case you are not sure.

Initially, ballpoints were very exciting writing implements, at least for our cousins across the pond; nonetheless, it took some time for them to figure out exactly what was the point of a point with a ball on it? Not surprisingly, initial sales were extremely low. They finally did cotton on, however, and throughout 1946 hundreds of people were queuing up to buy them, despite the fact that just one biro cost around $150 in today's dollars. Can you imagine buying a pack of twelve at $1,800 – I can't! As a matter of fact, I get lots and *lots* of letters from criminals using biros. These days they can only use the inner ink reservoir; the plastic outer casing is taken away from the cons because of its usefulness, referred to earlier, as a weapon (shank) with which to stab other inmates or the prison guards – something our László never intended it to be used for. I get Christmas cards from killers too; mostly handwritten, or occasionally a typed letter, as was Peter Sutcliffe's wont. Some crayon cartoons on the envelopes. 'Charles Bronson' (Charles Arthur Salvador), does it. Phillip Carl Jablonski once did, for he died some time ago.

Some of the homicidal scribes featured within these pages vehemently profess their innocence. Others glorify in their heinous crimes. The now deceased Harvey 'The Hammer' Louis Carignan would send me reams of stuff about his rapes and murders. At one time he used a typewriter called 'Clyde', but that broke. When I asked him why he called it 'Clyde', he stoutly replied: 'That's one of my pearls of wisdom. The answer is amongst [*sic*] secrets I hold that I'll never reveal to anyone.' I firmly responded with: 'Okay, Harvey, so you will call your next typewriting machine 'Bonnie', correct? So fuck you, too!' Indeed, as one of his prison guards – correctional officers who can never correct any of their charges – at the Minnesota Correctional Facility (MCF) in Stillwater, Minnesota, told me: 'Sir, I had never seen a typewriter fly before. It went straight outta the window. Mr Carignan was truly pissed because we didn't have the funds to repair it.' Nonetheless, not to be deterred from producing further pages of what amounted to drivel, Harvey resorted to using a pen.

As an aside, your author enjoys etymology. 'Pen' derives from *penna* (Latin for 'feather') through to *penne* (Old French) and thence to *pen* (Middle English). How the Italians turned a writing instrument into a penne pasta dish only the 'Saint of Writing', aka Catherine of Bologna OSC, might know. But wait a moment: maybe it was a bolognese?

Putting his serial killing aside for a moment, you would have probably liked Harvey. He spoke in a very soft, grandfatherly voice, yet – resembling a character from *The Planet of the Apes* – he was an immensely strong guy. Some fifteen years ago he could do one-arm pull-ups for ten minutes without breaking sweat. I went to a zoo once and saw some apes doing the same thing. It was well worth the quarter of a banana I tossed them. And this is another strange thing: the chimpanzee and bonobo are said to be genetically our closest living relatives – certainly with my late mother-in-law – because we share as much as 98.8 per cent of their DNA (but then we share about 90 per cent with cats). In the context of this 'Tree of Life' stuff, quite obviously the missing 1.2 per cent covers an ability to read, write, vote and use the internet, which must have taken the wrong branch at some time.

You may be shocked by the contents of Harvey's letters, but those from female killers can be just as horrific, or even more so. On that note, we will very briefly consider Joanne Dennehy. Dennehy, a manipulative British serial killer who despatched three men, also attempted to stab to death two male dog walkers in broad daylight, after which she licked their warm blood from her blade. Step aside Rose West, there's another psycho-bitch on the block and she is most certainly the most dangerous female inmate held within the 'British Correctional Estate', as the Home Office describes its prisons. Of some inconsequential note, these institutions are most often farmed out to private companies who treat their inmates as 'clients'. And get this: these firms get paid bonuses for the amount of time cons are allowed *out* of their cells (or 'peters') than in. Later, we'll examine letters from the upscale Melanie McGuire, aka 'The Ice Queen' – articulate, cogent and a million miles away from the horrific crime she committed, but she's in a US prison and that place is a hellhole.

> That's not a red lipstick kiss, Chris. That's menstrual blood.
>
> Keith Hunter Jesperson: to the author, referring to a letter from one of his countless murder groupies

Dubbed by the media 'The Happy Face Killer', interstate 'mother trucker' Keith sent taunting correspondence to police adding a 'smiley' ☺. This Canadian-born American monster wrote hundreds of letters to me, as he will to you if you should show even the *slightest interest* in his life from foetus stage until the day you contact him. He will expansively expound on backhoes, and how mean and cruel his pa was in insisting that as a fresh-faced kid he spend much time out in the wild enjoying healthy pursuits: fishing, shooting small game, making a log cabin and learning how to use a bow and arrow. You will not even have to mention his murders, because he will boastfully go on and on about them – especially if you include a photograph of some busty blonde Russian model and hint that it's you. Of course, as his hundreds of supportive pen friends will rail that I really should not suggest such a thing, but why not? Think about this for a moment. If every reader of this book sent Keith a letter along with an alleged selfie of a 'Miss Rock Your Socks Off Tatiana Hotski', while complimenting him on his rugged looks, detailing their own avid interest in backhoes, Big Mack trucks and whether his pecker really is the size of a Californian redwood, they *will* get a response. Whether the American paper industry will be able to supply his stationery needs is another matter entirely.

On a more serious note, Keith once reviewed one of my books, *Talking with Serial Killers*. No other multiple murderer has done this before with any true-crime author. He sent the book back to me, annotating page by page where I'd got things wrong and giving me his own professional psychological analysis [quotation marks removed] on the killers featured throughout my book. I mean, one could not make this up if one tried!

So, with all of that done and dusted, in this book we will focus not so much on what these killers say – their penmanship; the way they structure a page, or even whether they choose to write with a pen or to type; it is what's missing that counts. Then, when you compare these written offerings with what we know as fact about each offender's criminal antecedents, I hope that you might come to understand a little more about the murderous instincts that lie deep within their modus cogitandi.

Psychopaths Using Pens

You really should learn to use your own English grammer [sic] effectively. I'm sick and tired of correcting yours [sic] errors. You dont [sic] learn do you [missing a ? mark]. My lives [sic] story is very important and your readers should appreciate what I have done.

KEITH HUNTER JESPERSON, RANT IN THE FORM OF A LETTER TO THE AUTHOR CORRECTING YOURS TRULY ON MY GRAMMAR

Quite why we should 'appreciate' what Jesperson has done remains a tad unclear. However, what one *can* appreciate when researching, writing about, then visiting heinous killers of any ilk, are the road trips involved. Gig Harbor, where we filmed the once dishy VerLyn (Veronica Lynn Compton) at the Washington Corrections Center for Women (WCCW), is set among the pine-clad San Juan Islands in north-west Washington State. Taken in the round, this area is breathtaking. It is as if America imported lots of Norway's fjord water and around this planted many trees. And they do the best clam chowder at the local Tides Tavern, where Frazer and I spent two lazy evenings eating buckets of blue crab, drinking ice-cold beers, pledging to be friends till the end of time (until the following morning, when sobriety called for serious business) in the course of getting femme fatale VerLyn to spill the beans about her sordid and almost murderous relationship with the psycho-twisted serial killer Kenneth Alessio Bianchi, and her previous penpally plans to open a mortuary with the serial killer Douglas Daniel Clark aka 'The Sunset Slayer', and have sex with the dead.

Nevertheless, if you *are* keen to visit serial killers in the US you'll need to pack a liking for travel – lots and *lots* of travel. It's nothing like buying a day-return rail ticket and visiting hubby having a comfy time in HMP Woodhill, Milton Keynes. In the states, most always you are entering 'The Twilight Zone'; places where, like anywhere else in 'The Land of the Free', you stand a very good chance of being caught up in one of the country's daily, de rigueur mass-murder events or perhaps far worse: having to attend one of Donald Trump's fascinating and eloquently choreographed mass-produced redneck 'Make America Great Again' (MAGA) stuffed rallies.

During some tumbleweed-strewn road trips to interview killers, we interviewed greet-and-meet cops and visited crime-scene locations. Small-town cops wearing Stetsons and packing heavy heat are very proud of their crime scenes, you know. They insist on being filmed precisely where some mother-in-law was chopped up, in a case probably dubbed 'The Granny Axe Murder', or pointing to a row of Tommy-gun bullet holes in a bank's ceiling. At one place near Wichita

Falls, we filmed a local sheriff proudly holding his Remington twelve-gauge, but we signally failed to tell him that he was standing atop a fire ant hill. Of some minor interest, Wichita is quite famous: it boasts the 'world's littlest skyscraper' – the narrow, four-storey Newby–McMahon Building. Make of that what you will.

Yes, dear reader, we had to drive dusty, arrow-straight, meltingly hot long-haul roads, such as in Texas to meet death-row inmates Henry Lee Lucas and Kenneth Allen McDuff. To come a-calling in places dubbed 'cities' yet where the population numbers just a few hundred. Rosebud, for example, where Texas Longhorns have the right of way, and guess what – most of them have a 'Boot Hill', a misnomer if ever there was one. The deceased back in them thar good ole Wild West days were never buried boots-on because, and you'll doubtless have already guessed this, the boots were removed by the undertaker to help pay for his undertakings. Any lead he found in the corpses he recycled, selling it to other gunslingers to make more bullets, which inevitably brought in more clientele – an eminently sound, environmentally almost green business practice, it seems to me.

I certainly digressed there so please forgive me as I momentarily went off-piste, so let's get back with the programme. The following (complete with original spelling mistakes) is a letter sent by Clyde Barrow to motor mogul Henry Ford. After it was published in the national press, sales of Ford V8s rocketed, in the best marketing wheeze in automotive history.

Tulsa Okla
10th April
Mr. Henry Ford
Detroit, Mich.
Dear Sir:—
While I still have got breath in my lungs I will tell you what a dandy car you make. I have drove Fords exclusivly when I could get away with one. For sustained speed and freedom from trouble the Ford has got every other car skinned and even if my business hasen't been strickly legal it don't hurt enything to tell you what a fine car you got in the V8 –
Yours truly
Clyde Champion Barrow

Dubbed by the media 'The Death Car' – more formally, a 1934 Ford Fordor Deluxe sedan – the automobile in which Bonnie and Clyde died is now parked up on a plush red carpet next to the main cashier's cage at Whiskey Pete's Casino, 100 W Primm Boulevard, Primm, Nevada. Come to think of it, this V8 must have been the first automobile in auto history to have through-and-through air conditioning: 167 air vents in total – not including the shot couple who were well ventilated with bullet holes too.

That is a very American thing to do, is it not? I cannot think of any British, European, or any-place-else country on planet Earth where one goes into a casino for a flutter, complete with gratis free snacks, to be confronted by a 'death car', and right up close and personal to a cashier's desk where one throws one's hard-earned money into a trash can. And all the while, the clerk gives one a wry smile and says: 'Thank y'all. You have a nice day, y'all, and ya come back soon, y'all hear,', while she's really thinking: 'Thanks for being a losing dummy and paying my wages.'

Now back to whether it is the desire for the thrill of the fear these killers induce, or in trying to understand how their evil minds work, or where their bullet-peppered cars are presently parked, we find ourselves inextricably, weirdly fascinated by the stories of the killers who wreak havoc in our communities. We are fixated by the likes of the bank-robbing, shoot-'em-up gang led by Bonnie and Clyde outrunning the law, a motley mob with a sexy young tartlet posing over the hood of a souped-up Ford V8 with a Thompson submachine gun. They wrote many love letters to each other, too. Frazer and I visited the site of one of the banks they robbed when making a TV documentary about Henry Lee Lucas. It's now a café, but one of its outside walls still has the bullet holes from their raid – a memento of the day when Bonnie and Clyde made a cash withdrawal in a 'not strickly [*sic*] legal' sort of way!

If you ask me, I think that the couple's letters to each other are *very* romantic. You can find a few of them online. Oodles of *real* love; evangelical, deep-seated tenderness dished out in spades. One can almost feel Bonnie's heart thumping as her adoration for Clyde flows unabated onto each page. None of this E.L. James *Fifty Shades of Grey* love malarkey here. Nothing erotic, seedy or explicit. Clyde Barrow and Bonnie Parker were no Christian Grey and Anastasia Steele. These days such written appreciations of a loved one come by way of a text, Messenger or WhatsApp as in: 'Hey hun. Fancie a curry tonite and a quick fuck under the pier. Luv U', which to my mind leaves something to be desired, and is most certainly not designed to knock anyone off their feet, unless their IQ is about six.

If you do decide to read Bonnie and Clyde's correspondence, you will find it is very much like the quilled letters exchanged between high-society Lord Nelson and Emma, Lady Hamilton; the latter having climbed the social ladder using her 'charms'. Her sequin-embroidered curriculum vitae included roles as a model, maid, actress and dancer. She began her career moving in the less salubrious circles of eighteenth-century London, opening her legs to a series of wealthy men and culminating within Lord Nelson's britches – when he wasn't sinking just about every French and Spanish man-o'-war ever built with cannon fire, that is. Yes, Bonnie and Clyde's letters prove that they enjoyed a low-key sexual enterprise based solely upon gunslinging, pumping red-hot lead into lots of innocent folk with discreet hints of some shagging thrown in between these very naughty events. My authority on this is – as might be expected – the 1967 biographical crime film starring Warren Beatty and Faye Dunaway.

Perhaps the first issue we should get our heads around is that the letters featured throughout this book are written by people bereft of morals. They are penned by homicidal psychopaths, some sadosexual psychopaths with a few one-off killers and a wild card being an oddball thrown in for good measure. They are devoid of conscience. Their character profiles prove that where any sense of right and wrong should exist, there is a black hole. They have no concern for others; are so reprehensible that they abduct, torture, rape and commit serial homicide just for the fun of it. Then, when finally behind bars, many of them miraculously find Jesus Christ and/or entice some halfwit women to fall in love with them; sometimes it even ends in marriage. It works vice versa, with men being just as foolish too.

> Christopher, I promised the authorities that if they let Art out of prison I will make sure that he keeps taking the pills then you can be the Best Man at our wedding.
>
> Clara Neal, serial killer Arthur Shawcross's fiancée: during a filmed interview with the author, September 1998

Once a criminal psychopath always a criminal psychopath. Psychopathy can be defined as a neuropsychiatric disorder marked by deficient emotional responses, lack of empathy, and poor behaviour, all of which, unfortunately, often result in persistent antisocial deviance and criminal behaviour, and in their letter writing as well. These people have been found to have weak connections among the components of the emotional systems in their brains. It is also claimed by professionals much brighter than me that psychopaths are not good at detecting fear in the faces of other people. I strongly disagree with that. Many of the serial killers I have interviewed gained a great sexual kick out of terrifying their victims to death. Serial killer Michael Ross could only fulfil his sex needs if the victim fought for her life. He told me that he felt cheated if they just went limp, thus, the more passive the victim, the less excitement the killer receives as a sexual reward. Psychopaths, specifically sado-psychopaths, get pleasure from hurting or humiliating others. We will see this in Phillip Jablonski as he relives his murders in ink.

While there are those who will differ with me, I state that sexual psychopathy *cannot* be cured with pills or any form of medication because more often than not this disorder is ingrained into these killers' formative years by bad parenting, poor diets, disruptive schooling, familial abuse and a whole raft of other issues related to the nature and nurture debate. All of which the child begins to accept as being the norm. We will see how this can happen when we examine some of these killers-holding-pens later.

> I hated all my life. I hated everybody. When I first grew up and can remember, I was dressed as a girl by my mother. And I stayed that way for two or three years. After that I was treated like what I call the dog of the family. I was beaten. I was made to do things that no human bein' would want to do.
>
> Henry Lee Lucas (1936–2001)

There is no empirical evidence to prove that criminal psychopaths are more intelligent or less intelligent than most of us. With their absence of empathy and the blunting of other affective states, they exist across cultures and ethnic groups. It's been estimated that approximately 1 per cent of males and 0.3–0.7 per cent of females could be classified as psychopathic. Rose West, Cathy May Wood, Joanne Dennehy and Melanie McGuire are among this 'deadlier than the male of the species' breed. When you read McGuire's correspondence, this lack of empathy leaps from the pages. An innate ability to manipulate and control others stands out with most of them. One can go online and find out just how many psychopathic killers have been released from mental institutions after receiving years of medication and psychiatric counselling, after the shrinks, who should have known better, and some half-wit parole board have rubber-stamped the release papers, signing off: 'In our professional opinion, the patient is now cured and fit to return to society.' Then, what happens? Yes, you've guessed correctly – the freed man goes homicidally ape. Take just two examples: Arthur John Shawcross (US) and arch-poisoner Graham Young (UK). Both of them were freed from mainline prisons or mental institutions to kill again and again. In Henry Lee Lucas's case, he didn't want to be freed and he reiterated this when I interviewed him while he was still on death row at Ellis Unit, Texas. I can understand that when a one-time murderer's tariff expires, then release might be the right thing to do – if, and only *if*, he or she has shown solid signs of rehabilitation. However, once a sexual psychopath *always* a sexual psychopath. So I would urge a major rethink by governments: never mind the thirty-year tariff – life should mean natural life with no quibbling about it.

Some among us may be inclined to think that psychopaths – most especially serial killers – have a superficial charm. Ted Bundy, Michael Ross, John Cannan and John 'J.R.' Edward Robinson are regarded as good-looking men, in some quarters. That said, any high intelligence that such individuals may have is deeply undermined by a litany of crippling character flaws: poor judgement and failure to learn from experience, pathological egocentricity and incapacity for love, impulsivity, grandiose narcissistic sense of self-worth, pathological lying and manipulative behaviour. And in any case, many serial murderers have extremely low IQs and are ugly specimens of manhood – witness Henry Lee Lucas, although I must admit that his handwriting was quite neat, that's if someone didn't put pen to paper at 'Enry's behest.

> When they put me out on parole [from the Ionia State Mental Hospital], I said I'm not ready to go. I told them all, the warden, the psychologist, everybody that I was going to kill.
>
> Henry Lee Lucas: to the author at interview, death row, Ellis Unit, Huntsville, Texas, February 1996.

Lucas was literally dragged protesting and screaming out of the gates and thrown into the road. The next day, the body of a young girl who had been raped and beaten to death was discovered just under a mile away.

If we look at psychopathy through the other end of the behavioural telescope, we can identify 'recidivism': a tendency to relapse into a previous condition or mode of behaviour, especially into criminal behaviour. It describes criminals of all sorts who despite spending periods behind bars cannot refrain from committing crime once they have been released only to be arrested, over and over, ad infinitum. These characters know what they are doing is wrong, yet they simply don't care about the consequences to their victims, their own kith and kin – and themselves, come to that. Simply put, they never learn from the errors of their ways. Low-level recidivists include impulsive shoplifters and drivers who continually break the speed limits; moving up the scale, we get to burglars, sex offenders, rapists and serial killers. We will see much of this warped psychopathology in the letters that follow, so bear with me please.

A more recent example closer to the British home was the release from a life-licence tariff of British double child-murderer and rapist Colin Pitchfork. He was the first killer in criminal history to be convicted using DNA profiling after he murdered two schoolgirls in 1983 and 1986. He was given a thirty-year minimum term and despite massive public protests he was granted parole in June 2021. On 19 November 2021, he was arrested and returned to prison after being seen by police stalking young girls in Portsmouth – and he'd only been out of jail since the start of September, for God's sake! The Parole Board wrote to me stating that they *had* to release Pitchfork, which is patently untrue. He had being conning the prison's psychiatrists, falsifying regular polygraph tests and boasting about his murders to his fellow cons, all of which the Parole Board were very much aware of, and this being so, I would certainly dock their wages, do you agree?

What I am now about to propose will deeply offend everyone who leans so far to the left they might be inclined to topple over. But let's get real, now. Imagine that you were the parents of Pitchfork's victims – Lynda Mann and Dawn Ashworth, both aged fifteen – and thirty-some years after you'd lost your precious daughter to a craven sex monster, you see press photos of him out on day release, parading himself around the city of Bristol wearing expensive trainers, a smug smile from ear to ear. Then follows a national outcry because he is due for release on licence, wearing a tag of course. Out of the prison gates, he is provided with an all-singing, all-dancing multi-geared cycle courtesy of HM Government, fancy clothes, given *free* accommodation at the taxpayers' expense with more benefits than most, and then starts following young girls in your town or city. If one of those murdered girls had been my daughter, I would have wanted him executed from the get-go. Sadly the Parole Board doesn't see it that way. But then, none of those pen-pushers have lost a loved one that way. Period!

Graham Frederick Young

To give the reader some initial insight as to what to start looking for in an offender's correspondence (and an insight into a total botch-up by psychiatrists and the Home Office), we need look no further than a small sample penned by serial killer Graham Young, aka 'The Teacup Poisoner' (1947–90). Young had been confined in the Broadmoor mental asylum since the age of twenty for poisoning his parents and a sister. However, despite the concerns of many of the nurses, just eight years later – during which time he is widely believed to have killed another patient and *is* known to have attempted to poison hospital staff with bleach in their tea urn – on 4 February 1971, the blinkered authorities set Graham free on the recommendation of the hospital's shrinks.

Almost immediately, Young sought employment, applying for a job at John Hadland Ltd, a company in Bovingdon, Hertfordshire that specialised in high-speed photographic and optical equipment. The firm's stocks of extremely toxic substances were more than substantial. In his initial application letter, Young wrote: 'I previously studied chemistry, organic and inorganic, pharmacology and toxicology.' All fake hyperbole with huge red flags. By way of a reference, the hospital psychiatrist, Dr Udwin, provided Hadland's with the following letter:

> This man [Graham Young] has suffered a deep-going personality disorder which necessitated his hospitalisation throughout the whole of his adolescence. He has,

> however, *made an extremely full recovery* and *is now entirely fit for discharge*, his sole disability now being the need to catch up on his lost time. [Author's italics]

One could cynically suggest that Dr Udwin meant 'lost time in killing people' but I won't suggest anything of the sort; nonetheless he wrote his letter to John Hadland not on Broadmoor stationery but his own, so the company was not aware that this 'hospital' was a nuthouse containing some of the most dangerous individuals in the UK. With Mr Hadland reassured, Young was given the job as an assistant storekeeper with access to enough lethal substances to kill most of the country's population, and he wrote the following letter to thank the firm for accepting him. I quote verbatim:

> Dear Mr John Hadland
> I am pleased to accept your offer, and the conditions attached, thereto, and shall, therefore, report for work on Monday, May 10th at 8.30 a.m.
>
> May I take this opportunity to express my gratitude to you for offering me this position, notwithstanding my previous infirmity as communicated to you by the Placing Officer [Dr Udwin]. I shall endeavour to justify your faith in me by performing my duties in an efficient and competent manner.
>
> Until Monday week, I am, Yours faithfully, Graham Young

Young repaid his gratitude to Mr Hadland by killing two of his employees and attempting to fatally poison others. But what does the tone of that brief letter smack of? It's obsequious, ass-licking, over-flowery – especially when the first paragraph would have been more than sufficient, with something like: 'Cheers, mate, I will start on Monday.' Hidden between the lines however we find a man who likes to hear himself talk, perhaps expansively, probably a 'Mr Know-All', like Donald Trump even, so taking what's on the page and what's hidden between the lines, in Young's letters we should instantly sniff an arrogant, jerry-built, boastful individual (Donald Trump again). I can confirm this, because once settled in at Hadland's, Young held forth on all matters concerning toxicology: what he didn't know about ratsbane, hemlock, deadly nightshade, datura, henbane, monkshood and vomica one could write on the back of a postage stamp. As for expounding on the unpleasant effects following ingestion of corrosive drain cleaner, battery acid, prussic acid and every other lethal substance known to mankind, or an 'A to Z' of the periodic table of elements, he knew it all. And it was this that *finally* – after a very long time – led to suspicion falling upon him and his arrest.

Young got a perverse kick out of people falling ill; watching and gloating as they writhed around in agony, and leaving the staff at Hadland's – and previously the doctors and nurses at Broadmoor – completely in the dark as to the cause of these terrible symptoms. Being a homicidal voyeur, Young then had the gall to advise the attending medics and a canny police officer on what that problem might be. It's mind-bending, isn't it? Here we have a fully emerged psychopath more or less pointing a finger at himself with the shrinks bickering among themselves as to whether or not the problem lies in their county's contaminated water supply, radiation from some unknown source or some red berries, or even laurel leaves from a bush.

> We have a cure for sexual psychopathy and serial killers. We strap them down on that gurney there and inject the goodnight juice. Hurt? Of course it hurts. It's like having acid pumped through your veins.
>
> Death row warden, Neil Hodges: execution suite, 'The Walls Prison', Huntsville, Texas, to the author at interview

In the UK we have something like a polite note being passed to a sexual psychopathic murderer saying: 'Hi, there, the Parole Board are delighted to inform you that your prison tariff has now expired and all of us at the Home Office apologise for having detained you so long.'

Way to go, bro! These stone-cold American killers know all too well what the ultimate penalty could be if they get arrested for committing first-degree aggravated homicide: a fry-up in an electric chair, a good dose of toxic drugs given as a bolus injection or 'The Long Drop'. Therefore, quite effectively they are committing judicial suicide, with the state merely providing the terminal means to dispatch them.

Selecting which of the homicidal ink-slingers out of my vast collection of letters to include in this book has been a momentously difficult task. There will be critics who will say that I have not included a 'Mr So-and-So', even a 'Mrs So-and-So & Sons'. On that score, I can only reply that I will include in a sequel those individuals I've left out this time around.

One thing the reader will quickly notice is the complete lack of contrition among these killers. In my face-to-face, up-close-and-personal interviews, and/or correspondence with around thirty serial killers and mass murderers, I can say that never ever once has *any of them* exhibited a flyspeck of remorse.

> I was born with the devil in me. I could not help the fact that I was a murderer, no more than the poet can help the inspiration to sing [...] I was born with the evil one standing as my sponsor beside the bed where I was ushered into the world, and he has been with me since.
>
> Herman Webster Mudgett, aka H.H. Holmes or 'The American Ripper' (1861–96)

On the rare occasions that a monster has expressed any form of remorse, it's accompanied by a crocodile tear or two with some sackcloth and smoke-blown ashes into my yard to gain my sympathy. This charade is phoney. If they appear to be upset, it is because of the unfortunate fix they now find themselves in – some often having just been moved to the death-house suite a few short steps from the electric chair or lethal injection gurney. You will see this writ large in some of their letters to me.

A fine example of this 'hollowness' is the two-faced shifty, sly Ted Bundy's filmed interview with author and evangelical Christian, Dr James Dobson. The reader can find it on YouTube. Look at Bundy's face: his expression as fake as a hooker's smile, the occasional flickering glance up into Dr Dobson's eyes to see if his bullshit is being believed, that Dr Dobson is being taken in. Many of my colleagues and guests who attend the annual CrimeCon event in London will spot this false-presenting in a heartbeat. So, please watch this interview with Dr Dobson then can you see Bundy's fake mask of suggested normality, the phoney contriteness, the blame-shifting onto his early exposure to pornography? Ted's psychopathological mind working flat out in pathetic mitigation as his end draws nigh, when his head will be shaved prior to being strapped down hard into the electric chair after a tampon has been stuffed into his rectum and an elastic band pinged around his penis to prevent his urine from shorting out the electrode strapped to his leg.

When we watch a live criminal trial on Court TV or YouTube, we often see a defendant apologising to the judge, with his attorney laying on mitigating bullshit faster than a cook ladles soup into a bowl. These killers do not mean that they're sorry at all. One wonders if they even understand what that adjective means; besides, as with Bundy, you can see pretence written across their stony faces, and throughout the following letters, you will spot the pretence too, with no mention of 'I'm sorry' too.

Judges have long since cottoned on to this, as is clear from the collected accounts of the first trials at the Old Bailey, which were published in 1674. During one later murder case, the defendant, pleading to be spared, begged: 'M'lud, please don't top me. I'd like a prison sentence best.' The judge, Sir Horace Edmund Avory, was 'thin-lipped, utterly unemotional, silent, humourless, and relentless towards lying witnesses and brutal criminals' according to *Brewer's Dictionary of Phrase and Fable*. Among the legal fraternity he was dubbed 'The Acid Drop', Wrapped up in ermine and as cold as a wintry day, he glared at the prisoner in the dock and replied: 'I don't give you what *you* like I give you what *I* like.' He donned the black cap, read the dread words, after which he did what all murder trial judges did in those days – he snapped off the nib of his pen (a symbolic act signifying that he'd never use the same pen again) and ordered the guards to 'Take him down.'

I like Judge Avory, don't you too? He's my kind of guy. Pity there are none like him on the benches today, hanging the illiterate little asswipes who beat old ladies to death to steal their pension money just collected from the post office. Oh, my gosh. I sound a bit like grumpy Victor Meldrew from the British sitcom *One Foot in the Grave*, do I not?

Moving swiftly on. Many years ago at the Federal Correctional Institution in Tallahassee, Florida, I interviewed the grossly obese Cathy May Wood on camera for our *The Serial Killers* TV series. Along with Gwendolyn Gail Graham, Wood was the other half of the killing tag team dubbed the 'Lethal Lovers' by the media, because during the ice-cold winter of 1987, they burked (i.e. suffocated by kneeling on their victims' chests, pinching their noses and forcing their hands over dry mouths and pursed lips) five elderly residents of the Alpine Manor nursing home in the homely Walker suburb of Grand Rapids, Michigan. I also interviewed the scrawny, self-harming Graham at the Women's Huron Valley Prison in Michigan.

Cathy Wood was released from prison on 16 January 2020. Graham will only be freed wearing a cardboard coffin. Meanwhile, Wood – the prime instigator – whistled a plea-bargain deal to get herself a lighter sentence, oozing regret, to the point of tears with phoney facial expressions that she'd hoped would melt anyone's heart, but as soon as she left the interview room, my crew and I overheard her snigger and say: 'I bet I fooled those fuck-suckers in there!' And what a fine example that is: the crew and me had no idea what was going through her mind during the interview, yet now we see Wood presenting as someone she patently was not, with pretence writ large over her podgy face.

So there is a parallel example of what I mean when I talk about reading between the lines of a letter. While the smug expressions on a killer's face might appear sincere enough, what's hidden behind the fake mask that he or she wears tells us a great deal more.

Another thing I hope to reveal in most of the following letters – and this also links to their psychopathologies – is that they love talking about themselves. If they write about their crimes, most often they do so in an off-hand, boastful sort of way. These types are extremely manipulative congenital liars through and through. This makes studying their correspondence even more fascinating when trying to get to grips with their twisted mindsets, especially when they vehemently plead innocence, as we'll see later on with John 'J.R.' Edward Robinson, aka 'The Slavemaster'. One should also be mindful that in cases such as these, and across the lengthy periods of correspondence that I've had with them, the more they put pen to paper the more they forget what mitigation they'd written beforehand. Pathological liars have to have excellent memories, but they do not!

Also nicknamed the 'Bodies in Barrels' serial killer, Pecksniffian to a fault John 'J.R.' Robinson was a 'multiple presenter'; a great dissembler who constantly stole other people's money, with a personality as crooked as a three-card trick, he could change his colours at the drop of a hat. It seems that he truly believed that he'd portrayed himself as an honest, hard-working businessman who had been wrongly accused of serial murder; the very thought of being involved in extreme BDSM (bondage and discipline, dominance and submission, sadism and masochism) activities had never crossed his mind, he claimed repeatedly. Yet when corresponding with a former female FBI agent (who used a fake name and photograph as part of a honeytrap), he played out a very different part of his Dr Jekyll and Mr Hyde mindset, all too soon revealing his true nature. Of course, he was big time into bondage and all other BDSM stuff. He wallowed in it up to his neck – as you'll discover for yourself when you read his letters later on. And what he suggested his female penfriend should do with some golf balls wouldn't go down very well with the stewards and committee of the prestigious St Andrews Golf Club in Scotland, one can bank on that!

> Man is not what he thinks he is, he is what he hides.
>
> (Georges) André Malraux

And André hits the nail on the head for while an offender's handwriting might indicate something about his or her character, this can be merely a small part of their psychological narrative. Quite often a killer will reply to different recipients in various ways, and this applies to handwriting styles too. That's not to imply that they have true split personalities or a multiple personality disorder. Rather, this is their cunning manipulation at work: tailoring their letters to suit whomever they are corresponding with, in order to receive in return what suits their own needs best. British serial killer Joanne Dennehy is a prime example. She would write just a couple of grammatically perfect letters to me, great penmanship too with not an expletive on the horizon. Yet when writing to some of her pit-bull-terrier-owning, brain-dead fans, or her imprisoned murderous cohort, Gary Stretch, she wrote bespoke to suit their moral compasses and intelligence – or lack thereof – using language that would have made any 1920s New York longshoreman go blue in the face.

So let's change tack for a moment. Let's take a more detailed look at a subject I raised right at the start of this book. All of us true-crime-minded folk know about Dr Edmond Locard's 'Exchange Principle' which broadly states that any contact between two items will result in an exchange of microscopic material. This certainly includes fibres, but extends to other microscopic materials including hair, pollen, glass fragments, paint, bodily fluids and DNA. In forensic science, this principle holds that the perpetrator of an offence will bring something to the crime scene and leave with something from it. With the great gift of hindsight, this might seem patently obvious, but it was Dr Locard who first figured this out in 1940. I now suggest that we *could*, if we so wished, extend this idea beyond physical forensics and into the world of the killers' writings featured throughout this book. In their letters they are bringing something 'physical' (i.e. their written words) while, without intending to, leaving their conscious and subconscious thought processes concealed between the lines – an alternative 'exchange principle', in other words. Thus, if we take the time to interpret their dual-mix psychological code, and compare it with the 'known facts' about their crimes, it will be of some value to us in understanding more about them – perhaps more about psychopathy in general, dare I say.

Neville George Clevely Heath – a Letter too Far

They're weak and stupid. Basically crooked. That's why they're attracted to rascals like me. They have all the morals of alley-cats and minds like sewers. They respond to flattery like a duck responds to water.

NEVILLE HEATH, HMP PENTONVILLE, LONDON, PRIOR TO HIS EXECUTION

From just those few lines, one can immediately smell arrogance in extremis. The writer is unrepentant. That he's also a narcissist and misogynist is patently obvious. And they come from a man about to meet his doom; he is not trying to eyewash us, as did Bundy.

By way of a brief background, during the night of 20 June 1946, a drunken Heath sadistically beat, whipped and murdered thirty-two-year-old Margery Gardner in his room at the Pembridge Court Hotel in Notting Hill, London.

> Even without the 17 lash marks the girl's injuries were appalling. Both nipples and soft breast tissue had been bitten away and there was a seven-inch tear in her vagina and beyond.
>
> Home Office pathologist Professor Keith Simpson

The lash marks had been made by a leather riding whip with a diamond pattern weave; nine lashes were across the back between the shoulder blades, six across the right breast and abdomen and two on the forehead. The young woman's body had been bound hand and foot, the right arm pinned beneath the back. In the pathologist's opinion, the wounds to the vagina were due to a tearing instrument. In the fireplace was a short poker, which Professor Simpson believed may have caused the internal injuries. He surmised that Margery met her death by suffocation, either from a gag or from having her face pressed into a pillow. 'If you find that whip, you've found your man,' Simpson told the police.

Realising that the law would soon be on to him, Heath packed two suitcases into which he put Margery Gardner's bloodied clothing, the scarf he used to gag her and the cloth that had tied her wrists. He washed the riding whip, putting that in too before fleeing to Brighton. And he had very good reason to leg it: already, a wanted notice, along with his photograph, was being circulated to every police force in England. Two days after the murder, Heath sent the following letter to Scotland Yard:

> Sir,
>
> I feel it to be my duty to inform you of certain facts in connection with the death of Mrs Gardner at Notting Hill

Gate. I booked in at the hotel last Sunday, but not with Mrs Gardner, whom I met for the first time during the week. I had drinks with her on Friday evening, and whilst I was with her she met an acquaintance with whom she was obliged to sleep. The reasons, as I understand them, were mainly financial. It was then that Mrs Gardner asked if she could use my hotel room until two o'clock and intimated that if I returned after that, I might spend the remainder of the night with her. I gave her my keys and told her to leave the hotel door open. It must have been almost 3 a.m. when I returned to the hotel and found her in the condition of which you are aware. I realised that I was in an invidious position, and rather than notify the police, I packed my belongings and left.

Since then I have been in several minds whether to come forward or not, but in view of the circumstances I have been afraid to [...]I have the instrument with which Mrs Gardner was beaten and am forwarding this to you today. You will find my fingerprints on it, but you should also find others as well.

[Source: *Murder Casebook 15*, Vol. 1 Part 15 – elsewhere with slight variations.]

When we compare this letter, and Heath's attitude to Margery Gardner in particular, to the way he expresses himself in one of the last letters he penned before his execution (*see* the epigraph to this chapter), we find something interesting: he is intimating that the dead woman was of loose morals at once subconsciously revealing that he is also like-minded. Heath is also attempting to paint himself as a hapless victim 'by association'; a jolly decent, hail-fellow-well-met, who was trying to accommodate Margery and who now finds himself in rather a dreadful fix because of it. The police, however, knew that Heath's appalling record of past crimes stretched way back: bigamist; arch-conman; fraudster; thief; wearer of military uniforms he was not entitled to wear; the list was almost endless. The police never received the whip in the post, nor did they believe a word of his bullshit story, so Detective Superintendent Tom Barratt was not impressed with the letter, which had been posted on 22 June 1946, postmarked Worthing, 5.45 p.m.

A taxicab driver named Harry Harter told police that he had dropped off Heath and Mrs Gardner at the Pembridge Court Hotel, where the man was registered as 'Lieutenant-Colonel N.G.C. Heath'. Police knew that Heath held no such rank – and he'd paid the cabbie 2s 2d for the 1s 9d fare. Harter recalled that both were highly intoxicated and they had their arms around each other as they staggered through the front door.

> He stood out from other men, tall, blond proud and arrogant as a Nazi. He played I'm-hard-to-get. So I did. I won.
>
> A woman from Cambridge who refused Heath's oily advances

My book *Talking with Psychopaths and Savages: Beyond Evil* contains a detailed chapter on Heath's narrative, but the lady above sums his character up perfectly by describing him as 'arrogant as a Nazi'. This underpins every single line of his correspondence from the death cell and his letter to the police, which he would have been far better off not sending at all –

indeed, why he took away some of the crime-scene artefacts is anyone's guess.

Psychopaths such as Heath are control freaks, and here we find him being stupid enough to believe that elite Scotland Yard detectives would buy into all that he'd told them. But again, it is what is concealed between the lines that should interest us, because there we can see his way of thinking as clear as day. Assuming the moral high ground, he denigrates Margery Gardner, at once giving the police information known only to her killer and themselves, so apart from telling the police more or less what they knew already, he is trying to appear calm and sincere in an effort to convince them that he is telling the truth and to get the heat off his back. However, the police were now aware of his extensive criminal rap sheet that for most of his adult life he had been a con artist with a habit of assuming false identities; yet, so ingrained was his pathological mindset that Heath truly believed that law enforcement would buy into his story as hundreds of people had done before – but the police didn't!

On 3 July 1946, Heath met twenty-one-year-old Doreen Margaret Marshall, then serving with the WRNS, in Bournemouth. Four days later, her body was found in woodland at nearby Branksome Chine. She, like Margery Gardner, had suffered appalling injuries. The pathologist, Dr Crichton McGaffey, noted marks of attempted strangulation. Her throat had been cut twice. One rib had been broken and the others bruised, suggesting that the killer had knelt over her or jumped on the body, all of which shows a total hatred for young women in general. Abrasions on her wrists suggested that her hands had been bound. The hands themselves bore a number of defensive knife wounds, as if she had been trying to deflect the knife blows. Both of Doreen's nipples had all but been bitten off.

When Dorset police started to make enquiries, this arrogant, narcissistic man had the nerve to stroll up to the nearest police station to tell an officer that, in passing, he'd met Doreen the previous day, and that she'd had dinner with him at the Tollard Royal Hotel on the evening that she'd vanished. 'I walked her part the way back to her own hotel,' he told Detective Constable Souter, 'and I have not seen her since.' The sadosexual Heath was arrested that evening. The riding crop and some of Margery's clothing were found in his suitcases in the left luggage office at Bournemouth railway station. Nonchalant to the end, Heath sat calmly in his cell. When Albert Pierrepoint, the public executioner, arrived, Heath reportedly said: 'Come on, boys, let's get on with it.' He accepted the traditional offer of a glass of whisky to steady the nerves, adding: 'While you're about it, you might make that a double,' before, with a stiff upper lip, he strode unassisted to the trap to meet his doom.

The Right Bait

All manner of sin and blasphemy shall be forgiven unto men.
MATTHEW 12:31

Once again praying that I do not incur the wrath of Our Lord – although I am cast-iron guaranteed forgiveness and redemption anyway – let it be said that prison ministry pastors, and some members of the Parole Board good people they may be, all too frequently become sucked in by these killers who have suddenly turned to God. These murdering psychopaths, who have probably never seen the inside of a church in their entire lives, start attending prison religious services and writing letters expressing remorse having 'seen the light', with repentance for their sins jam-packed into all four corners of the prison-issue notepaper. When we examine the correspondence written by serial killer John 'J.R.' Edward Robinson later on in this book, we will quickly realise how these evil men and women are able to con almost anyone given half the chance. Of course, most

God-fearing folk do, or strive to, seek goodness among their fellow man, and why not? It is natural for us to look for the good in people, not the bad.

> I want to get right with God.
>
> Gary Ray Bowles, kidnapper, torturer, rapist and serial killer: letter to the author

Those good people who strive to save the lost souls of monsters such as the sexual psychopath Gary Ray Bowles are on a losing wicket from the outset. They are duped into believing – and they truly *want* to believe – what these born-again redemptionists write and say while not having an inkling as to what is concealed between the lines, or what is actually going through these criminals' manipulating minds.

Kenneth 'The Hillside Strangler' Bianchi, a sadosexual serial murderer – the man who raped and tortured *at least* two twelve-year-old schoolgirls and is now a (self-declared) ordained priest – belonged to so many churches that he lost track of what denominations they were and which pastor was to visit him next. To earn a few bucks, Bianchi even wrote his essay: 'Sociological Theoretical Thesis: My Word on the Word'. What a ream of garbage that was too, yet members of many churches and religious outreach groups read his bullshit and literally queued up to offer succour and spiritual guidance to prepare Bianchi to be greeted by God with open arms 24/7. Indeed, so enamoured with Bianchi's newfound faith were well-meaning Mr and Mrs Dorothy Otter, they wrote to the Parole Board, pleading with deep-seated, holier-than-thou Christian conviction: 'Ken has found The Lord in all sincerity. If he were to be released he would be welcome to stay with us and our two young daughters whom he would get on very well with.'

And, you betcha he would!

I corresponded with Bianchi for a few years before I interviewed him at the Washington State Penitentiary in Walla Walla, Washington State. Then we had a falling-out, with me giving him payback time with some not so diplomatic correspondence of my own. Everywhere I went with my TV crew, I sent him picture postcards from the locations of his killings, along with the words: 'I bet you wish *you* were here.' I even sent him one from Gig Harbor: 'Hi, Ken, just visited with one of your accomplices VerLyn Compton Wallace in the Washington Corrections Center for Women (WCCW). Interviewed her for a TV documentary and bro, didn't she just shit in your nest. Then I went steelhead trout fishing with your assistant governor. She's got a cabin out here, done some varmint shooting ... so how's your day been?'

Sometimes I can be a bit naughty too!

As one might imagine, Bianchi was not impressed. In the good spirit of reconciliation I have since written to him, without even having received the courtesy of a single reply. Yet on 15 May 2021, he sent the following email to a lady pen-pal of his after they'd had a slight tiff:

> I'm lying on my 3 inch mattress which rests on a concrete slab. V tired. Busy day, meals, shower, tier porter job morning and afternoon, time to respond to multiple emails from my contact in England who has been working on things for years. Today I'm feeling my age [70]. I get that you get V angry, but what you say is how you feel

> within. Words cannot adequately express how much I hate and detest Berry-Dee. For you to equate me to him is not only how you feel, but beyond insulting. Plus, it was your contact, Angelique, who most likely caused him to text you. If what you said was not how you feel, you would not have said that during your rant.

You win some and lose some, as the following quote attributed to the poet John Lydgate, and later adapted by President Lincoln, sums up (and my critics should take note): 'You can please some of the people all of the time, you can please all of the people some of the time, but you can't please all of the people all of the time.' So if any reader is of the mind to berate my syntax as shockingly awful, I shall roundly thank him/her because I have been struggling for years to get a smidgen of praise for my syntaxical [*sic*] achievements – allegedly☺.

So, let's look again at Bianchi's email. What does it tell us from what we have learned thus far from the examples of Graham Young and Neville Heath? Bianchi's first few lines are an effort to elicit sympathy. Bless him, he is lying on a three-inch mattress that rests on a concrete slab. I have peered at Bianchi through his bars and seen his cell ('house' in US correctional parlance), so this much is correct. But what about his numerous victims who now lie rotting in their graves and who will never get a chance to get 'V tired', eat meals and have a busy day, let alone ever have the luxury of taking a shower again? Neither will his deceased victims be responding to emails, writing letters or sending tweets.

Then there is a sudden switch in Bianchi's tone. Feeling his age at seventy, he rails against me. He detests and hates me, then he lets rip with this: 'For you, V, to equate me to him is not only how you feel, but beyond insulting.' What an immoral bigot Bianchi is, to then sign off by blaming 'V' and a TV documentary-maker called Angelique for allegedly breaking his confidence. As for his contact in England 'who has been working on things for years', I can tell the reader that this 'contact' is one half of a half-brained tag team trying to overturn his Bellingham murder convictions for the double murder of Washington State University co-eds Diane Wilder and Karen Mandic, even though he has already sunk his own boat – all of his appeals long exhausted. And, this once again proves my point, with 'V' having tried to explain the true facts of Bianchi's rock-solid convictions to those wannabe TV-documentary-making halfwits who are lobbying for his release, and the Bible-thumpers who promise to invite him to live with them and their nubile daughters – they just don't understand that even *if* Bianchi were to be freed from the Washington State Penitentiary, the moment he stepped outside of the gate he would be arrested by LA homicide detectives and extradited to California, where he would serve another life sentence for the 'Hillside Stranglings' that earned him his sinister nickname.

So, what if you decide to write to a serial killer? Well, to start with you will need to use the right bait, simply because quite often it is very difficult to get these people to open up in correspondence – let alone for you to receive a reply – because they are highly suspicious at the best of times. They will only entertain you if there is something in it for them, in the form of money or some other benefit that appeals to their egotistical senses.

If one is writing a book about one of these monsters, or

maybe a chapter within a book, a magazine article or researching a TV documentary, one has to thoroughly research their criminal narratives and their modus operandi as much as possible – even going way back to their formative years. And among all of this info, if you are on the ball, you will find something that might trigger a favourable response.

I look at this 'angling for a response' as a fisherman might; a beach-caster slinging his limpet-baited hook into a roiling surf to entice a sea bass, or a fly-casting laird on the banks of a Scottish river meandering through a heather-carpeted glen. It is all about what bait to use, and how one presents that bait to catch a decent fish, you see. The predatory pike for example: they are greedy SOBs, snatching pretty much anything that swims past, and they'll bite your fingers if you're not careful. Some killers are the same. Tell them straight off that you think that they are innocent. Tell them you intend to write a book about the miscarriage of justice they are suffering; go as far as saying that a major UK TV broadcaster is interested, with maybe even some cash in it for them at the end of the day, and they cannot fail to rise to the surface and take your literary bait as fast as a mousetrap snaps shut. Of course, you are telling them a bucketful of lies, but the easiest folk to deceive are the deceivers themselves. You can take that to the bank, because once locked up in prison these killers become just a number in the correctional system and any attention they can get from the outside world massages their egos.

Other fish are cautious. Carp have to be because they often live to sixty years plus and, just like me, they put on a lot of weight during that time. Another reason carp can become the fish equivalent of a sexagenarian is that the angler who has hooked a specimen has to net it, weigh it, then put it back into the water. Thereafter, the carp slowly dives under a bed of water lily, muttering: 'I really must give up eating those boilies, the scent of fishmeal still drives me crazy.' I really can't see the point in fishing for carp, anyway. They swim slowly around a self-contained lake, are highly addicted to those boilies (flavoured bait) and, providing the angler can drop a load of them on the fish's nose, it is more or less guaranteed to bite. It goes without saying that many serial killers have a similar mindset, especially if they are really (in)famous and have lots of people writing to them week in, week out. Your lure has to be first-rate. These killers are cautious, as was 'J.R.' Robinson, who saw my bait, sniffed at it, swam around it but refused to reply until I eventually figured out his warped mindset and presented him with a tasty bullshit lure he could not resist: offers of money – sacks of it. As you will see later, Robinson took some reeling in. The results were amazing; I was electrified – which, indeed, Robinson should have been – but in Kansas nowadays, they get 'the goodnight juice', aka lethal injection. They stopped using 'Old Sparky' some time back. It may have been because some inmate caught on fire and the witnesses threw up over each other, I'm not sure really, but when you learn what J.R. did to his innocent victims, then read his letters, I am sure that most of my readers would have queued up to pull the switch.

Arthur John Shawcross, aka 'The Genesee River Killer'

Shawcross liked fishing too, especially the Black River at Watertown in upstate New York, and much later the Genesee River, Rochester, 150 miles south-west, and fishing was to become part and parcel of his modus operandi and murderous modus vivendi.

Unlike an elderly carp, Arthur didn't live to a ripe old age. He died of natural causes, aged sixty-three, in 2008, while serving 250 years to life. I spent several years writing to him and trying to get him to agree to be interviewed on camera, my bait being a phoney teaser of some funds coming his way. Eventually I received this blunt response:

Dear Christopher
I WILL SEE YOU.
Sincerely
Arthur Shawcross

91-B-0193
P.O. Box AG
Fallsburg, N.Y 12733-0116
U.S.A.

I replied and then came this. As with all the letters reproduced in this book, it's quoted verbatim, including the capitals:

DEAR CHRISTOPHER,
THANK YOU FOR THE LETTER. I WOULD DO THE 30 MINUTE INTERVIEW, BUT CAN YOU TELL ME IF THERE IS A CAMERA INVOLVED OR DO WE TALK TOGETHER? WHICH EVER IS OK. YOU HAVE SPOKEN OF FUNDS AND THEY ARE MUCH NEEDED, MY WIFE IS IN A BAD WAY RIGHT NOW. SHE IS SICK WITH THE FLU-CHEST-COLD. PLUS HER JOB IS UNSTABLE FROM ALL THE PUBLICITY THAT HAS GENERATED AROUND ME. EVERYONE IS TRYING TO GET ME TO SPEAK TO THEM BUT I WAIT. THERE IS MUCH STILL GOING ON IN THE CITY OF ROCHESTER, NEW YORK. PEOPLE WANT MY OPINION. YOU CAN GET IT PLUS WHAT MY THOUGHTS ARE.

WHAT ARE THE QUESTIONS YOU'D ASK OF ME? AS LONG AS MY LAWYER UNDERSTANDS AND WHAT I CAN ANSWER.

NOW THEN, PLEASE HAVE THE FUNDS SENT TO MY WIFE ROSE AND SHE WILL DISBURSE

THEM FOR BECAUSE OF TAXES.

DO NOT SEND ANYONE TO BOTHER HER.

ROSE M. SHAWCROSS

RD #3 BOX 274

ONEONTA, NEW YORK – 13820

UNITED STATES OF AMERICA

THANK YOU.

RESPECTFULLY

ARTHUR J. SHAWCROSS.

Reading between the lines of that letter, we can instantly see that my phoney reference to funds coming in his direction paid off. He is also playing the sympathy card with his wife Rose having the flu; that her job is unstable because of all of the morbid publicity surrounding his case. Then he throws in the notion that people want his opinion, but that he will wait. Signally, he fails to mention why people want his opinion, or his thoughts, for here he is spinning hogwash and trying to make himself appear more important than he realistically is. He also mentions that he needs to talk to his lawyer (although he didn't have one at the time) before contradicting himself and forgetting all about Rose's flu, because in truth he wants the cash disbursed to him and for her to dodge paying taxes.

Thereafter, Arthur's letters came thick and fast, all followed in short order by mail from Rose and his long-time lover Clara Neal, whom he was about to bigamously marry, 'no matter what the law is' as he put it to me.

What I found particularly galling, in equal measure to the content of Shawcross's letters to me, were the letters both Rose and Clara Neal penned without any reference to the many women and two little kiddies whom he had previously raped and killed while Rose was living with him in Watertown and him bonking Clara circa the same time. Karen Ann Hill, aged eight, was raped vaginally and anally, after which Shawcross had pushed her body into a drainage pipe on the banks of the Black River. Jack Blake, aged ten, was also killed by Shawcross, who took him fishing along the same river.

Rose stuck like superglue to her husband throughout his fifteen-year prison term and she resumed their physical relationship after he was released and while he was murdering prostitutes in Rochester, New York, and screwing Clara Neal while also using her car during his killing spree. Most of Shawcross's Rochester victims were dumped close to, or in the slow-moving waters of the Genesee River. One corpse was gutted like a fish; he cut out the vagina of another victim and ate it while driving Clara's car. 'It was frozen from the creek,' he wrote in a letter to me, 'so I thawed it under the car heater, chewed on it a bit, then I threw it outa the car window. Went down to Dunkin Donuts and chewed the fat with cops talking about the serial killings [...] Coz I had shiny black shoes, they thought I was an undercover cop. Funny I think.'

It was as if neither Rose nor Clara believed that 'Art' had killed anyone. That surely proves that they had a total lack of moral compass and were plumb-dumb stupid. Both women wanted to get hold of as much money as possible without a single thought or mention in their correspondence about the terrible deaths Arthur had brought upon so many of his innocent victims and the grief he unloaded on their next of kin.

On 23 April 1993, Rose Shawcross dictated this letter to me, which was posted from P.O. Box 453 in Omerta, New York, and the grammar is all hers:

> Dear Christopher.
>
> Please find enclosed a copy of the letter that you sent to Arthur Shawcross
>
> On November 9, 1992.
>
> Art says that he has written to you, but received no answer. I am having a friend of 20 years, write this letter to you. She also take me to see Art, once a month. Recently, we have missed going for 2 months as I have no money. I work in Omerta, N.Y., as a Certified Nurses Aide, doing home care. At first I was getting 50-60 hrs a week until the company found out who I was. They started cutting my hrs until I could not pay my rent or go and see Art. They were giving me 12 or 17 hrs a week, sometimes 20 hrs. I have had to leave the small apartment I had in half of a mobile home, and moved to a room in Omerta.
>
> The busses stopped running, so I had to hire a taxi to take me to work, this I could not afford.

Let's take a breather here to try to fathom out the mindset of this woman, whose husband's killing time was as much concern to her as water off a duck's back. Despite all that he had done, not only to his victims but after having heaped everlasting shame onto her too, she's still complaining that her working hours have been cut down to the degree that she's unable to visit this piece of human scum in prison as often as she'd like to. What follows says it all:

They started offering me jobs 25 miles away from where I lived. I couldn't take them. When I told them I didn't drive, and I couldn't afford a taxi, they said, 'Well why don't you buy a care [*sic*] and learn to drive? Just thing, you could go and see your husband more often.'

My family kept after me to change my name, but, I refused. They are alienated from me.

Art loves to cook, so when I do go down to see him, I take coffee, salad foods etc. Now, if I can get enough money to go see him, I have to go empty handed.

Art has had at least 12 offers for an on-camera interview, but he has refused. He wanted to take you up on your offer, as, we read the Murder Casebook, *Monster of the Rivers*. We thought it was well written. [I did not contribute to the article, although I may have referred to it when I first contacted Shawcross.]

We had a very rough winter here. I had to walk on some of the coldest days. I couldn't breathe, and I fell on the ice. I have a breathing problem. As you know, I am a heavy woman and I have phlebitis.

We would appreciate hearing from you. Thank you

Yours sincerely.

Rose Marie Shawcross.

Rose Shawcross never received so much as a dime from me. A couple of years later, on 4 November 1994, Shawcross's fiancée Clara Neal cottoned on to the possibility of some cash flowing her way. Again, the grammar and spelling are all hers:

Hi, Christopher
How is my Very good Freind doing these days Fine I hope as for myself just doing the same Not yet able to go see ART which you probley know it real hard for me to do only thing I still don't have no car to go in, and he is going crazy to see me before Winter starts. So we can Disguse our Business in person with each other about our money situation and most of all our wedding photos For Spring. Oh yes I ask Art if he would like for your family to bee there at our wedding and he said he would love it too. Christopfer if there is any way for you to bring a camera to make some Pictures O sure would be grateful to you and your Family I am looking Forward meeting your wife and children, yes, Christopher some way the paper here in Rochester got the word out about our interview so they came all the way out here to my trailor they wanted to know everything I said and where you people were from wanted to know where we met and all that JAZZ I told them Plain out no more enterviews ever because everything they even printed was HOG WASH about Art because he never killed anyone. They even ask me if art and I got Married yet I said how he is still married to Rose I am not dumb. They ask me if I still go see him I said yes when I can so did you contact the News Paper when you were in Rochester that they knew about you or did some of my Nosy Neighbors Report to them I don't know [...]

Time for you and me to come up for another gulp of fresh air because Clara, a mother of at least eight children with circa twelve to sixteen grandchildren, hadn't quite finished:

> [...] but there is something offel Funny now the Lady that brought me in for the enterview wont even talk to me now so Iam sorry about the Phone No and that you cant call me. But I hope real soon Arts money From the Service will start coming in to our bank as soon as it does I will get a Phone on here in my own trailor. Then you can call me any time to let me know how things is in your country and I can let you know about me and art how our plan is coming along so all I can say is if you want any enformation from me you will half to rite me a little sorry no phone. Oh yes Christofer what did you do with my pictures I have got them did you take them to England or did you have them here at the Motel if so they said they did not have them Im very unhappy if they are destroyed so please rite and let me know soon.
>
> Your Friend
> Clara Neal
> Ps. Sorry for the miss spelling
> Your name and having to change it.

As mentioned previously, one can get a picture of someone's intelligence, or lack of, through their writings, so I am obliged to tell the reader that this author met both Clara and Rose in the flesh, so to speak, therefore, with my hand on my heart I cannot say that in either case the phrase 'stimulating dialogue' was on the table. Clara's reference to Arthur receiving money from the 'service' proves that she was totally unaware, or too thick to know, that his Army pension had been stopped years ago. As for the photos? Well, yes, I did return them – to the Rochester PD, as a matter of fact. And it was one of those photos with Shawcross wearing a red sweatshirt that helped me and the police close the cold case of murdered Kimberly Logan. My website includes photos of me with Captain Lynde B. Johnston and homicide detectives Billy Barnes and the ever-smiling Lenny Boriello down by the side of the Genesee River where Shawcross dumped so many of his victims' terribly mutilated bodies. So thank you, Clara. Inadvertently you helped clear up one of your lover's murders.

Clara and Rose are, like Shawcross, now deceased, and remain so to this very day.

Phillip Carl Jablonski, aka 'The Death Row Teddy'

The only good woman is a dead one.

PHILLIP CARL JABLONSKI

Thanks for that info, Phil. As an aside, 'Jablonski' is a Polish word derived from the root *Jabłoń*, meaning 'apple tree'. Some say it was originally used as a surname for someone from an apple tree orchard – that would be an 'orchardist', it seems to me. It is also possible that 'Jablonski' was derived from the town of 'Jablonowo' near Mlawa. Polish in root and in origin, but let's see just how far from the 'Jabłoń' Phillip Jablonski fell.

One of the first questions I am always asked while giving public talks, podcasts or during TV interviews, is: 'What makes a serial killer tick?' This is a simple enough, off-the-shelf stock question proposing no definitive answer. Each murderer is as different from another as is a nub of teacher's chalk and one of Poenaru's fountain pens. I can, however, confirm, as will the

FBI, that a grossly dysfunctional childhood can, or will play, no small part in turning some children into thoroughly rotten adults; thenceforth they *can*, over time, metamorphose into serial rapists and serial murderers.

Sticking with the theme of fruit, it should be noted that in many families that have spawned serial killers, and where there are several siblings, usually only one of them turns out to be the rotten apple in a basket of otherwise perfectly good Granny Smiths.

At this point, may I introduce you to a 6-foot 2-inch, 200-pound hulk. The creature we are about to cast our eyes over was thirty degrees below trailer-park trash, yet it would be fair to say that Phil loved writing lots of words, yet nouns such as 'redemption' and 'mitigation' never once existed in his stunted vocabulary. To be frank, this guy could never say 'sorry'.

The correspondence sent to me by Phil from death row in San Quentin State Prison arrived in white envelopes upon which he – or someone else – drew rather cute pictures using coloured crayon: a cuddly teddy bear or some Walt Disney cartoon characters, that sort of stick-down-one's-throat-to-gag-upon yuck. But let me assure you that there was nothing cuddly or endearing about this guy at all, even when he informed me 'and I writ my own biography', but I suppose we can forgive him for that minor grammatical error. What was less forgivable, however, was the number and quality of the psychiatrists called to give evidence in his defence, and those who had treated him beforehand.

And here's the thing; most of the psychiatrists called by Jablonski's defence team to give evidence at his trial would have read (or should have read) the head-shrinker's bible: the

Diagnostic and Statistical Manual of Mental Disorders. For the reader's edification, *DSM* is the go-to reference for psychiatrists and psychologists worldwide.

Time to digress a tad and cutting to the chase, *DSM* (which from time to time is updated – we are now on *DSM*-5-TR) is a sort of trainspotter's guide to every known or yet-to-be-discovered mental illness, malady, unsound-of-mind affliction, round-the-bend, up-the-fucking-pole, sandwich-short-of-a-picnic scenarios that anyone could imagine or even invent. Trust me when I tell you that *DSM* is *the* book for the psychiatrist, the couch head-shrinker, and just about every psychologist, psychoanalyst, psychotherapist, psychologist who can actually understand it. This is Freudian, Jungian, Adlerian, Gestalt psychology versus psychiatry jack-off-hard-on literature. It's about intellect – to be specific to wit the absence thereof. The pages – and there are lots and lots of pages, with lots and lots of very big words – are comprehensively hedge-your-bets explicit about vacuity, brainlessness and up-shit-creek disordered moronic behavioural traits. It is all – or struggles to be – about what goes on inside one's grey matter, because the contributing authors of *DSM* are well into lack of cognition, absence of perception, even an active psychogenesis, ad infinitum, the science – or signally the lack of science – concerning what goes around in the human mind, if very much at all.

And guess what? All of this is *not* a science; it's about as far away from being a 'science' as one can get, unless one calls science a hotchpotch of educated/uneducated guesswork, off-this-planet lateral thinking and flights of psycho-speculation with a handy seasoning of 'dunnos' thrown in for good measure. We will see this writ large in Jablonski's case, as sure as eggs is eggs.

And what I'd like to add here is this scintilla of common sense. If you dear reader had in mind to visit a ~~nuthouse~~ (strike out, insert 'secure mental health facility') and spotted a convicted killer claiming to be Napoleon but mistakenly wearing a policeman's helmet, at once chained to a wall because he bounces off the ceilings during teatime, then you don't need to read any of the edition of *DSM*, to figure out that he isn't right in the head. Alas, much the same thing cannot be said about the many doctors who had professional opinions about Mr Jablonski.

> One day ... just one day ... we might be able to find just two psychiatrists who can agree with each other.
>
> Prosecution psychiatrist Dr Dennis A. Philander: throwing his hands up in dismay following Harvey Carignan's first trial for serial homicide

What I am struggling to say here is this: shrinks are not the sort of people us sane folk should barbecue with – nor are funeral directors or accountants, when it comes down to it, at least that's my opinion.

The other thing about these mind-probing folk – as well-intended as they may be – is that not many of them are much ever able to agree with another colleague on someone's state of mind, let alone their own states of mind when it comes down to it.

Many US psychiatrists charge big bucks to entice some person with mental-health issues to lie on a couch for five-and-twenty minutes in what are called 'counseling sessions', which more often than not further car-wreck their patient's life when they're shown the bill – plus tax. And all this while Mr Shrink's own life may itself be fraught with problems. Although I cannot confirm it, I've heard that most American psychiatrists treat other psychiatrists as patients, ad infinitum.

As for psychiatrists being good judges of character, it may interest you to know that while in Los Angeles – and while he was killing numerous young women – Kenneth Bianchi not only applied for a job with the sheriff's department, but using credentials stolen from a psychology student he conned a genuine card-carrying psychiatrist into allowing him to use one of the shrink's vacant offices. That takes the biscuit, don't you think?

It would be very difficult for anyone to find a worse case of psychiatric incompetence than what follows. Did Phillip Jablonski throw the psychiatrists a well-calculated homicidal curve ball that they did not see coming? Was not the writing all over the wall? Were they blind to the fact that they were dealing with a human time bomb? Perhaps a more important question to ask is: were any of these professional men and women held accountable for what later transpired? The answer to the latter is a big countable noun '*no*, not any of them'.

> Her boobs had transplants. When I bit into them it didn't taste like milk.
>
> Phillip Jablonski – letter to the author

Schizophrenic to the nth degree, Jablonski was all but sub-human; a sort of hillbilly gone real mean ornery bad. He was not the sort of chappie you'd want a young daughter to date, nor a widowed mother-in-law come to that, nor even your granny if push comes to shove. Can you imagine you and your partner, as responsible parents, arriving home after some evangelical door-to-door knocking/Bible-thumping to find your apple-pie daughter reading a letter. The scenario might go something like this:

> You: Hi, Sweetness and Light. Wow, you look so happy this evening. You have received a letter, I see. Have you finally been accepted into the Holy Sisters Order of St Disorder Latter Away-Day Saints?
>
> Her: No, Mommy and Pop, I am thrilled because this letter is from my penfriend Phillip. He tells me he's coming to visit with me. He's just getting out of ...
>
> You: ... out of ...
>
> Her: ... Yes, out of some place called the Atascadero State Mental Hospital. Phillip and some of his buddies found Our Lord in there. I even met Jerry Brudos and Charlie Manson there last week. Very devout is Charlie, he's got something like a crucifix carved into his forehead.
>
> You: Phillip is such a nice name, my child. It's like Philip the Apostle but with an extra 'l'. Is your Phillip the patron of joy and humour?
>
> Her: When he's not sedated, he's a ball of fun. But the doctors say Phillip is much better now because he has apologised for hacking his wife's head off. Besides, he has repented. Can we make up a bed for him in the spare room? He'll be here tomorrow.

Of course, I made all that up, but it is not so far from the truth as we'll shortly discover.

Phil once wrote to me: 'Christopher, do you know John Christie [the British serial killer]? A friend of mine who was in the police, sent me a photo of him. Me and him almost look like brothers.'

What more can I add than this: Phil was not mad in the legal sense, as defined by the M'Naghten Rule which was codified in the 1840s in response to the attempted murder of the British prime minister Robert Peel. The assailant, Daniel M'Naghten, shot Peel's secretary, Edward Drummond, by mistake, but was found not guilty as he was deemed to be insane at the time. A public outcry led to the creation of a more rigorous legal definition of madness. For his part, Phil knew the difference between right and wrong, but by the time you have arrived at the shrinks' so-called professional conclusions, you will have already got this in spades. Why? Because all of my readers are living in the *real* world, not on some planet a million light years from reality.

Let us start with some of Jablonski's back history (or 'narrative', to use a noun that professionals bandy about a lot on TV these days). From there we'll take a look at his correspondence before moving on to his horrific nightmare-inducing crimes. And we'll end – ashes to ashes, dust to dust – with his just place, hopefully in hell.

> All women are fuckin' whores.
>
> I ripped off her nose with my teeth. I ate her eyes while I was fuckin' that whore, bitch wife. Are you married Christopher?
>
> Phillip Jablonski: letter to the author

He didn't mince his words, our brown-eyed Phillip Carl Jablonski, who was born prematurely, weighing less than five pounds, on Thursday, 3 January 1946, in Joshua Tree, San Bernardino, California. His parents were Nettie (*née* Miller) and Phillip Jablonski. They'd moved there in August 1945 from Flint, Michigan, while his mother was pregnant with him. There were already two children, Phyllis and Louie.

> The trip took two months because the Chevy's front end was out of alignment and so family had to constantly replace its tires and tires on their trailor [*sic*]. My family arrived in California with no money and had to live in a friend's house.
>
> Phillip Jablonski: letter to the author

As events later transpired, it was not only the Chevy's tyres aka 'tires' that were out of alignment, but Phillip's mind too. And as this book is a 'road trip' of sorts, I feel duty-bound to inform you that Flint, Michigan – and Flint has some import with regard to Jablonski – was *the* go-to place to visit if one's entire family had an overwhelming desire to catch Legionnaires' disease. In 2014, a water crisis began after the city switched its water supply from Detroit's system to the Flint River. A cost-saving, cash-back-pocketing move by a corrupt governor and local politicians resulted in inadequate treatment of the water supply, resulting in foul-smelling, discoloured, off-tasting water being piped into Flint homes for eighteen months. It brought about brain damage, skin rashes, hair loss, itchy skin and pretty much every other ailment known to humankind. Indeed, President Obama – taking only White House-brand bottled water with him – paid a fleeting visit to Flint to try and calm everyone down and met many of the local dignitaries, did lots of grip-an'-grins, then left hastily to allow the County Drain Commissioner, Jeff Wright, to announce: 'See folks, nothing to worry about, the water is fine.'

On a related note, I have visited Russia many times, specifically St Petersburg, Samara and the former mining town of Buzuluk in the Orenburgskaya Oblast. Turn a tap on in Buzuluk and the water has a rather eye-pleasing soft cadmium-orange hue. In Flint, however, the ante went up by a considerably eye-watering amount; colour varying according to which toxic chemicals were in the city's water supply at any given time – anything from phthalo green to shit brown or Prussian blue, along with some teeny-weeny live things bugging around and trying to crawl up the side of one's glass.

And here's the thing. Flint's water woes had been evident for more than a century. The river flowing through the heart of the city served as an unofficial waste-disposal site for treated and untreated refuse from the many industries that sprouted along its shores, from carriage and car factories (including that of General Motors) to meatpacking plants and lumber and paper mills. And that ain't all. The waterway also received raw sewage from the city's waste-treatment plant, agricultural and urban run-off, and toxins from leaching landfills. And yes, not surprisingly, the Flint River caught fire twice. This contaminated water contributed to a doubling – and in some cases the tripling – of elevated blood lead levels in the city's children, imperilling the health of its young generations. To put it another way, Flint's children, and thousands of adults, would be a lot healthier today if they'd upped sticks and trooped en masse to a Thames sewerage outfall pipe to spend a year taking in something far more beneficial.

Lead poisoning damages brains, and without any doubt the

Jablonskis' brains were never much up to scratch at the best of times. And what an interesting road trip the family had, taking two months to cover a distance of 2,200 miles – a journey that usually takes around 30 hours.

According to Jablonski, on the advice of a doctor he was raised on goat's milk, and he volunteers that he didn't start walking until he was sixteen months old. On a more serious note, the official record does show that his father was abusive. Phillip writes: 'He loved to beat his wife and children. My mother loved to be abused physically and sexually,' although that latter comment is most certainly untrue. A sister, Patsy, was born in 1948, a brother, Albert, followed in 1949 and Nettie Jr arrived in 1950.

(Ed note: In a letter to the author, dated 12 March 2008, Phil writes, and the spelling and grammar are all his):

> 'O-TO FIVE YEAR OLD'
>
> My family first house in California was in Severance Street [it's 'Avenue', bro] in San Bernardino. The area was semi-rural at the time, made up of lower-middle-class of which my family were among the poorest.
>
> My parents sleep in one bedroom and my sisters slept in the living room. Us boys slept in the dining room, which had been converted into a bedroom for us. We didn't have a phone, and my parents raised out own chickens, pigeons, and rabbit for food. My parent would leave me and Patty [it's Patsy, Phil] with a neighbour, Oroll Crum. The neighbor was my parent best friend babysitting for us, while my parent went shopping or went to pay bill.
>
> Shortly after I turn five years old Oroll Crum and his

> wife Barbara wus babysitting as normal. But everything was about to change between us and them. Soon has my parents step out of their front door and bearly outside their, a hand was put around our mouths and I was pick has was my sister into a shape bedroom, and while Oroll carry me he whispered in my ear saying: "Nothing to be scared of. Your sister is teaching a adult game between little girls and women. She will be a woman soon and you little boy will soon be a little man. It's normal for a man to teach a boy about being a little man." I heard a loud slap and my sister crying.
>
> Then Oroll Crum pulled my pants off followed by my underwear and his cold hands off over my small butt. And he made me turn over on my back and his hands spreading my butt cheeks.

Then in graphic detail he describes the most disgusting level of child abuse performed on him and Patsy, and how he was anally raped time and again. 'That night we told our Dad what happened. He confront them and Crum said he never touch one of us anyway. So me and my sister was seriously beaten for telling out rages lies [*sic*].'

The next time the Crums babysat for him and his sister – and this will come as no shock to the reader that there was a *next time* among these families of in-breds – Jablonski claims that he knew he and his sister were in for trouble:

> He [Crum] beat us mercilessly until our little butts was bright red and bleeding. And we were made to crawl and was kicked in our butts ... [He added:] ... they tied us

> up and around our ankles and hung us upside down and swing us back and forth. Sometimes our heads would hit together. We never mention it to our Dad again. If we mentioned it to mother she'd tell our Dad and we would get another beating. One of Crums' favour games was making us play doctor and nurse. Make us play with each other with our hands or licking each other all over.

According to Jablonski: 'They had their way with us for nine months then they moved to another state.' He ends this letter with a dismissive: 'I'll close for now and then start from 6 years to 8 years old. Take care Chris. Phil.'

I have spent eons wading through correspondence from many notoriously twisted serial murderers and sadosexual killers and, for the most part, these offenders have a penchant to make up stories in an effort to mitigate their crimes and try to elicit some sympathy. Yet, somewhat surprisingly, all that Jablonski says turns out to be mostly true. He might have been prone to exaggerated and depraved descriptions, but I have read the case notes for his trial: *The People* v. *Jablonski* (courtesy of Stanford University Law School's library: https://scocal.stanford.edu/opinion/people-v-jablonski-33578, Harvard School of Law's Case Access Project and other reputable online sources) and can confirm that a number of witnesses corroborated his accounts of an abused childhood. I should add here that I am indeed indebted to the documents arising from the court cases, *The People* v. *Jablonski* and, to a lesser extent, *Jablonski* v. *United States*, for much of the material in the account that follows of Jablonski's multiple murders most foul.

At *The People* v. *Jablonski* his sister Patsy claimed that their father was a bullying alcoholic who abused his wife and children; he called his wife and daughters 'whores', and grabbed their breasts and those of their girlfriends; neighbours called as witnesses confirmed that he was a brutal, cruel man who beat his wife and children – all of which Jablonski quite independently detailed in his correspondence with me. When his parents had sex, his father would beat his wife or try to strangle or suffocate her while the children looked on. This abuse bears all the hallmarks of the way Peter Kürten and Henry Lee Lucas were raised. All three men turned into sadosexual murderers. The British serial killer Frederick West suffered extreme abuse from his father too.

It was Phillip who got beaten the most, because he would come between his parents to try to prevent his father hurting his mother. When Jablonski Sr was in a bad mood, the children would run away and hide from him, their mother signalling them when it was safe to return. There are echoes here in the narrative of the now executed Michael Bruce Ross, the Connecticut serial killer, who sent me a letter while on death row in Somers Prison:

> It's hard for me to tell you what was wrong with my family because I don't know anything different. That's how I was raised. I was beaten sometimes but I don't think that was it. It was more emotional abuse, an' like I mean with my dad when we were beaten, we would go out an' pick up a stick from the garage where we had a wood pile. An' what you would do was to go out and you couldn't pick one that broke 'cos if it broke he'd get pretty mad. But, you didn't pick yourself a club. You

> know, you didn't want to get the hell beaten outa you. An' so I had my own stick put away, hidden away in the back so that people coming in to get firewood wouldn't inadvertently take it. But I mean there is something wrong there when a kid goes to the wood house and picks up a stick; his own special stick for getting beaten. And, he hides it so no one accidentally takes it. And, you know Chris, if you got beat you didn't scream because my father just got madder.

NB: I am not suggesting for a millisecond that what Michael Ross or any of his ilk say or write in a similar vein can be mitigation for the terrible crimes they have committed – far from it. However, innocent kids who suffer such physical and emotional abuse can become hard-wired to seek some form of revenge as they grow older. I do not think that anyone will disagree with me on this. Did Michael Ross express any remorse of his crimes? The answer is 'No'! He revelled in it all during my TV filmed interview with him, and in his letters too. What you got from Michael Ross was as advertised on his homicidal tin. In his filmed interview he said:

> Chris, you could show me an array of the girls I raped and killed an' I wouldn't recognize any of them. It's like one of those old black and white flicker movies. Faceless. I feel nothing at all. You ask me what I did with them? I used them, abused them, raped them. I strangled them and dumped their bodies like so much trash. What I got a kinda kick out of at trial was the medical examiner who could not explain the multiple bruising around the

> dead girls' throats. That because they struggled so much, an' my hands got cramp. I had to stop and massage my hands before I reapplied my grip. What else do y'all wanna know?

Michael then smiled and started to giggle, so much so that the tears rolled down his cheeks.

But back to Phillip. There was violence in the Jablonski family on an almost daily basis. Police were frequently called to the house but refused to intervene. Jablonski Sr was also cruel to animals. He always carried a gun, as Phillip and Patsy confirmed, with which he would threaten them as he berated them for their worthlessness, telling them they had not deserved to be born and did not deserve to live.

Patsy also confirmed that Phillip was sexually molested by a neighbour when he was four or five years old, which backs up Phillip's claim about Mr Crum (the reduced form of McCrum). Crum, she said, also sexually assaulted her. Two local children, Dale and Janice Rearick, were present when this molestation occurred.

A number of the defence witnesses at his trial, who had known the Jablonskis for many years, agreed that the family were among the poorest of the poor in a lower-middle-class neighbourhood. The portrait they painted of Jablonski Sr was grim. One witness described him as 'the meanest man' he ever knew; another said that when he was a child Jablonski had run over his puppy and did not even bother to stop. He shot his neighbours' cats if they strayed onto his property, slaughtered chickens in a sadistic manner and once killed the family pet – a pig – for dinner. A former daughter-in-law affirmed that he had once snatched her month-old infant from her and fed the baby hot sauce.

Witnesses for the defence told the jury that as a youngster Phillip was a 'nice person' who 'was quiet and kept to himself'. He was described as being a very anxious child, 'scared all the time', and as 'a thin, pale, ill-looking and lonely child who cried all the time'. His sister Patsy said that he was a quiet child, and that she and another brother, Albert, used to call him 'Goody-Two-Shoes'. However, Phillip would take out his aggression on Patsy and Albert, and hit them when their mother and father were out of the house, although he would get upset when their parents were gone for a long time, and would dissolve into tears, lamenting, 'They never loved me. They always hate me,' he would say. Phillip 'cried about everything'.

One person called to give evidence, however, recalled that he saw Phillip and his sister Patsy having consensual sex on two occasions when they were teenagers. 'The two bragged about it,' she said, 'and thought it was funny.'

Patsy testified that when she was fourteen years old, Phillip – then aged sixteen – came up behind her, put a rope around her neck, threw her on the bed, and said: 'I'm going to get some of that off of you.' She said that her brother had an erection and that she thought that he was going to rape her, but then he suddenly stopped and began to cry. When she told her parents about the incident, their father beat Phillip.

Such an extremely dysfunctional childhood like that beggars belief. Pretty much from the get-go, he was being psychologically indoctrinated into becoming a very dangerous adult.

Backing up a tad, at the age of six, Jablonski started first grade at Arrowhead Elementary, and walked to and from school each day. 'A rail track ran through part of the neighborhood,' he writes, 'a water train would travel through four times a day. Neighborhood kids would lay pennies on the metal slug on the tracks and came back later to find the flattened coin or metal slug on the track and pick them up.' Searching through Jablonski's letters, sometimes penned in italic script or in bold capitals – sometimes a twixt-mix of both – can dizzy the mind. I really tried to find something of interest regarding his schooling, but my hopes were dashed when he suddenly went off his own rails and started, somewhat undiplomatically, calling the prison mailroom staff 'a buncha fuckin' illiterate incompetent ass holes [*sic*]', just because they put the wrong stamp on one of his letters.

Having spent more time visiting American prisons than might be considered healthy, I have found that in the main, US correctional officers have very high IQs; circa 70ish I would say tongue-in-cheek, however down in the Lone Star State it's a rare event to find one with an IQ significantly higher, so Phil may have had a valid beef there.

Nonetheless, he writes about those early days, almost as if he were reliving them as a child: playground and class activities; local haunts where he and his kiddie peers liked to spend their weekends and evenings. He mentions his fascination with the fire department, the flood-control department and bulldozers. Then, in a flash, the mood of his writing darkens once again, switching from happy to angry. To me, that indicates a schizophrenic personality disorder, almost as if he is having an angry conversation with himself:

> One evening a bulldozer operator ask me if I would like to take a ride with him on his bulldozer. I said 'sure'. He

gave me a hand up and had his hands on my belt and loosened it and unzipped my pants. I know if I didn't get away he was going to rape me. It was two years since I was raped the first time. I wiggle and twisted but he grab me between my legs and squeeze my balls and I screamed. He told "Stop wiggling or I will squeeze a lot harder", so I stop wiggling and he pulled my pants and underwear down around my ankles and position between my legs and spread my butt cheeks ...

There can be no doubt that Mr and Mrs Jablonski were dysfunctional parents, perhaps even 100 per cent in-bred morally out of sorts, as Phillip hints at here:

My family raised chickens, rabbits and us children were expected to help butcher the animals and during the task our Dad would tease us by slinging blood on us, or pulling the tendon of a dismembered chicken's leg to make the claw move, while he chased us around the yard. We had a pig. We kept it as a pet, not to eat or sell. When it was fully grown we'd ride on it, but then my Dad butchered it and forced us to eat it. Many families in the neighbourhood raised chickens and killed them. My Dad would not merely wring the neck of the chicken, but tearing the head off watching the decapitated body run around the yard until it killed [*sic*] over.

On the same page, he reverts to some inane writing about playing marbles and mentions the home-built scooters the kids had; how they all made roller skates out of wood and small wheels. Clearly Phillip didn't excel at school, because he was held back from entering the second grade to join his younger sister. When his father learned of this, he thrashed him and sent him straight to bed after dinner, so Phil says.

Throughout Jablonski's letters, he records multiple allegations of rape. In the case below, however, it was one of his teachers (name removed for legal reasons) who was in the firing line. (I note here that this teacher must have moved into the Crums' house after they moved out.)

> The teacher who lived next door would come over and set on our porch and drink beer with my Dad and listed to radio and watch us kids play. My Dad mention during one of their communications about my bad grade, and the teacher said all I needed was someone to set down with and take the times to explain to me and just go over my class work and homework, and I would be just fine. He said that he had extra time to tutor me in his free time.
>
> So next night my Dad told me to gather up my books and any class work or homework and he was taking me next door for the teacher.

That evening, Jablonski says his assignment was reading and writing. That the teacher promised he would walk him home. 'The teacher said, "Now that we are alone, I've been eyeing you and like what I have seen. The special way you fill your pants and fantastic how it would be to have you in bed with me."' Once again, what followed in Jablonski's letter is a sickening account of the abuse he suffered over the next two hours. He rounded off this account by adding: 'He [the teacher] said before he was done with me, I would be looking forever in pleasing any man in bed. I would be gay forever.'

Phillip's letters ceased at this point because after several years of sporadic corresponding with your author, sick and tired of the abuse they were receiving from Inmate #C-02477 3EB 84 JABLONSKI. P.C., the prison stopped posting out any more of his letters – his postal sell-by-date had expired, at least to me, it transpires.

Alice McGowan

> She [Alice] abandoned me. Like her, her mother was a slut.
>
> Phillip Jablonski: letter to the author

Jablonski met his first wife, Alice McGowan, in high school. He enlisted in the Army in 1966, became a sergeant and served two tours in the Vietnam War, receiving the Vietnam Service Medal. Upon his return to the US in 1968, the couple married and moved to the 'Lone Star State', and it was here while living with his parents that Jablonski started to develop violent tendencies.

On one occasion during sex, he placed a pillow over Alice's face and attempted to suffocate her into unconsciousness. Another time, he grabbed her throat and strangled her until she actually became unconscious. Once, he went into the bathroom while she was bathing and tried to drown her; once, when she was pregnant he began to strangle her until his mother intervened, begging him to stop. Not surprisingly, Alice left her husband. If she hadn't, he would most probably have killed her.

Jane Saunders

That Saunders woman was a whore, like my own mother.
Phillip Jablonski: letter to the author

Tch, tch, Phil, but of course, she was no such thing, however if the truth be told, Jablonski met a Jane Saunders in November 1968 and on their first date he raped her – an offence she didn't report to police because she was afraid of him and felt ashamed. She fell pregnant and when he was discharged from the military suffering from 'schizophrenic illness' they relocated to California in July 1969.

As might be expected, their sex life was marked by Jablonski's violent behaviour. On one occasion, when they were having intercourse and Jane wanted to stop, he pulled out a pistol and threatened to shoot her. He hit her with the butt of the gun and she passed out. When she regained consciousness, he was raping her. The next time, despite her objections, he tied Jane to a bed while they were having sex and left her there before smothering her with a pillow – as he had done with Alice McGowan. Terrified that if he killed her their children would be left alone with him, somewhat belatedly she left him in 1972. Shortly before she fled, he became so angry that he threw a frying pan filled with hot grease at her. The pan missed. She picked it up, knocked him out and then, with her two children, she ran for her life. As might be expected, she never looked back.

Marsha Strain

> Strain. Know her? As I recall I have no knowledge of her at all.
>
> Phillip Jablonski: letter to the author

Marsha Strain and her husband became acquainted with Jablonski when they bought some dogs from a company for which this sex beast now worked, training security guard dogs. He delivered the animals to the Strains' home and taught the couple how to handle them. On 17 December 1972, he turned up unexpectedly, even though (or probably because) Mr Strain had asked him not to because he would be at work and his wife would be alone in their house. After wheedling his way into the place, Jablonski and Marsha discussed a problem with the dog. He told her to watch from the bedroom window while he worked the animal outside, then suddenly he crept up behind her, put a knife to her throat and ordered her to undress, threatening to kill her children unless she complied.

The loving mother of two was now subjected to a terrifying ordeal. First, Jablonski raped her at knifepoint. During the assault he struck her in the face with the handle of the knife, fracturing an orbital bone around her eye. Then, with her eight-month-old baby in the room, he tied Marsha's arms and sodomised her. But then the dog started barking. He told Marsha to go and bring it into the house, and that if she didn't return he'd kill her children. Once outside, with great presence of mind, she ran to a neighbour's place. The man of the house grabbed his gun and ran into Jablonski as he tried to leave. The sheriff arrived and Jablonski was arrested. Weakly, he told a detective:

'I don't know why I did it … My wife just left me ... I didn't know what I was doing at the time ... I just wasn't myself ... I figure to myself, under a doctor's supervision that it would never happen again.'

But of course, Jablonski would have murdered Marsha; he could not afford to leave a living witness who could identify him.

Mary McGovern

I have already dug your grave.

Phillip Jablonski: to Mary McGovern

Before we embark on this part of Jablonski's narrative, the reader might wish to sit down and pour oneself a stiff drink, and it goes like this.

Mary became acquainted with Jablonski while he was serving time in prison for the rape of Marsha Strain, and through her participation in a prisoner letter-writing programme organised by her prayer group in Zionsville, Indiana.

Sadly, a multitude of Our Lord's disciples believe that they can redeem these 'lost souls' and help them into 'The Light', even though an ever-growing number of totally verified cases prove otherwise. These good-minded folk really have *no idea* how a manipulating psychopath's mind works; they simply do not have a clue. If one of my loved ones had been abducted, raped, tortured, killed and dumped like so much trash, perish the thought that some Bible-thumper would subsequently visit that piece of human scum, taking him candy bars and other goodies, then read a lot of 'Our Lord forgives all' biblical passages to him so that when he applies for parole, Rev. Goodwill and his wife, from some hick town such as Milton Turdwater, Georgia, can vouch for his integrity. But Mary went one step further.

After Jablonski was released from prison, Mary McGovern accepted his offer to visit him. She agreed on one proviso, making it crystal clear that she wasn't interested in having sex with him and that her stay would all be about the scriptures – and she could do some knitting while she was there too. But he was pulling the wool over her eyes. On the third day of her visit, Jablonski told her that because she was so sincere about helping him to find God, he was going to be honest with her. He explained that the week before he'd dug a grave for her and offered to show her the hole in the ground. She declined – wouldn't you? – and he added, 'but because you are kind to me, I've decided not to kill you'.

How generous of you, Phillip. What an evangelical chappie you turned out to be after all!

> God moves in a mysterious way, His wonders to perform.
>
> William Cowper: 'God Moves in a Mysterious Way' hymn (1773)

I mean, you could not make this up if you tried. When you take into consideration the fact that Mary knew all about Phillip's crimes, that he wanted to show her the grave he'd conveniently dug in advance for her, and with the lecherous twinkle in his eye indicating that he wanted to get his rocks off, one might have thought that any right-minded person would have fled his home faster than a lightning bolt. Not so in Mary's case.

Perhaps with Luke 23:34 ('Father, forgive them, for they do

not know what they are doing') resonating through her mind, she stayed another night and on the fourth day of her visit he woke her up and demanded sex. She refused. Eventually, to placate him, she allowed him to tie her hands and feet together with her knitting yarn, thinking she could break free if necessary. After he tied her up he left the bedroom to return with a glinting straight razor of the type that mafiosi use. Mary thought that he was going to kill her; instead, he shaved her pubic area, then took a photograph before pressing a pillow over her face. She played dead. He stopped and left her alone on the bed. The next day, after Mary came up with the pretext that there was an emergency at her daughter's home, he allowed her to leave.

I betcha that 'Benevolent Mary' never entertained a similar prayer group outreach programme again. 'God moves in a mysterious way, His wonders to perform' indeed.

Melinda 'Linda' Kimball

In February 1977, thirty-one-year-old Jablonski tells us that he met forty-eight-year-old Linda Kimball. By August, they were living together. That December, she gave birth to a daughter they named Meghan; Linda's mother, Isobel Pahls, conveniently lived nearby. So far, so good. But that's about as good as it *would* get.

On the evening of 6 (or 7, accounts vary) July 1978, Isobel Pahls was awakened by Jablonski, clad only in undershorts, lying on top of her. He held a knife to her throat and told her that he had come to rape her but could not because when he'd looked into her face all he could see was Linda's face. Terrified,

Isobel managed to escape and ran to a neighbour's home. She spoke to the police and reported having been receiving obscene phone calls and 'other malicious acts', which the police believed Jablonski was responsible for. Pahls, who later stated that she had spoken to a Dr Kopiloff at Loma Linda Veterans Affairs Hospital after the assault, spoke to the police and discussed the possibility of Jablonski receiving psychiatric treatment, but, out of concern for her daughter, did not press charges against him. Not long after, Phillip agreed to be examined at the Loma Linda VA Hospital. It is here in Jablonski's narrative that the wheels really started to fall off his already unstable wagon.

Taking some initiative, a cop called the hospital to be informed that a Dr Kopiloff had been assigned to treat Jablonski. Kopiloff was unavailable, however, so the head of psychiatric services, a Dr Berman, took the call.

The officer told Dr Berman of Jablonski's prior criminal record, and described to the doctor Jablonski's recent violent criminal behaviour towards Isobel Pahls. He added that, in his view, Jablonski should be treated on an in-patient basis at the psychiatric hospital. Unfortunately, Dr Berman forgot to pass the policeman's words on to Dr Kopiloff, who later stated that had he received the information, he would have hospitalised the mentally disintegrating army veteran, even, if necessary, without the patient's consent.

The omission by a preoccupied doctor to relay just a few words had heart-breaking consequences, for now it was only a matter of time before Jablonski would go nuclear. Let's remind ourselves of how Jablonski had manipulated Mary McGovern with his alleged newfound love of Our Lord. 'Contrition'. 'I've seen the Light,' while pre-digging her grave. Can you see into his warped mindset more clearly now? Because in what follows, you will see him use the same twisted psychopathology to run rings around several highly paid psychiatrists.

> I am very concerned about Phillip's behaviour, but I love him.
>
> Linda Kimball: in a private meeting with Dr Kopiloff

On Monday, 10 July 1978, Linda drove Jablonski to the VA hospital. During the interview, Kopiloff discovered that his new patient had already been imprisoned for five years for raping his wife, Alice McGowan, and that he'd also raped Marsha Strain. Kopiloff also learned that just four days before the interview, Jablonski had tried to rape Isobel Pahls. Jablonski then enlightened the doctor by telling him that he had undergone psychiatric treatment in the past. He refused to comment further, however.

Kopiloff felt that his new patient had an 'anti-social personality' and regarded him as being 'potentially dangerous'. He advised that Jablonski should hospitalise himself. Phillip declined. Kopiloff concluded that there was no urgency in the case, and that it wasn't appropriate to forcibly hospitalise Jablonski. The latter was to return for another appointment in a fortnight's time.

In 1983 Isobel Pahls, on behalf of her young granddaughter, Meghan Jablonski, brought a legal case arguing that the negligence of doctors at Linda Loma VA Hospital in failing to obtain hospital records of Jablonski's prior treatment meant that they wrongly discharged Jablonski who later killed Meghan's mother. The medical records were obtained, and produced, for *Jablonski by Pahls* v. *United States* (transcripts of which may be found online). They revealed that in 1968, Phillip Jablonski had received 'extensive psychiatric care' at an army hospital in El Paso. That hospital's records reported that he had a 'homicidal ideation' towards his then wife (Alice McGowan), that on numerous occasions he had tried to kill her, that he'd probably suffered a psychotic breakdown and that further violent behaviour was highly likely. The icing on this particular slice of fruit cake was that he was 'demonstrating some masculine identification in beating his wife as his father did frequently to his mother'. The diagnosis concluded, in part, that Jablonski had a 'schizophrenic reaction, undifferentiated type, chronic, moderate; manifested by homicidal behavior toward his wife [...] this is a highly dangerous individual, who, if in the future shows such tendencies again, and refuses voluntary psychiatric in-care, must be hospitalized against his will.'

The clock was now ticking. A day or so after Jablonski's interview with Dr Kopiloff, Mrs Pahls telephoned the doctor to complain about the two-week delay in Jablonski returning for his second interview. She threatened to call the police again. Kopiloff persuaded her not to. However, to placate her, he brought forward the date to Friday, 14 July, when Linda drove him to see Kopiloff and his supervisor, Dr Hazle. Although he revealed that he'd experienced episodes of violent anger for as long as he could remember, Jablonski again refused to be admitted as an in-patient. This time Kopiloff concluded that his patient exhibited an 'anti-social personality disorder with explosive features'. Dr Hazle went several steps further. He believed that the man was 'downright dangerous' and stated that his case represented an 'emergency'.

Yet, and only God knows why, *despite all of this* the two shrinks still believed that there was no basis for involuntary hospitalisation. (NOTE: in the UK, Section 3 of the Mental Health Act allows for a person to be admitted to hospital for treatment if their mental disorder is of a nature and/or degree that requires treatment in hospital. In addition (and this is the important part of Section 3) it must be necessary for their health, their safety or for the *protection of other people* that they receive treatment in hospital (author's italics). However, once again, no effort was made to seek out Jablonski's prior medical tests – which could have so easily been achieved by contacting the Army. Instead, Jablonski was scheduled for more psychiatric examinations and sent home, holding a prescription for Valium. A third appointment was booked for Monday, 17 July.

While the second interview took place, Linda Kimball was waiting in the hallway, probably praying that the next time she saw her man he would be wearing a straitjacket and chained to a wall. Upon hearing the quiet discussion through a partly open door, she broke down, as well she might. A third psychiatrist, one Dr Warner – the chief of the mental health clinic – heard her and invited her into his office, where she confessed that she no longer felt safe around Jablonski. Although compassionate, Dr Warner advised the terrified woman in measured tones that if she was frightened about what he might do, and that if the psychiatrists could not establish grounds to hospitalise him against his wishes, she might consider keeping away from him altogether.

Linda took Warner's advice. She left Jablonski and moved in with her mother, who was by now sick and tired of the whole sorry affair. Doubtless she felt that if the police had proved themselves all but useless in dealing with the rages and deviancy exhibited by Jablonski, the medical profession had surpassed them by miles. That she hadn't even filed a sexual assault complaint against Jablonski didn't seem to occur to her.

At about eleven on the morning of Sunday, 16 July, Linda returned to the apartment she had shared with her common-law husband to pick up some nappies and other items for baby Meghan. There, Jablonski attacked and murdered her, and as murders go this one was well below bottom drawer. He beat her, raped her, stripped her, slashed her and – after death had mercifully intervened – he cut off her ears, ate her eyes, and finished it all off by abusing the sexual organs and anus of the corpse (the more lurid details are from Jablonski's correspondence, in which he gloats over his crimes).

A few hours later, Linda Kimball's body was found there. Her shirt had been pulled up, her trousers and underpants pulled down, and her bra ripped up. Her wrists tied together, she had been beaten up and stabbed – and then strangled with a man's belt: the cause of death was found to be asphyxiation.

Eileen Millsap

Now on the run from the police, Jablonski would have been in need of money, and an advertisement he spotted in a local newspaper presented an opportunity to enter someone's property and rectify the matter. He went to the home of Eileen Millsap, ostensibly to look at the stove she was selling, but, finding her there alone with two small children, he took out a knife and, threatening to cut the throat of her three-year-old son, pushed her into a bedroom, and made her undress. In front of the two children, he threw her down and assaulted her, tightening his grip round her neck until she blacked out. When she regained consciousness, he had left, having stolen her card case and purse, later using one of her credit cards to buy petrol for his car (which would have helped police track him down).

Jablonski was arrested in Arizona eleven days later. Police found a note in his handwriting that read: 'Killed to date, Linda Kimball, common-law wife. I told her she would never raise Meghan alone or leave me alive. She begged me not to kill her. You screamed but it was cut short.'

Had the US judicial system had any wits about it, it would have ensured that the US penal system would have gobbled Jablonski up never to see the light of day ever again. But this was not to be, for – wait for it – in 1982, he met and married forty-six-year-old Carol Spadoni after she had answered a lonely hearts newspaper ad he had placed while serving time. Don't these people ever learn? Why can't they find someone half-decent outside prisons instead of shopping for a spouse behind high walls and razor wire? Are they stark raving bonkers?

Nettie (*née* Miller) Jablonski

> CDCR recognizes visiting is an important way of maintaining family and community ties.
>
> California Department of Corrections and Rehabilitation: website

While serving his prison sentence for the murder of Linda Kimball at the California Men's Colony in San Luis Obispo, Phillip did some family and community tying of his own: his parents were on a seventy-two-hour family visit in July 1985 and Jablonski lost his temper because Carol Spadoni had not come with them, so in a fit of pique he seized his mother, choked her with a shoelace, put his hand over her mouth and dragged her into the bedroom of the family visiting trailer. She managed to cry out and his father came to her aid.

Despite a momentary lapse of good judgement inter alia attempting to murder his own mother on prison property, Jablonski was released on parole in September 1990 for 'good behavior'. The Department of Corrections prepared a release programme study report in which it was noted that he was a 'Category J psychiatric inmate who had received treatment including medication'. The report also noted that a staff psychologist was very concerned about Jablonski's parole and warned that, although in remission, he could become 'psychotic' at any time. I myself prefer the more professional psychiatric term 'going thermonuclear', as in predicting that Jablonski's brain nuclei would, as so many times before, fuse at high temperatures, and go 'BANG'.

Jablonski's original parole plan required him to seek mental-health counselling, which he eventually did – once more at the Loma Linda VA hospital – and also that he attend a government training course.

A couple of months after his release, on 30 November 1990, a psychiatrist at the VA hospital, Dr Sylvia Winters, undertook an assessment of Jablonski's mental health. He told her during their session that in the previous six weeks he'd been hearing voices and seeing faces, just as he had before he killed Linda Kimball, and added that he'd stopped taking the medication he had been on while in prison. He also told her that helicopters flying above the hotel where he was now living were making him nervous, and that he was having nightmares about a friend who had died in Vietnam when a helicopter, on which they both were, crashed. He claimed a flashback to his time in Vietnam was what led to his attack upon his mother when she visited him in prison, and also blamed his experience in Vietnam for his murder of Linda Kimball, saying, 'I thought my wife was Vietnamese when I strangled her.'

It should have been quite obvious to Dr Winters that Jablonski was a tick, tick, ticking time bomb. She knew all the details surrounding Linda Kimball's murder and that psychiatrists at Loma Linda VA had naively deemed him to be neither homicidal nor suicidal. Despite all that she had heard, however, she believed him when he claimed that he no longer wanted to cause harm to others, and that should the warning signs come back then he would get in touch with his parole officer. Yeah, right!

Dr Winters concluded her examination of Jablonski with a tentative diagnosis of schizophrenia and possible post-traumatic stress disorder, prescribed some medication and referred him to the specialist Post-Traumatic Stress Disorder team at the hospital. Interestingly, however, Dr Winters suggested to Nancy Witney, a clinical social worker attached to the Post-Traumatic Stress Disorder Team, that she 'might take some precautions' for her own safety when Jablonski arrived for his appointment; and she also wrote to his parole officer, telling him to be sure that Jablonski did not sleep in a room with others for fear of his having another Vietnam flashback.

So back to Carol Spadoni.

In April 1991, Carol lived on Sanchez Avenue, Burlingame in San Mateo County with her seventy-two-year-old mother,

Eva Petersen. Carol's relationship with Jablonski had begun after she answered a personal ad he had placed in a newspaper. Yes, you read that correctly – convicted killers in the US can do such things. They were married in 1992 – not in a church with a tall spire, nave, vestry, bridesmaids and some rosy-faced vicar, but behind the grim walls of San Quentin State Prison, where he was, at the time, incarcerated.

Eventually, Carol saw the light and wanted to end the relationship with Jablonski; she'd confided in a friend that she now found him 'weird'. In fact, she was shit-scared of him, and had every reason to be, and by this time he had been transferred to the California Medical Facility (CMF), Vacaville, where he was being treated for schizophrenia.

To claify matters, if one is completely criminally off-the wall, CMF is the place to be. Charles Manson gave his first-ever TV interview in CMF. Bobby Beausoleil, Ed Kemper, Donald DeFreeze and Jim Gordon, among many other unhinged minds, have been housed there. So, if you ever receive a letter from a man giving his address as Vacaville, CA 95696, do exercise due diligence for heaven's sake. Ask, at the very least, for a curriculum vitae; or, as they say in the antique trade, 'good provenance'; or in the parlance of the motor trade, the full service history with receipts and a current MOT.

I am using these two analogies here simply because one does not want to buy an expensive 'genuine circa 1762 Chippendale dressing table' only to get it home and find a well-hidden stamp on its underside bearing the legend 'Made in China, 2020'; neither does one want to buy a 'one careful owner' Jaguar E-Type to have it grunt to a halt in the middle of a motorway. Metaphorically, this is precisely what those who fell for Jablonski *didn't* do. They simply believed every word he wrote to them, that deep down he was a misunderstood cuddly teddy bear.

In the summer of 1990, as the date for his release approached, Jablonski had some of his belongings sent to the address Carol Spadoni shared with her mother Eva Petersen in Burlingame. It was clear from this that he intended to move into their home, and they were very alarmed. Eva phoned Richard Muniz, a friend of Jablonski's and former fellow inmate at San Quentin prison, with whom the women had become acquainted. After his release Muniz, who had settled in Sacramento, had remained on friendly terms with the two women, and Eva, who was scared – I mean *really scared* – of Jablonski and didn't want him anywhere near them, now asked Muniz if he could come to their place and remove Jablonski's belongings. This the obliging Muniz did, storing the items in his garage in Sacramento. Meanwhile, Carol Spadoni had spoken with Robert Paredes, Jablonski's parole officer, and told him how afraid she was of Jablonski and that she did not want him living with her.

Phillip Jablonski was released from CMF Vacaville in September 1990; Muniz was there to meet him, and drove him to Sacramento, explaining that his possessions were now at his place as Carol and Eva wanted nothing more to do with him. Jablonski was not too pleased to hear this, so he spent that weekend with Muniz before going to meet Paredes at his office in Indio, Riverside County, where he would learn the terms of his parole. He was not permitted, Paredes told him, to travel more than fifty miles from his home without permission, and he was *absolutely forbidden* to go to Burlingame or to try to meet up with Spadoni or Petersen. He was also ordered to join a counselling programme at the Loma Linda VA hospital.

That Christmas, Jablonski asked for leave to go to Sacramento to visit Muniz and to obtain a driving licence. Before giving him permission, Paredes spoke to Eva Petersen and explained what Jablonski wanted to do, assuring her that the man would not be allowed anywhere near Burlingame or indeed inside San Mateo County. Petersen raised no objection.

The shit was soon to hit the proverbial fan.

Jablonski spent a week with Muniz in Sacramento, all the while moaning about Eva's influence over Carol, and how they were frustrating his plans to move to the city himself, which he felt had held back his employment prospects. Jablonski returned from Sacramento with a bee in his bonnet, a driving licence and a 1965 Ford Fairlane. In January 1991, he signed up for auto classes at a local community college.

Fathyma Vann, aka Fanny Hansen

Among his fellow students at the automotive course were Fathyma Vann, a newly widowed thirty-eight-year-old mother of two, and a man called Jim Lawrentz, who later told police that Phillip always tape-recorded the lessons and was 'very intelligent', which somewhat speaks for Lawrentz's IQ, too, Anyway, about halfway through April 1991, Jablonski learned that Lawrentz owned a small gun and asked if he would sell it to him – knowing full well that as a convicted felon he was forbidden by law to possess a firearm. Lawrentz demurred at first, but two days later, probably unaware of Jablonski's criminal history, changed his mind and sold Jablonski his .22-calibre RG-14 revolver and bullets.

On 22 April, Jablonski informed his instructor, John

Tamulonis, that he had to go to the doctor's and would miss the next day's class, assuring him that he would be back for the following session. Later on the same day, Tamulonis saw Jablonski with Fathyma Vann.

Jablonski did not return to the college. Nor did she.

That evening, Jablonski gave Fanny a ride home from class. The next day, her body was found in a ditch by a road in the desert outside Indio. It was horribly mutilated with stab wounds in the neck, abdomen, vagina and rectal areas. The ears and nipples had been cut off and the eyes lacerated. On the back cuts and scratches appeared to read 'I [heart shape] Love Jesus'. The cause of death was a gunshot wound to the head.

By way of an afterword, Fathyma's daughter, Yolonda Robinson-Vann, who, with her sister, became an orphan following the death of her mother, later told of having a chilling premonition when, aged nineteen, she met Jablonski for the first time. In an interview with Fox News in 2020, she revealed:

> She introduced me to him. And immediately, without even saying 'Hi' to him, I said, 'If something happens to my mother, I'm going to come looking for you.' [Jablonski replied] 'Well, you don't have to worry about me doing anything to her. You should worry about her doing something to me.' And I said, 'Well, we shouldn't have a problem. 'Cause if you don't mess with her, she's not going to mess with you.'

Yolonda added:

> Just the way he stood there and was looking at my mother,

> there was just something about him that didn't sit right in my stomach [...] My kids always wanted to know about their grandmother. But when you go online and put her name in Google, his face pops up. And you have to remember, I had a conversation with this man. I felt like I was given a warning and I hate the fact that I didn't listen. I still wonder, had I not told him anything about messing with her, would she still be alive today? Or was he already plotting to kill her? I live with that.

Yes, Yolonda. All of my thousands of readers will feel your grief. We are parents too. What *you* saw was something in Jablonski that the shrinks and the cops didn't see – it was streetwise common sense.

Carol Spadoni and Eva Inge Petersen

On 23 April 1991, not even a year after Jablonski had been released on parole, Carol Spadoni and her mother Eva were murdered in their Burlingame home in San Mateo County, California. In fact I would not hesitate to say that they were 'over-murdered in extremis', if it comes down to it.

Carol Spadoni and her mother had been in the habit of meeting a friend, Robert Galindau, regularly for coffee and doughnuts at a coffee shop. When more than once they failed to turn up and didn't answer his phone calls, Galindau became worried, and early in the morning of 26 April he drove round to their house. There was no sign of the women; he noticed several newspapers piled up outside the front door and also a couple of parcels. Round the back he found a few starving cats in a pen, at which his concern became one of serious alarm. He called the police.

When Officer Frank 'Slim' Pickens of the Burlingame Police Department arrived, he first of all knocked at the front door. There was no reply. He checked the windows: there was no sign of a break-in, but he did find that a side door to the garage had been left unlocked and went in, followed by a fellow officer. Across the garage was the open door to the kitchen; on the garage floor in front of him was the body of a woman. She was all too clearly dead. The two officers moved, guns drawn 'tactical style', into the house, where they found, on the living-room floor, a second body, again very obviously dead. The spare, factual prose of the descriptions of the bodies as cited in the trial documents gives a chilling picture:

> The first body found was that of Eva Petersen. A towel had been folded over and pushed into her mouth and a bullet had been shot through the towel. Petersen was naked from her waist down; her sweatshirt and brassiere had been pulled up above her breasts and around her neck. There was another bullet hole above her right breast and a stab wound in her neck. There were also cuts around one of her nipples and around her right eye; the cut to her nipple could have been made with a knife, and the cut to her eye may also have been made by a knife. Blood smears on the kitchen floor indicated that she had been dragged across the kitchen. The stab wound to her throat had been made while she was still alive. The cause of death was the gunshot wounds to her head and chest.

Worse than the state Fathyma Vann's body was left in. And it gets nastier.

> The second victim was Carol Spadoni. Her body was found in the living room, dressed in a nightgown. Her nose and mouth were covered with duct tape wrapped so tightly it would have cut off her breathing except that she had been stabbed in the throat creating a functional tracheotomy. She had a bullet wound behind her right ear and three stab marks in her abdomen. Additionally, half of her right breast was sliced off, exposing a silicone implant. There were also stab wounds to her vagina, and her intestines were protruding from her anus as the result of a laceration. The cause of her death was the gunshot wound with the stab wounds and duct tape suffocation as contributing factors. Because decomposition had begun to set in, the pathologist who examined the bodies could not determine if any sexual assault had occurred.

The hunt now began in earnest for a homicidal psychopathic killer.

Investigators found on the kitchen table a journal, its final entry on 23 April 1991, and envelopes addressed to the women by Jablonski, while a letter addressed to 'Mrs Carol Jablonski' in his handwriting was found in a bedroom.

Back at the police station, a computer check showed that earlier Jablonski had been stopped by a traffic cop in Burlingame for failing to yield right of way. The officer, who was unaware that Jablonski was in violation of his parole terms, reported no signs of intoxication or nervousness in Jablonski.

Further investigations involved a search of Eva Petersen's bank records, which revealed a cheque for $200 made out to Jablonski and purportedly signed by Petersen – the signature, however, did not match that on Petersen's bank card. A cashier at the bank where the cheque had been cashed later identified Jablonski as the individual who had cashed it on 23 April.

Yvette Shelby

Some thousand miles on, on 25 April, now on the run following the Vann, Petersen and Spadoni murders, Jablonski pulled in to a service area in Wyoming. Seeing Yvette Shelby there, who had stopped to let her dog out of her vehicle, Jablonski, for some unexplained reason, reached for his pistol and threatened her with it as he got out of his car. She was fortunate – the gun slipped from his grasp and fell to the ground, and she was able to get back in her car and quickly drive away. She stopped at the next service station and phoned the police. Using a remarkable lack of common sense, the cops who pulled him over didn't even radio the call in. Jablonski, on parole and illegally in possession of a firearm, explained that the gun was for personal protection and had fallen out as he was getting out of his car. The officers accepted his explanation, told him to put the gun in the car's trunk, and let him continue his long interstate drive.

Margie Marie Rogers

On 27 April 1991, the body of fifty-eight-year-old Margie Rogers was found in the service area store where she worked, in Thompson Springs, Grand County, Utah. She had been shot twice in the face with a .22-calibre gun. Her shirt had been pulled open and her bra had been tugged up over her breasts. There was $153 missing from the till – presumably taken by the killer.

This was to be Jablonski's last kill.

The next day, a Kansas Highway Patrol Trooper spotted a car with its bonnet up in a service area in McPherson County, Kansas, and stopped to check on its driver. Not satisfied with the driver's response, he ran a quick check on the vehicle's registration, learned that there was a warrant out in California for Jablonski, and, calling for back-up, arrested Phillip Jablonski.

When they searched him, the police found $710 cash in his wallet, alongside a cheque for $90 drawn on Eva's bank account and a credit card in her name. There was also a small address book in the wallet, in which Jablonski had written the names, addresses and dates of birth of Eva Petersen and Carol Spadoni. Beneath each name were the words 'Death, April 23rd, 1991'. At that time, the dates of the murders had not been publicised.

In Jablonski's car, officers found a loaded .22-calibre revolver beneath the driver's seat, and a box of .22-calibre cartridges. Bullets removed from Eva's body matched the rounds in the revolver; the bullet recovered from Carol's brain was too damaged to be conclusive, but it did match the rifling characteristics of the revolver. The police also found in the car duct tape similar to that used to gag Carol; an electric taser; homemade wire handcuffs, and a sheath from which the knife was missing; the latter showed signs of what seemed to be blood. Also recovered was a holdall containing blue trousers stained with human blood and semen. There was a black leather belt found in the car, on the inside of which the words 'Carol

Jablonski 4-23-1991, Burlingame, California' and 'Eva Petersen 4-23-1991, Burlingame, California' were written in ink. The handwriting was later resolved by an expert to be Jablonski's, as was the writing in the address book.

What makes these terrible homicides even more horrific was a cassette tape found in the car, on which Jablonski had recorded what he did from his arrival at the victims' house: he described shooting Petersen, fondling her breasts, sodomising her, having sexual intercourse with her and trying to gouge her eyes out. He described shooting Carol through the brain, binding duct tape around her mouth and nose, stabbing her in the throat, slicing open a breast and stabbing 'her ass and pussy'. According to his taped account, he then moved their bodies, had something to eat and a shower, and then, before departing, fired a shot through a towel he had stuffed into Eva Petersen's mouth.

So back to Jablonski and your author. One of his pen-pals wrote to ask if I would correspond with Phil as he was writing a book. My interest piqued, I dropped Jablonski a line. That said, having met and corresponded with so many manipulating serial killers over the years, one kind of gets a sniff of something being not quite right when someone claiming to represent a convicted felon sends one a letter out of the blue. Death-row inmates, or those serving extremely long tariffs for committing the most awful crimes, are not allowed by their respective departments of corrections (DOCs) to go fishing for any kind of money-making venture, so they are cute enough to get someone on the outside to do this for them.

Jablonski was straight out of the starting blocks in replying. His correspondence was written on both sides of lined, buttercup-yellow prison-issue paper, sometimes using quite neat capitals throughout, at other times flowing italic script, sometimes a mix of both. Unlike so many inmate correspondents he did not cram his writing onto the page. He justified his text, with paragraphs short and to the point, all in all making for an easy, albeit disjointed, read. Overall, on the face of it I *quite* liked his style. The envelopes in which he placed his correspondence featured very well drawn, crayoned cartoons. Assuming they were his work, in better times perhaps he could have found his calling as a children's book illustrator, even for a Teddy Bear story, but, alas, Phillip opted for a different route, taking five lives and committing a string of dreadful sex offences to boot.

My suspicions increased with the different style of writing Phil used. Furthermore, even a blind forensic document examiner would have noted that *before* the envelope was addressed to me the cartoons, which always took up at least one-third of the paper, were drawn and coloured first with Jablonski's address on the left-hand-side, noting the different styles of penmanship. It's all very confusing so maybe Phillip Jablonski is a Dr Jekyll and Mr Hyde. Maybe he didn't draw the cartoons after all!

Phillip JABLONSKI, C-02477 3EB 84, San Quentin State Prison, San Quentin, CA, 94964, USA

While the envelope was addressed to me in capitals on the right-hand side, below is an earlier letter from 28 January 2008 that he sent to me, penned in reasonably competent script and in which he feigns surprise that I'd written to him at all. As cunning as foxes these guys and gals are. Published verbatim is a taster, so see if you can smell a rat here:

> Dear Christopher.
> Received your surprising letter. I am only acquainted with a few true crime authors in the states. I had a newspaper reporter write a autobiography about my crimes and it wasn't in the market long. Maybe at the most less than a year. Its first appearance for sale in Australia and then in the States. Many of my pen pals who read it thought it completely boring and a lot of shit, full of half-truths and numerous lies and crap. There was little investigative work done by him. He got most of his information from Court reports. I did do an interview with him on paper and not a thing I wanted appeared in the book.
>
> What are the titles of some true crime books you writ [*sic*]? Are any of them in book stores in the States? Do you know John Christie? I believe he is a famous killer in the U.K. I believe he killed his wife and prostitutes and burned the bodies. A friend of mine who was in the police, sent me a photo of him. Me and him almost look like brothers.

Having told me that he looked like John Christie's brother, and that some unnamed newspaper reporter had written his autobiography when he should have said 'biography', and adding that it 'was full of crap', he upped the ante a bit with:

> Will be glad to assistance you in writing my side of the story. Your letter was wrote on Jan 3, 2008, my birthday by the way. With all the work I am going to be putting into the project, what am I going to get out of it? <u>Just curious!</u>' I would seriously like IWC Media to do a TV documentary about me.

Nice try, Phil. Subtly fishing for a few bucks already. Goodness gracious me, now it's a TV documentary you want too – you're no shrinking violet, are you? And all that work you are going to have to do. Such a shame to put you out while you lie on your bunk twenty-three hours a day. But please go on:

> Have you ever heard of the 'Death Row Survey' here in the State. They publish a magazine titled 'Stuff'. My interview was selected to be published in the 'Stuff' magazine and I was to receive a copy of the magazine with my interview in it. It's called 'Maxim' in the U.K. I was wondering if you ran across the magazine and read the interview?
>
> By the way I have son name [*sic*] Christopher, who is doing time in Michigan for child rape. I guess you could say he is following in his father's footsteps.
>
> I have no remorse for murders, rapes or pumping young adolescence boys and girls I did [*sic*]. I am proud of raping my slut sisters and mother. Maybe my slut mother will rot in hell. They died in 1986. Beside the murders you might have read about what I committed. There is a few that are unsolved at this time. And a few are over twenty years old.
>
> I'll be looking forward to working with you on this project.
>
> Take care
>
> Phil.

Let's take a breather here shall we, and maybe have a cup of tea. I really wanted to tell him that *Stuff* magazine is for electronic geeks. In no way is it associated with *Maxim*, either. Why an electronics mag would do a death-row survey beats the hell out of me, unless they were advising electric-chair operators and refurbishers on how to service 'Old Sparky', or Alabama's 'Yellow Mama' or 'Old Smokey' (New Jersey and Pennsylvania), that is.

The same letter now went on a bit more, this time underneath his previous and most courteous sign-off (we can call this an addendum), starting in script followed in capitals dated 2/28/08, and here things go grammatically downhill faster than former ski-jumper Eddie 'the Eagle' Edwards. I reproduce it here, verbatim:

> If you cant read the handwriting, I'll be glad to PRINT MY PREPARED TO YOUR INTERERDUCELY LETTER ON DATE OF THIS LETTER BUT OUR ASS HOLE MAIL ROOM PUT I INCORRECT POSTAGE ON THE ENVELOPE SO I HAD TO BORROW A STAMP TO RE MAIL THE LETTER TO MAKE SURE THIS LETTER REECH YOU. I REAL KEEN ON WRITE MY SIDE OF THE STORY. I HOPE YOU STILL INTEREST IN ASSISTANCING ME.
>
> I AM A INDIGENCE INMATE SO I HAVE TO DE PEND ON THE PRISON FOR MY POSTAGE, WRITING SUPPLIES, ETC, ETC.

We are not quite out of the woods yet, because guess what? He then reverted back to script, with:

> Just some information you possible haven't seen on the inter-net, there is a book write about my crime entitled

'DEADLY URGES' by BARRY BORTNICK. Also enclosed is a poem wrote about one of my murder victims. The nigger I torture and brutally tortured and rape, sodomy and shoot to dead. Anything about me on the internet is I am Bisexually and proud of my sexually originally (Miasspelled [*sic*]). Again I hope that you my reply [*sic*] to your letter I received on February 19.2008 that you mailed on January 21, 2008.

I again like to express that I am really keen on getting my side of story out to the public with your assistance, and I hope you didn't think I am pulling a con for on about asking for $50.00 to cover postage and for writing paper, etc, etc. Kindly try to understand our mail room is must [*sic*] of uneducated and inefficient ass holes. I would sent you the envelope the return to me that the mail room put incorrect postage on. But I am filing an appeal to get the matter corrected if they can read before I am contacting my lawyer about the matter.

Take care Phil.

As you will have now gathered, with serial killer Phillip Jablonski there is some very good news and buckets full of bad news; the former being that he died, of 'unknown causes', aged seventy-three on 27 December 2019, in his San Quentin State Prison death-row cell. However, as late as 1994, he was still using a website asking for men and women to write letters to him, in which he described himself as a 'Death Row Teddy Bear'.

Now comes the fun part. Jablonski's actual words in describing himself on this website are detailed below:

I ask your indulgence male and female and promise to he as brief as possible allow me to introduce myself as 'Death Row Teddy'.

I am 58 years old. My DOB is January 3rd 1946.

I have been on death row for 11 years ((Aug. 1994).

I am seeking for a female/male Teddy Bear.

I once lost my heart scarcely used by one careless owner.

As I last saw it was thubbing [*sic*] in your direction.

Caucasian male – seeking an open minded male/female for unconditional correspondence on mature and honest level, that has a caring heart to create a special friendship build from the heart.

Why choose me?

I am a professional artist, photography, amateur poet, writer, masseur, college educated, not a rude person, like to party, travel. My home town is Joshua Tree, CA. I am very understanding and loving. I believe in giving a second chance. People describe me as a gentle giant.

I love cats, dogs, parrots and teddy bears.

What I like in a friend? I like to travel, party. Someone who is mature and wants an honest friendship. Someone who is able to discuss personal issues on a mature level and is not scared of Frank [*sic*] discussion.

Jablonski would not be travelling and partying with anyone, anytime soon. As for discussing personal issues on a mature level, he signally failed to mention that five of the women with whom he 'discussed personal issues' ended up mutilated and in their graves.

At this point in Phil's love-seeking soliloquy, I would like to stop for fear of boring my readers; however, I simply cannot resist what follows:

> What I miss the most: Traveling, photography male and female company, giving massages, partying, walking in the rain, romantic walks along the beach, romantic candlelight dinners, cuddling in front of a roaring fire.
>
> Lets share our thoughts and feelings (good or bad) lets learn about one another freely and watch our friendship bloom like a rose and be as strong as a castle wall which can't be broken.
>
> A loving heart is worse then a mountain of gold [*sic*]. Love communicates on any subject or issue. Write me please you won't be disappointed.
>
> Don't let my situation stop you from writing me. Pick up your pen and pay me a visit ... if possible, please send me $50 for my stationary [*sic*] and stamps, and you will get a guaranteed response ... sincerely, Phillip.

But here's the rub. Scores and scores of women answered Jablonski's ads, and all as a result of an effort by him and some scammer on the outside to hoover up as much cash as they could. Indeed, while his hideous rap sheet was readily available on the CDCR's death row website, along with his mugshot, so enamoured with our Phillip were these ladies that he actually received several offers of marriage. I tracked two of these halfwits down.

'Miss A' (name removed for legal reasons) is from Hastings – the once genteel Edwardian/Victorian, silver-spoon-born-in-one's-mouth seaside resort, not far from the *original* Brighton, which for American readers is in the UK. An *extremely* substantially built woman, 'Miss A' writes to countless serial killers and mass murderers, using her social benefits for airmail stamps, many biros and lots of stationery to court at least one of these homicidal maniacs in an effort to entice him into wedlock. What funds she did have left over she sent to Phillip Jablonski – a total of circa £600, all told – and she was broken-hearted when he passed away. 'Christopher, don't be heartless. You don't even know how much I adored Phillip,' she wrote in a letter to me. 'We thought in exactly the same way. His letters touched my soul. But don't let my grief upset you or your work; I am now writing to [serial killer] Gary Ray Bowles. With a reverse twist on the late actor and comedian Benny Hill, she finished with, 'He likes big women so he tells me. Do you?'

Next up was 'Miss B' (name removed for legal reasons at my publisher's lawyer's advice and *not out of choice*). She hailed from Wisconsin, and *actually* visited Phillip while he was still in CMF Vacaville. Obviously, 'Miss B' had the upper hand in the courtship stakes over 'Miss A' because she met him in the flesh. Love at first sight was the order of the day. But let me ask you – and you can check this out for yourself when you take a look at his photos online – would Phillip have been suitable for casting in *Baywatch* or even as one of the Chippendales strippers, come to that? C'mon my dear lady readers, pretty please take a peek at the now late 'Romeo Phillip' and drop me a line with your thoughts. I'm easily found on Facebook Messenger, so, God's truth, I would love to hear your opinions.

I don't know how old 'Miss B' was back then. I don't even know whether or not she wore high-power spectacles, either. I don't know if she had any religious leanings. I have not a *single* clue as to how many dollars Jablonski fleeced out of her – though I would hazard a guess that it was a tidy amount going by how easily these women get fleeced– even though she lived way up in Oregon, some 670 miles distant from California. Well, love conquers all obstacles, or so they say. She did confirm that he was the 'most handsome man I have ever cast my eyes upon and his poetry [shown and dated 2000, with a cartoon of some chap looking through a mirror, by Jablonski, text verbatim below] entered my heart.'

Phantasm
I have dreamed a dream
A dream of wisdom and pain
Where all in this made up world seems right
I know what I have done
And yet, I can take comfort in those acts
As they have set me free,
Free like a bird in the dream
Drifting to places unknown
Always searching
Always looking
For answers
To questions
That others are afraid to ask
But not afraid to answer.

Detalles de la sepultura desconocidos
('grave details unknown')

Melanie Lyn McGuire, aka 'The Ice Queen'

Beauty lies in the eyes of the beholder.

PARAPHRASE OF A STATEMENT MADE BY THE GREEK PHILOSOPHER PLATO

There is something magnetically alluring about femmes fatales, including the killer breed. Especially the more intelligent and better-bred women – although among the homicidal criminal ranks they are a rare species indeed. For further reading, my book *Talking with Female Serial Killers: A Chilling Study of the Most Evil Women in the World*, might give the guys pause for thought!

In the US, any up-market partners that these up-scale gals put into a grave are mostly for double-indemnity insurance purposes; tending to be dentists, doctors or other well-paid professionals with life insurance policies the size of the Federal Reserve. By contrast, British female killers rarely murder their spouse or partner for monetary reasons; it is far more common for them to do so out of jealousy. And, again, only a very small proportion of those women who commit murder are serial killers.

And so to Melanie McGuire, who is not a serial killer, but could be said to be a serial letter-writer. And that is my excuse for including her in this book.

On 23 April 2007, thirty-four-year-old Melanie Lyn McGuire was found guilty of murdering her husband some three years earlier, by first drugging him and then shooting him, dismembering his body and disposing of it in three black rubbish bags, placed in three identical suitcases and dropped into Chesapeake Bay. She received a full life sentence.

> This is a defendant who puts on a face and shows the people before her whatever it is she wants to show. I don't know who the real Melanie McGuire is.
>
> Assistant State's Attorney Patricia 'Patti' Prezioso
> at Melanie McGuire's trial in 2007

With so many letters from killers in my collection, choosing which, and written by whom, to select for this book has been no mean task. The now executed serial killer, Robert Joseph 'Bobby Joe' Long a distant cousin to Henry Lee Lucas, penned dozens of porn-driven filth to my confederate 'Kate' in a honey-trap sting set up by me and her. (I am still working with Kate even today; the choice of name is hers.) But as I am sure my publishers would agree, putting this disgusting material – even with the heaviest of edits – into the public domain would be a bridge far too far. For my own purposes, it certainly gave me a very detailed picture of this man's utterly depraved mind.

If it is a case of judging a person's character by the quality of the material that they are reading – which would make my readers not only astute, highly intelligent but dear friends of mine for life – it would be fair to say that Melanie McGuire was more eclectic in her reading than some other killers I could name: she favoured a mixed bag of stuff, including some conspiratorial literature, as we will see in due course. But the same cannot be said of Bobby Joe Long. In his letters to 'Kate', he promotes *Bizarre Magazine* and *Draculina*, graciously listing an entire catalogue of his must-reads, while also recommending suppliers and giving her the addresses and zip codes for the websites QSM Mail Order, Redemption, *Rose Comics* and *Centurion* magazine. After that, he prints in bold black ink – and it should be noted that this was his first letter to 'Kate', who'd merely asked if his crimes had a sexual element to them, mentioned that she would be interested in him as a person and asked about his literary preferences:

> ... AND BE SURE TO SIGN AN AGE STATEMENT, AND I THINK THEY'LL ALL SEND YAH SOME CATALOGES YOU'LL FIND ... INTERESTING ☹. WHO KNOWS, MAYBE EVEN SOME 'STUFF' YOU'VE NEVER SEEN BEFORE!
> HAVE YOU NEVER WATCHED A HARD CORE XXX RATED, GRAPHIC 'FUCK-VIDEO'??? IF SO, WHAT DID YOU SEE THAT MOST 'INTERESTED' YOU? IF NOT, WOULD YOU LIKE TOO?

At this point I am sure my readers will know 100 per cent where Bobby Joe Long is going next. Among the varied subjects up for discussion are:

> WHO WOULD YOU LIKE TO "TORTURE AND RAPE ... KILL? ... KITTEN, XOX. I WILL CALL YOU "DARK KATIE" . I FIND THIS EXTREMELY INTERESTING. I HOPE YOU WILL SHARE IT WITH ME, AND NOBODY ELSE. THAT'S MEAN A LOT TO ME, PEANUT!

From here on in his perversions plunged downhill, to rock-bottom into an abyss of sexual depravity. Kicking off with:

> I LIKE SHOPPING FOR WOMENS' CLOTHES. I HAVE A LOT OF OUTFITS – AND SHOES TO WEAR, THAT I'D REALLY LIKE-REALLY-REALLY LIKE TO SEE YOU IN ... CAN YOU CUT OFF A LOCK OF YOUR HAIR ... 10-15 STRANDS UP ABOUT 2 INCHES FROM YOUR HAIR LINE AT THE NAPE OF YOUR NECK ... BUT I'M 'DISAPPOINTED', BECAUSE I THINK THAT YOUR LITTLE PUSSY IS STILL 'CHERRY' ... MY TITTIES ARE I THINK BIGGER THAN MY VIRGIN PUSSY KATS.

Former nurse Melanie McGuire, in contrast, stands almost atop so many others for she has oodles of wit and humour in spades. She can be blatantly flirtatious, calling me 'Christopher', 'Chris', 'Chris my darling' and 'my love', as suited her mood. She almost weaves a spell. One cannot help but like her because she can have oodles of charm and style, too.

SBI #00319833C McGUIRE, Melanie, corresponded for many months. She is enigmatic to a fault; even her handwriting seems to beguile the reader. Her penned words have a rhythmic sequence that flows easily onto the page with not a grammatical error to be found. One could say that her syntax is nigh-on perfect, unlike mine, so some of my critics say. So I was soon able to imagine – just from her correspondence – why men found this petite nurse so attractive. Scores of her female patients adored her too. And, as will soon become apparent, for 99.99 per cent of her life Melanie never put a step wrong. She wasn't a drinker and would never have failed a field sobriety test. But for 0.01 per cent of her life she went bad, and I mean ape-shit, flying well over *The Cuckoo's Nest* seriously bad!

For this once pixie-faced, 5-foot 3-inch, 121-pound mother of two killed and then chopped up her husband. The media dubbed her 'The Ice Queen' because she appeared so cold and emotionless throughout her entire trial proceedings. In her heyday, no one could have said that Melanie was unattractive. Today, however, after more than fifteen years behind bars, life has chewed on her.

There is an old saying that 'one should never judge a book by its cover'; similarly, 'all that glitters is not gold' and 'beauty is only skin deep'. You might apply all three to Melanie McGuire, in different ways. Let's take 'one should never judge a book by its cover' first.

She has been judged by some – such as newspapers local to her – to be one of the most notorious femmes fatales in the criminal history of New Jersey (the 'Garden State'). That is the cover of her life's narrative that we see at first blush today. But if we were to read into her history, perhaps we might discover a decent person, albeit one who has now become a lost soul. I will let my readers decide on this.

'All that glitters is not gold?' As mentioned, for the vast majority of her life she did glitter. Most of those who knew Melanie felt that she sparkled from within, from her heart even. We can't take this away from her either.

'Beauty is only skin deep?' Physically, Melanie McGuire modestly says, she had no outer beauty; her manner is self-effacing, but it was what lay beneath the surface that drew people to her. 'Little Melanie was a powerhouse of energy,' one of her former patients explained. 'She would do anything for us. She was so loving, sweet . . . made me feel like I was her sister.'

Shortly after her conviction on 23 April 2007 for killing her husband, Melanie cropped up on my radar. She had become a media sensation, with journalists and authors clamouring for her exclusive red-top story. If I wanted a piece of this better-baked all-American homicidal pie, I had several obstacles to overcome:

1. Melanie was incarcerated in New Jersey, 3,500 miles from my home on England's south coast.
2. She was in mega demand from writers and journos far closer to her than I would ever be.
3. There would be every chance that if I did arrange to visit her she would cancel the meeting at the last moment, leaving me and my film crew high and dry – as had happened while making a TV documentary with another incarcerated killer from the 'Garden State', the now deceased James Allen Paul, who committed three murders in New Jersey, Vermont and Connecticut:

> Yeah, so what. I did agree for you to interview me. Now I've changed my mind. So fuckkk off.
>
> James Allen Paul: to the author,
> Trenton State Prison, New Jersey

Actually, I did get to meet James Paul for a moment. We had been filming a TV documentary with my late, dear friend, Connecticut state homicide detective Mike Malchik – the lead cop in both the Michael Bruce Ross and James Paul serial killings. I had hauled my film crew all the way to Trenton (now New Jersey State Prison). They parked up outside while I went inside to sit down on the right side of a bullet-proof glass screen, only for this pasty-faced serial killer to tell me to 'Fuckkk *off!*'

Absolutely no class at all. We made the programme without him.

As for Melanie McGuire? Finding myself in a bit of a quandary about the distance involved, and also considering that I am related to Scrooge, I decided that some thinking time was needed. So, after dinner I put on my Sherlock Holmes houndstooth deerstalker, lit my calabash pipe, sat back in my captain's chair, took a swig of Sherlock's favourite tipple – the 'Gloria Scott' port – and did what they call 'musing' before the shrill ring of my telephone rudely brought me to sensibility.

Okay, I made all of that up, but I did have what some people call a 'eureka moment'. If I were to even stand a chance of catching and landing this little fish, I needed the right bait. I did a little bit of research and discovered that not only did she try to feed her murdered husband to some bigger fishes (in that she chucked the suitcase containing his dismembered body into the Chesapeake Bay), she was well educated. In point of fact,

Melanie had graduated from Middleton High School South in the top 50 per cent of her class. She went to Rutgers University, graduating with a bachelor's degree in 'statistics' as she called her double major in mathematics and psychology, then went on to get a nursing diploma. This was when the dime dropped. Unlike James Paul, 'Our Mel' would appreciate a classy approach, so it was time to do what some university students do – as in carry out some thorough preparation.

Being the true-blue parsimonious tightwad that I am, I nipped down to my local stationers, where I asked the young assistant to remove three sheets of Conqueror laid cream paper from an unopened ream, and place them in a brown paper bag along with a matching envelope and a stick of red sealing wax. Then, with a, 'May I have a receipt please ... it's for tax purposes, you know,' I hastened out to flash my bus pass for the ride home. Back at my PC, I typed a short letter to Melanie, leaving her name and my signature to be added in ink. I smugly admired my handiwork. All that remained was to impress my family seal ('D') in wax below my signature, include photocopies of several of my book covers, along with a generous spray of Chanel 'Égoïste', and an airmail stamp. Into the post it went – and I didn't expect a reply until hell froze over.

As my grandfather, the very late solicitor Oscar Berry Tompkins, used to say while peering over his half-moon spectacles and nodding a head of the finest silvery spun hair: 'You'll learn, my boy, that you can wait ages for a bus then half a dozen all come along at once.' He was a tightwad too: tight-fistedness runs throughout our familial DNA. Oscar defended William Henry Kennedy, who, in 1927, with accomplice Frederick Guy Brown, shot to death a PC 489 George William

Gutteridge at Stapleford Abbotts in Essex. His client was hanged, but he was right about the buses. I didn't have to wait too long for Melanie to reply and soon her letters began popping through my letter box, often several at the same time.

'Glancing at a piece of handwriting for the first time is rather like meeting someone new,' writes Margaret Gullan-Whur, in *Discover Graphology: A Straightforward and Practical Guide to Handwriting Analysis*. She adds: 'We are bound to be aware of a unique essence: we receive impressions which, because they are unconcerned with reason or cause, evaporate quickly on further acquaintance.' Here, specifically with regard to Melanie McGuire, Gullan-Whur hits the nail right on the head. If one is *really* interested in graphology, then her book is a must-read. Intriguingly, she advises at first we should consider handwriting as a picture, and ask ourselves: 'Are its component parts well-blended, or do some aspects seem harshly exaggerated [...] is there one movement which regularly spoils the flow? Is the penmanship well-proportioned and clear, or is there a sudden contraflow testifying to a lack of harmony within the mind of the writer? Is it gracefully simple or fussily embellished?'

Then comes into play grammar. 'Is the person educated or lacking a fundamental grasp of English?' Margaret asks. Think back to when we studied a few of the letters from Phillip Jablonski. Aside from his totally screwed-up script, we most certainly witnessed a mentally disturbed mind using a pen. This is the lack of harmony that Margaret alludes to. There are regular moments where Jablonski spoils the flow, almost as if he is two characters, and this is confirmed by the psychiatric assessments he underwent – the shocking results of which were treated by doctors in an offhand way, resulting in them more or less giving

Jablonski a licence to kill. Yes, Phil was schizophrenic, but pathologically he was much more than that, was he not? To me, he brings to mind the image of a boxer in a ring fighting himself, something all too evident in his writings.

Not so with Melanie Lyn McGuire. Her handwriting seems completely at odds with the horrendous nature of her crime; that said, her letters show no genuine regard for her children, who adored their dad. The other thing worthy of note is that she avoided like a pinprick of sarin any discussion about the crime for which she received a natural-life prison term. When I eventually pressed her on the subject, she stopped writing to me altogether. This rejection may have been because at that time she was still pleading her innocence and appealing her sentence, even though the evidence against her was overwhelming. Perhaps she was (indeed, is) living in a state of pathological denial.

Melanie's first letter to me was dated 26 January 2008:

Dear Christopher.

I apologize for not responding to your first letter. While I am indeed interested in telling my story and the events totally, and in depth, to a reputable news outlet, I am currently involved in appealing my conviction and sentence. As a result, I must defer to my appellate counsel and their advice regarding the matter.

At this time we are having some difficulty with our telephone communications, and I've not been able to contact them directly. I realize that contacting me via conventional mail is less than expedient – as a result, I'd like to provide you with the contact information of one of my closest friends, Allison Li Calsi, as I speak to her daily, and she might function as an intermediary.

Thank you for contacting me – again, my apologies for not responding sooner.

Warm regards

Melanie McGuire.

As I am sure the reader will agree, a polite, measured letter, that was too. So I replied, pointing out that I was *not* a 'news outlet' – just a minor italic slap from me to put her in her place, so to speak.

Considering Melanie's alleged reluctance to say very much because of her upcoming appeal, she replied much faster (indeed, by return of post) than I'd anticipated. Dated 8 February 2008, here's her next letter, at once proving that a splash of Chanel 'Égoïste' can work a treat – with the ladies only, I stress!

Dear Chris.

Thanks so much for your letter. I continue to be amazed that your correspondence seems to find me with greater expediency than that of my own family, who live a mere few hours away. I also smiled when I read your comment (and the postman's) about my penmanship, imagining the conversation: ('... yes, but this incarcerant can write'). I should warn you that I have what many consider a fairly caustic sense of humor – it's proven itself to be a good coping mechanism, especially in my current environment.

You needn't have pondered my astrological affiliation – my birthdate is on my DOC 'factsheet' where you

> obtained my contact information ☺. I was born Melanie Lyn Slate on 8 October 1972. My parents divorced when I was 5. My mother remarried shortly thereafter, to a gentleman named Michael Cappasaro, and I have a younger brother called Christopher. My biological father and I had sporadic contact before he died on 26 Feb 1987.

Melanie then went on to explain that having graduated in 1994, she waited tables, during which she met another waiter, William T. 'Bill' McGuire. 'I was attending the Rutgers School of Pharmacy at the time,' she writes, 'ironically housed in the same building as the Stats Dept.' She had been 'less enthusiastic about the major' she had chosen, even 'taking a number of psychological and educational courses', so at the age of twenty-two she had made the decision to enrol in the Charles E. Gregory School of Nursing in the autumn of 1994.

It is now that Melanie hit her stride. She tells that she excelled there, graduating, second in her class, in 1997. Not long after, she befriended all-American hunk James 'Jim' Finn, who would soon become a famous American football fullback playing for the Chicago Bears. To add some spice to her story she says: 'We had a bit of an on and off relationship.' I tentatively wrote back to ask Melanie what had attracted her to James Finn. In reply, she wrote: 'I am not the football type – being more of the conspiracy theory/science fiction type.'

Subliminally here, Melanie was giving us a clue to what would follow later, so take note of those words, then think about what is so often hidden between the lines of a letter and the thought-processing system – in her case her modus cogitandi, for here she is making a teeny-weeny slip of the tongue as will become apparent later. Football or not, she and Finn kept in touch – and he would become a state witness in her subsequent trial.

Melanie also told me that she was from the 'shore'. Seafood was her favourite, 'French cuisine the more the better and foie gras I can die for.' She also likes her books – certainly a better class of literature than that of the aforementioned Bobby Joe Long who was up to his neck in hard-core porn reading material:

> My favourite authors are: Stephen King; Janet Evanovich (selected works); P. G. Wodehouse; Martin Amis; Haruki Murakami; Hugh Laurie, and Matt Beaumont, he's so hilarious. I intend to read 'Duma Key' by Stephen King, 'The War against Cliché' by Amis, and 'The Gnostic Faustus' by Ramona Fraden [*sic*]. That's quite a few, I know.
>
> Alas, time for group therapy, so I'll close for now (and before, somewhere in my DC, my appellate attorney has a grand mal seizure). Let the healing begin (yes, that's sarcasm you smell). This should all be duplicative anyway, as I've channelled to your mailman all I wanted to say (the poor bastard).
>
> Love, Melanie.

Now you're talking, Melanie. (I'll vouch for Janet Evanovich; she's the bee's knees. Sir Pelham Grenville Wodehouse was the creator of 'Jeeves', the supreme 'gentleman's gentleman'. Ramona Fradon's book is way above my own head but I do get Hugh Laurie, as in *big time*. These are Melanie's words, not mine; Ramona Fradon is a graphic-novel artist.

To be totally honest with you, I was getting to the point where I started thinking: 'Why should I allow a damned good Agatha-type murder mystery get in the way of developing a lifelong, loving relationship with Melanie? Maybe Bill had gotten some well-deserved comeuppance?' Her correspondence came across as amusing, witty, well-read, with a *very* dry sense of humour, which is most refreshing in my line of work. I stress 'refreshing' because usually when trying to communicate with femmes fatales – perhaps a 'Black Widow' who has killed in quick succession three of her spouses by giving them drinks laced with antifreeze – I get something along the lines of: 'Before we start, how mucha yo's gonna pay me for my story. If not, yo go fuck yrseleves, an' wassat smell on the paper, it's stinking out my cell.'

> Melanie McGuire is just a powerhouse in a tiny petite little body. And she makes you feel like you're her only patient.
>
> Former fertility clinic patient on
> Melanie McGuire

> You felt that she was, you know, almost a girlfriend.
>
> Another former fertility patient on
> Melanie McGuire

While at nursing school, Melanie responded to an advertisement for ovum donors, and by the time she graduated, Melanie had undergone three such donations: 'treatment cycles which were anonymous at the St. Barnabas Medical Center', she wrote to me, adding, 'and in talking to the staff and head nurse there, they knew that my licensure exam wasn't far off, and they offered me a position as an ovum donor coordinator'.

Melanie tells us that she and Bill were by then an item (with Jim Finn being a fullback in the background so to speak), and it was Bill who encouraged her to accept the job offer. They became engaged in 1998, after which she had two more ovum donations – this time 'solely for research purposes'. The couple married on Sunday, 6 June 1999. She was twenty-seven, he was thirty-four. A week before the wedding, she learned that she was pregnant:

> I'd suffered a very early miscarriage about six months before that, I was thrilled but nervous. Later that year, the physician I worked with left St. Barnabas to form Reproduction Medicine Associates (RMA). I would eventually come to meet and work with Dr Bradley T. Miller there, and he still runs a successful practice in Morristown today.

And I'd put money on it that you are going to guess what happened next. Dr Miller was also an all-American hunk, and with three children, none of which proved an impediment, and he and Melanie soon indulging in some extra-marital bonking on the side. As for husband Bill, he was also having a bit, or even a few bits, on the side, too. Sadly, unbeknown to him he had less than five years left to live before becoming the contents of three brown suitcases that were *intended* to sink into the depths of the Chesapeake Bay – but oops-a-daisy, they floated.

During my correspondence with Melanie, and reflecting back on her formative years, I asked her whether she thought that the break-up of her parents' marriage when she was aged just five may have had any negative impact on her. She replied:

> I wouldn't necessarily say that my parents' divorce troubled me – I barely have a recollection of it, and I consider myself infinitely fortunate that my mother subsequently remarried to a wonderful man, who I truly consider to be my "real" father. However, I can and do acknowledge some pervasive abandonment issues – it would be disingenuous of me to say I wasn't affected by my natural father's absence (and occasional re-entry) into my life. I am reluctant to reflect on that and assign blame – I am an educated woman, and if it has power over me, it's because I allow it to.

At this point in our pen-pal relationship, it was becoming obvious that Melanie liked the attention of men. She liked her feathers stroked too – and who doesn't, I suppose? (She once wrote to me: 'Oh, I knew the Chanel immediately I opened your letter. It's my favorite men's cologne. You must be psychic.') So to reel her in just a tad further, I put it to her that she must be proud of her academic achievements. She responded in her typically humble fashion. Indeed, when I read what follows I wondered where, and at what point, she came up for air. She started with: 'Chris, dear Chris, my academic achievements are anything but interesting. You fascinate me. We could become soulmates. We could spend so much lovingly intelligent time, walking and talking about the finer things to be had from our lives,' ending with 'I must go now. It's lunch time. I wish I had a plane to catch.'

If Melanie had left it at that I would have been a happy man. But next came: 'but, I'll run through them if you like?'

'Oh, shit, here we go,' I mused once again. Throwing my bottle of 'Gloria Scott' port, calabash pipe and replica Sherlock Holmes deerstalker into a bin and replacing them with a twelve pack of Carlsberg Special Brew, two hundred Philippine rip-off Marlboro Reds and a pink papier-mâché hat that I'd kept from the previous Christmas, in a waste not, want not, sort of way. So here is the *exact* wording of what Melanie wrote to me:

> When I was in the second grade, someone thought it would be helpful to test my IQ. As a result I was placed into what was called a 'Gifted & Talented' programme (how politically incorrect – smile).
>
> [...] I was in this programme throughout grammar/ middle/high school, where I excelled even in a fairly competitive school system [...] I was amazing at stats, was a member of both the Spanish Honor Society and the National Honor Society and a drama club [...]
>
> [...] I was selected as an Edward Bloustein Distinguished Scholar intended to recognise the highest achieving graduating, high school students in or from New Jersey and to reward them with awards that are granted regardless of need [...]
>
> [...] then I went to Rutgers University, and got a 1.0 on the GPA scale my first semester to the acute distress of my parents. I discovered unchecked freedom – and parties [...]
>
> [...] I think I pulled a 3.0 or better each semester after that: Statistics major, Psyche minor, Religion Mini,

> but my initial fall from academic grace doomed me to mediocrity. I decided in my senior year that I wanted to pursue nursing, but I didn't have the credentials to switch majors at this point, so I completed my BA first at my parents' insistence.

She did not explain, however, how she killed and dismembered Bill, nor did she mention the three suitcases that she packed him into and threw into the Chesapeake Bay. Did I not explain from the outset of this book that corresponding with killers can be like wading through molasses?

In 2002, Melanie was pregnant; her second son would be William 'Bill' McGuire Jr. Meanwhile, her relationship with Dr Miller had evolved from two co-workers who flirted into a full-on *Sunday Sport*-type of affair. Indeed, Bradley would later tell the trial court that he bought two pre-paid cell phones for them to communicate and that they called each other ten to twenty times a day, 'even when we worked together' – although in different treatment rooms, we hope!

Now giving it the full *Fifty Shades of Grey* tin of beans, Nurse Melanie and Doctor Bradley fell deeply in love and started planning on how to leave their respective spouses, or so she says. Then, dammit, in 2004, just when Melanie decided to move out of their deluxe apartment and divorce Bill, her totally in-the-dark husband had just closed a deal on a more upscale home with a big yard for the kids. Then, to thank him for his alleged loving devotion to their marriage, Melanie killed Bill in what would ultimately become a cause célèbre.

The state claimed that Melanie's motive for killing Bill was so that she could start a new life with her boss Dr Miller without a messy divorce. During the seven-week trial, prosecutors relied on evidence of the affair along with testimony from a forensic expert. The latter stated that the black garbage bags containing the victim's remains that were found inside the three suitcases bobbing around in the Chesapeake Bay were microscopically consistent in every respect with the bags, filled with Bill's clothing, that were later discovered with one of Melanie's friends after his death. Despite all of her wit, intelligence and cunning, she had failed rule no. 1 in the *Murderer's Handbook*: get rid of every single piece of physical evidence involved in *any way* with the crime.

> He's charismatic. Bill has a sense of humor, a lot of '*Saturday Night Live*' type sense of humour. [...] He could pick on you but make you feel good about it at the same time.
>
> Jon Rice: Bill McGuire's best friend

Jon Rice had known Bill since they'd met in the Navy during the 1980s. When Bill and Mel married in 1999, the Rices were happy to take the newlyweds with them on holiday to the Bahamas. Then, in 2004, Jon and Susan Rice picked up on the bizarre story of suitcases containing parts of a dismembered corpse turning up in the Chesapeake Bay. At the same time, they were also engrossed in another strange tale, one that concerned the McGuires.

The Rices had just heard about the beautiful new home the McGuires had bought in New Jersey. Yet a few days later, Melanie phoned the Rices to say that she and Bill had had a terrible argument about their dream home just hours after signing on the dotted line. Melanie told them that Bill had got physical with her and stormed out of their apartment. Thus she broke rule no. 2 in the mythical *Murderer's Handbook*: attempting to transfer blame while not considering what the Rices might make of it. To them, Melanie's story simply did not add up. They knew that Bill loved his two sons, and had just signed up for a house with a spacious yard for them to play in. Jon was immediately suspicious. But Melanie insisted that he had left after hitting her and that she'd obtained a restraining order in case Bill slunk back.

In an effort to add weight to her phoney story she told a family court judge: '[Bill] told me I was stupid, and slapped me, uh.' The judge asked: 'Where did he slap you, ma'am?' Melanie replied: 'In the face.' The judge then asked a pointed question: 'Has your husband got a firearm or is there a gun in the house?' Melanie replied: 'No, ma'am,' to which the judge responded: 'That's fine. You are safe here.' However, what does not add up is the fact that immediately after the alleged assault, Melanie had failed to make an official complaint to the police, an issue that the judge completely overlooked. Moreover, she lied to the judge about that firearm, because just a few days earlier she had bought a gun. Mel loved tales of duplicity and deception, as suggested by her letters, but failed to differentiate between tales and realism.

While the Rices were unconvinced by Melanie's allegations, others were not. Speaking to NBC News in 2007, Melanie's friend Selene Trevizas, who had known Melanie for many years, said of Bill, 'I don't think he was a good husband . . . I don't think he was a great father.'

For years, she said, she'd thought that Bill was stressed by all his responsibilities. The good-natured banter between them had degenerated into verbal abuse from Bill. 'She was no longer fighting back. The arguing – it wasn't back and forth. It was more one-sided. She was just tired.'

Soon enough, people were starting to ask where Bill was. Selene and another friend, Allison LiCalsi, told NBC that Melanie had told them that Bill was a heavy gambler – so might he have gone to glitzy Atlantic City, lost a fortune he didn't have, got involved with the wrong people? 'Well, she knew that Atlantic City had always been a monkey on his back,' Allison said. 'But she also wasn't sure the extent of what he was involved with.'

The Rices thought it quite possible that their missing friend was in Atlantic City, perhaps gambling in the many casinos. When speaking to NBC News, they later mentioned that he used to go on trips to Atlantic City, and spoke of one occasion when he treated the Rices to a weekend there, and still returned home several thousand dollars better off. They were adamant, however, that Bill did *not* have a gambling problem or hang about with unsavoury characters. His chosen game, Jon explained to NBC News, was blackjack, and he was good at it.

With Bill now missing, the Rices began telephoning hotels in Atlantic City to see if they could get any information about his movements. As time went on with no news of Bill, they became more concerned. They did not immediately connect his disappearance with the strange story that was on the news – the one about the three suitcases found bobbing around in the Chesapeake Bay with parts of an unidentified man inside them. But one day Susan's attention was drawn to the television news and heard the reporter saying that the police had released a sketch of the dead male. 'I looked at the picture, and something about the military-style haircut looked familiar, so I compared it to a photo I had of Bill,' she recalled. 'I just remember that my heart just sank to my stomach.' She told Jon and they rang the Virginia Beach police.

When corresponding at length with convicted killers behind bars, I've noticed that over time they become trapped in their own way of thinking – more often than not they inadvertently reveal insights into their state of mind through slips of the tongue, or indeed in what they write. Over time, patterns of conscious or subconscious thought processing emerge. Let's focus on the modus cogitandi once more.

To all intents and purposes, the way we work and live our lives is inextricably bound by our modus cogitandi – it is human nature. Indeed, all animals desire to live within the confines of what makes them feel comfortable. Step out of our comfort zone and life becomes more uncertain – we are never truly happy when doubt enters our cosy lives. Everything we do, say or write, whether it's MO or MV, must, to my mind, spring forth from MC. Would you disagree? In that light, modus cogitandi is an issue that we should keep in mind as we read the letters penned by these evil people.

Let's return to Melanie's expounding on her academic achievement to the point of tedium. By relating that she is a dedicated bookworm of sorts, one fascinated with conspiracy theories, I suggest that she is subconsciously telling us – dressed up with a seasoning of pathos – just how clever she is. Her psychopathology does not permit otherwise, for she is trapped within her own learning-from-experiences. In reading the works of great storytellers, she becomes one of them in her own fantasy-driven world, a place where *everything* is possible for an educated woman like her – conspiracy theories into the bargain, for criminal psychopaths are the greatest control freaks of all. Along with zero feelings of guilt and exhibiting zero remorse, Melanie's true, manipulating mind will be revealed at the end of this chapter – and also her inability to be realistic – so I hope you'll enjoy every bit of the big reveal.

In a letter, Melanie writes:

> Did I have a 'bad' marriage? Yes. Was my husband abusive, be it emotionally, and/or physically? Yes. But I am responsible for staying and bending to his will on issues that I should have remained firm on. So, while I think things like a battered woman's syndrome do, indeed, exist and are appropriate affirmative defenses in some cases, I do place some degree of accountability on the 'victim', albeit limited. In my criminal case, I never waged an affirmative defense – my defense was always that of actual innocence.

That all seems very plausible, does it not? Although Melanie freely admits that her marriage was far from happy, suggesting elsewhere that 'Bill had a few problems – drink, gambling, and women on occasions', she was also quick to point out: 'I am not entitled to any righteous indignation about this as I, too, was unfaithful.'

If one were to take on its face what Melanie says as being sensitive and totally honest – which she wants us to believe – then one might sense that a *crime passionnel* might have taken place;

that in the heat of the moment, while trying to defend herself from an abusive husband, she had killed him. This could have been construed as second-degree homicide, or manslaughter as we have it in the UK. And, *had* this been the case and *had* she called the police with the body still in situ, then a state's attorney would have been extremely hard-pressed to charge her with premeditated murder. However, by now Melanie had already sunk her own boat with indirect admissions of guilt along with the three suitcases containing her husband that had remained floating on the water's surface, rather than obligingly sinking. It would become only a matter of time before motive, coupled with premeditation to commit murder most foul, was established. Attorneys for Melanie McGuire would later aggressively contest these allegations, arguing that their client had no motive to kill her husband – a man whom, they claimed, was involved in an extramarital relationship too.

And didn't Melanie say that she loved conspiracy theories?

So what had happened to Bill McGuire? He was last seen alive by Melanie on Thursday, 29 April 2004 – the day the couple had closed the sale on a $500,000 up-market house in Asbury, Warren County. Shortly after he disappeared, and over a period of days, three suitcases were found bobbing around in the Chesapeake Bay. Shock Stephen King horror: on opening, they revealed black plastic refuse bags containing a dismembered Mr McGuire.

In a case (excuse the pun) built entirely on circumstantial evidence, prosecutors theorised that Mrs McGuire had served her husband a celebratory glass of wine spiked with a sedative, then shot him to death – there were two bullet holes in him, after all. In a previous phone conversation with a friend, she had let slip that she had purchased the gun just two days before her husband disappeared. And of course, when she'd applied for a phoney restraining order she told the judge that the couple did *not* possess a firearm. Oh, Melanie, you really should have superglued your lips on that issue, as in when to speak and not to speak!

Police initially believed that Melanie had cut Bill up into four pieces in the shower using a saw. This caused a problem because investigators were unable – even using all the forensic CSI techniques available to modern law enforcement – to link the man's murder to his home in any way whatsoever. In her defence, Melanie claimed that the last she saw of her husband was on the morning of 29 April, after an argument over their new home. She said he drove off in his car and that that was the last she ever saw of him. At her subsequent trial, the defence suggested that his death may have been related to gambling debts. A letter (*see* later) allegedly written by a mobster from a major organised crime family in New Jersey had been sent to the DA; in it, the writer claimed that Bill McGuire owed a $90,000 debt to a Mafia family. This is why he was fed to the fishes in the true Cosa Nostra style, so the letter claimed.

In my opinion, she's a lousy actress.

Virginia Beach Detective Ray Pickell
(sometimes spelt 'Picalle') on Melanie McGuire

Now that the detective was able to confirm the identity of the dismembered body, he could try to find out who had so much wanted the man dead and had gone to so much effort to cover their tracks – a bit like covering over cracks with wallpaper which, when peeled off, reveals the flaws beneath.

Cherchez la femme: as in all such investigations the officer was particularly interested in speaking to the victim's wife, Melanie McGuire, for she was, he felt, best placed to help him. She must surely be able to tell him something that would give him a clue, he hoped.

He quickly dismissed Melanie's notion that Bill had been the victim of a gangland hit. From what the Rices said, Bill McGuire knew what he was doing and incurred no debts, or so they thought, so any suggestion of a large, unpaid gambling debt was ruled out. Pickell was more interested in the body itself: the almost surgical dissection of Bill's body was plainly the work of someone with medical knowledge, and this, the cop reckoned, was significant. What's more, it turned out that a blanket found in one of the suitcases was from a hospital; Pickell did some digging and discovered that Melanie was a nurse. 'She works at a doctor's office and those types of blankets were being supplied [there]?' Pickell asked NBC, rhetorically. 'Yeah, there's a lot of suspicion there.'

A week later, the sleuth was again interviewing the 'Black Widow', this time in her attorney's office with not just one lawyer present but two. The detective found it strange that she would need two lawyers present when all he wanted was to ask a few simple questions such as 'Did you ever own any brown matching luggage, which is now missing?'

In a knee-jerk reaction, she bluntly replied, 'No!' But to throw the detective off the scent, she volunteered that her husband's car might be in Atlantic City, New Jersey, and soon after that's just where police found Bill's blue 2002 Nissan Maxima. After

CSI examined the vehicle, they handed over to Detective Pickell a phial of white liquid – it was chloral hydrate – found with a syringe in the glove box. These items, along with the blanket, were significant finds. Chloral hydrate is a 'hypnotic', used among other things as a sedative prescribed in the short-term treatment of insomnia to help one fall asleep and stay asleep for a proper rest. When taken with any form of alcohol, this can lead to decreased mental and motor function. Symptoms may include excess sedation, confusion, loss of coordination and consciousness. Knock back a glass or two of wine spiked with this stuff and within twenty minutes one is living in the land of many, many fairies.

Police now searched the McGuires' home. It was spotless – and unfurnished, as Melanie had now vacated. As for Bill's clothing, Melanie told Pickell that she had, perhaps with somewhat indecent haste, passed them on to a friend. Pickell soon found them packed in black plastic bags identical to those that contained Bill's dismembered corpse.

As for the suitcase: the day after her interview in her attorney's office she told the detective that she and Bill *had*, after all, owned a matching three-piece set of brown Kenneth Cole luggage. 'I showed her a picture of one piece of luggage that was recovered from the Chesapeake Bay,' Pickell told NBC. 'And she identified that as the family luggage.'

But despite everything, there was no watertight evidence to pin Bill's death on his wife. The only thing Pickell felt sure about was that Bill had been murdered in New Jersey, not Virginia. So he opted to kick the can down the road. It was now someone else's problem, some other law enforcement's jurisdiction, to solve, to wit: New Jersey.

At the end of the day it's a horrible, gruesome murder.

Detective David Dalrymple,
New Jersey State Police

Dalrymple was the lead investigator in New Jersey, and opted to start with a different line of enquiry. He searched gun registration records and popped into gun shops, in the hope of picking up a trace of someone who knew Bill and had purchased a firearm. Bingo. He discovered that Melanie had bought a .38-calibre handgun on 6 April, just days before the murder. There was more to come. Police tracked down James Finn, the former on-and-off again boyfriend of Melanie's, who told them she'd been in touch to say she was worried about Bill's deteriorating state of mind and wanted advice on buying a firearm. Finn, a gun enthusiast, had informed her that she could get one within twenty-four hours from the neighbouring state of Pennsylvania. The cops got Finn to call Melanie and taped the conversation. Here is a short extract of that recording:

> Finn: Throw me a bone. Where's the gun?
> Melanie: The gun was in the lockbox when [Bill] first left … I put it into the storage unit … Of course, I went later and looked and it's not in there.

Which, of course, worked out well for her: no one could run forensic tests on a missing firearm. But hadn't she told the family court judge that the couple didn't have a gun? Indeed she had, so she was lying again, this time to James Finn, and inadvertently also to the cops listening in.

So what was the possible motive for killing her husband? In the course of their enquiries, the police contacted Dr Bradley Miller, Melanie's boss at the RMA fertility clinic. This turned out to be more informative than they could have hoped as they learned that Miller and Melanie had been conducting an affair for three years. And the doctor told the cops a lot more; relating an unconvincing story that Melanie had told him about how after the row with Bill, and her getting the restraining order against him, she had driven all the way to Atlantic City, where she had somehow managed to find his car and, out of vindictiveness, moved it to the out-of-the-way motel's car park. 'A security camera may have caught me doing it,' she told Miller. Tired out, Melanie said, she had taken a taxi home, and then, the next day, had taken another back to Atlantic City to fetch her own car, she said, and it was all smoke-blowing, all lie after lie, so now a sceptical Dalrymple checked with all the local cab companies and not one of them had a record of taxi rides to and/or from Atlantic City, a long journey that would have cost hundreds of dollars. Besides, if she was so exhausted, why didn't she simply book into an Atlantic City hotel that night? It just didn't add up. Melanie had also told Dr Miller another unconvincing story – that she had, coincidentally, happened to have been shopping for furniture in Delaware – which is not far from Chesapeake Bay – the day before the first suitcase was found.

Detective Dalrymple persuaded Miller to confront his lover in another secretly wired conversation, as reported by NBC News:

Dr Miller: The trip to Delaware. They [the police] want to know what you were going there for and what furniture stores you were looking for there and seem to believe that you went with your father.

McGuire: There was nobody else in that fucking car with me ... I think that they're ... when it comes to, like, the mythical second person. I think they're talking shit.

Dr Miller: I think they're either gonna come down on me or come down on your father. That it was, you know, the one that helped you do the murder.

Circumstantial though it was, the evidence looked damning: an affair; a string of lies; indirect admissions of guilt; missing gun; rubbish bags; unlikely trips; implausible explanations; wadcutter bullets, a syringe, a phial containing traces of chloral hydrate and a hospital blanket. What exactly did it all add up to? Would it all end with an arrest?

Let's start with the .38-calibre special. She had bought this handgun just two days before Bill's murder. He was shot by a firearm – once in the head, once in the body with wadcutter bullets – and the gun, according to Melanie, had conveniently gone missing from a locked storage locker *after* Bill had allegedly driven away from their home. She had told friends about the pistol after Bill's death; even then she shifted stories, saying that it was actually Bill who wanted the gun. Hadn't she told Finn that she wanted it for her *own* protection against her husband?

Forensic scientist Tom Lesniak carefully examined the McGuires' apartment and its few contents (for Melanie had moved out with her children) and also the rubbish bags that Melanie had with undue haste used to dispose of Bill's clothing. On examination, the forensic team's conclusion was that all the bags, those used for Bill's clothing and those the body parts were found in, were manufactured on the same production line *and* on the same extrusion run. Most suspicious, however, was what the forensics team did *not* find in their rigorous search of the apartment. It was dust-free, there was not a hair, no trace of blood or minuscule particle of skin – indeed no DNA material whatsoever – nothing at all to suggest that the McGuires, or, come to that, any person, had ever lived there before the McGuires' visits to the property and after it had been vacated. The obvious conclusion would be that the apartment, known to have been occupied by people until recently, must have been *very* thoroughly cleaned – a conclusion supported by a witness who stated that when she went round to the apartment there was a very strong smell of cleaning fluids and bleach.

'Who scrubs a bathroom wall when they're leaving an apartment?' the prosecutor, Patricia Prezioso, asked the jury, a question that she could have more forcibly put to them, for after all was said and done: wasn't Mrs McGuire a nurse who was an expert at cleanliness and hygiene, and this being the case she would be 'forensically aware'.

Melanie, however, was not out of the woods: more concrete evidence was found during the meticulous forensic search of Bill's car. Sifting their way through the particles of dust and bits vacuumed up, Tom Lesniak and his forensics team found microscopic traces 'that to me look[ed] like it could be possibly human tissue,' said Lesniak, as reported by NBC News. DNA testing showed them to be from Bill McGuire; and the medical examiner identified the particles as skin with associated fibrous connective tissue – and therefore from deep layers of the skin which would not normally be shed by a live human being.

This was a very significant find. The reader will remember that Melanie had already admitted moving the Nissan to the car park at the Flamingo motel that night. Prosecutor Prezioso said that it all added up. Melanie had picked up traces of Bill's tissue on the soles of her shoes before she had cleaned up and, that the particles had been transferred to his car when she had driven it to Atlantic City.

At the trial a computer expert told the jury about incriminating internet searches that had been made during the days before Bill's death. 'The search history, which was extensive, included searches for such items or topics as 'undetectable poisons', 'state gun laws', 'instant poison', 'fatal insulin doses', 'instant undetectable poisons', 'how to commit murder', 'chloral hydrate', 'neuromuscular blocking agents', 'sedatives' and 'Nembutal', *and* a local Walgreens (a major American pharmacy store chain). Chloral hydrate – a powerful but uncommon sedative – was of particular interest to the police because, as mentioned earlier, a phial of the stuff was found in Bill's car. Moreover, the Google searches led police to a branch of Walgreens and a prescription for chloral hydrate in the name of an RMA patient in the clinic where Melanie worked. It had been filled at the pharmacy just a mile from the day care centre where Melanie dropped off and picked up her children on 28 April.

With the noose tightening around her neck, the prosecutor pointed out that Melanie had access to the prescription pad and would certainly have in the past written out prescriptions for her boss, and sometimes signed them on his behalf. The prescription in question featured the signature of Dr Bradley Miller – Melanie's boss and lover. He was also the state's star witness. Under examination:

Prezioso: Sir, did you write that prescription?

Dr Miller: No, I did not.

Prezioso: Are you familiar with the handwriting on those two prescriptions?

Dr Miller: Yes.

Prezioso: And whose handwriting do you believe it to be?

Dr Miller: It appears to be Melanie's.

Melanie McGuire glared at her former lover. Her face crumpled up and the corners of her mouth dropped. Despite the fact that she had obviously forged Miller's signature on a prescription for chloral hydrate, in a letter to me this devious woman wrote: 'Bradley betrayed me. There is no decency in him at all.'

But the jury must have been privately asking themselves what had motivated the defendant to commit such a brutal, calculated crime. The answer was not long in coming.

In his testimony, Dr Miller told the court that he and Melanie had spoken of getting married and having children in the future but – possibly because Melanie was afraid that if she filed for divorce Bill would take their two sons and 'disappear' with them – they did not have immediate plans to divorce their spouses. Future plans, the prosecutor insinuated, that Melanie felt would never come true while Bill was still alive, at least.

Despite a spirited defence that revealed a few snags in the state's case, especially regarding the computer searches and the black plastic garbage bags, after deliberating for four days the jury foreperson announced that they had reached a unanimous verdict. McGuire was guilty of six of the ten counts. She was sentenced to two life sentences plus ten years for desecration of human remains and five for perjury. Her later appeals were unsuccessful, so she will die behind bars; most likely ruing the day she hadn't gone down the second-degree route, that she had shot Bill in self-defence, afterwards panicking and stupidly disposing of the body in the manner that she had.

The question we might now ask ourselves is: does Melanie Lyn McGuire really deserve to be dubbed 'The Ice Queen'? I reiterate: for the vast majority of her life – all but a week of it – she was a dedicated nurse who cared passionately about her patients and who wanted to bring children into this world. No one could fault her for any of that.

Melanie was unhappy in her marriage. As we have read from her letters, she admits that she should have left Bill way back. I also sense that here we find a well-educated young woman who was seeking the perfect husband – a stable professional man, whom she finally found in Dr Miller. Had she played it more sensibly, left Bill much earlier and played things with a straight legal bat, then that would have been the right thing to do. What would have been better: a messy divorce or a natural-life prison term?

It doesn't bode well to speak ill of the dead, but two issues have come to my mind over the course of this chapter. The first being that while a couple's relationship might seem all rosy to outsiders, one usually never knows what marital tensions exist behind shuttered windows and closed doors.

> Every failure teaches a man something, to wit, that he will probably fail again next time.
>
> H.L. Mencken: *A Little Book in C Major*, 1916

On Bill's gambling? Several of his friends were contradictory – one minute saying that Bill was not addicted to gambling then saying that he was a fanatic at blackjack; a 'high-roller' who fluttered with sometimes as much as $10,000 during a trip to Atlantic City, where he was considered a favoured client to the degree he gambled to such an extent he was awarded 'comp points' by his favourite casino with free perks thrown in. It would be right to acknowledge that he did win big *sometimes*, but we have no idea of his losses either for we all know gambling is a mug's game.

Whether or not Bill McGuire was a 'compulsive gambler' we will never know. In her letters to me, Melanie McGuire doesn't really touch on the subject. They were not a wealthy family by a long chalk and more than a family's financial health is at stake when gambling problems enter the picture. I know from my own research that Bill McGuire was ducking and diving, trying all sorts of shady business schemes and scams to make an extra buck. More to the point, thousands of gamblers live in a fantasy world, always dreaming of hitting the jackpot while losing their shirts at the same time, all of which can cause much domestic stress. So I believe Melanie when she claims that Bill was becoming more agitated and paranoid by the week. Perhaps some physical violence came into play. Melanie says that she was not sure if Bill knew about her affair with her boss, adding: 'very possibly he did'. She also claims that she placed her children first; that she adored her two young sons, that she wanted to raise them 'not losing a father at such early ages, just as I had done aged five'. But that is a somewhat strange statement to make when she did exactly the opposite in blowing away the kids' father; to deprive them of their dad and herself for the remainder of their lives.

Yes, she had been having an affair with the married Dr Miller. It would be fair to say that what both lacked in their respective homes *might* have been found in each other's arms. No terrible sin here, either – at least not unless one spends one's life living a puritanical existence, with one's nose stuffed into the Holy Book every minute of the day.

And what of Melanie McGuire's guilt? This chapter does not judge her, because a jury of her peers has already done so, with the state of New Jersey confirming that she committed a most heinous crime and without meaning to be crass here, a murder is a murder whichever way we judge such a crime. As is par for the homicidal course, this case bore all the hallmarks of sensationalism, which guaranteed headline-grabbing print. The petite 'Ice Queen' had shot her man, chopped up his body and thrown his remains off a bridge into the ice-cold Chesapeake Bay. It is almost too horrible to think about, is it not? However, as mentioned earlier, I believe that had Melanie come clean from the outset – confessed that she had shot Bill after a violent argument, had bought the gun a few days beforehand because she sensed he was going to hurt her, that she had obtained the chloral hydrate to calm him down, make him sleep, but then panicked, killed him and disposed of the body as she did – then she would have received a lighter sentence. In so many ways, Melanie dug her own grave using a treacherous spade of her own making, so what does my reader make of that?

Her defence argued that within twenty seconds either Melanie *or* Bill could have searched the internet on their home computer for information on gambling in Atlantic City, followed by a search for poisons. C'mon guys and gals, we can plain as daylight see that any suggestion that Bill was looking up Atlantic City's gambling venues does not hold water. He'd have known them and the locale like the back of his hand. Furthermore, it makes far more sense that Melanie, having checked out gambling venues her husband might be frequenting in Atlantic City – perhaps with a view to taking his car and then moving it to a different venue – should also then look online for a drug she could use to knock her husband out.

There are said to be thousands of individuals who painstakingly plan the perfect murder. However, they fail – to their cost – to plan the perfect getaway, for the devil is in the details. Melanie McGuire was too careful but plumb-dumb stupid at the same time; lacking streetwise common sense, she left a trail of circumstantial clues, none of which would have pointed to her guilt if they had stood alone. Instead, she left a trail of links that formed a chain of evidence so strong that no one could ignore their significance. Cold-blooded premeditation to kill was writ large over each blood-splattered page of her testimony.

If we follow the State's theory, then Melanie drugged her husband senseless while he was celebrating the purchase of their dream home with a glass of wine while their two boys were asleep in their beds. The next morning, after dropping off the kids at school, she returned home, placed a pillow over her still-sleeping husband's head, took out the revolver, shot him dead and then cut him up. Somewhat unfortunately, however, all of that leaves us with some other questions. Where was the blood splatter, if indeed he was shot in their home or even in their garage? Perhaps a pillow might have stopped the blowback, who knows? Could her thorough scrubbing of the apartment really have left not a single clue? Did she shoot him someplace else? How did this tiny woman drag her large, deadweight husband, dead or alive, into his car? And where did she dismember the body? For my part, there are a whole set of questions one cannot pair with answers, and this, as I am sure you will agree, sums up the dreadful enigma that still surrounds Melanie Lyn McGuire.

Oh, what a tangled web we weave,
When first we practise to deceive!

Sir Walter Scott, *Marmion: A Tale of Flodden Field* (1808)

Letters from killers are the central raison d'être for this book's existence, so I leave you with a lengthy letter typed by Melanie McGuire in the guise of a mobster and received by the State's attorney while she was on bail. It purports to explain why Melanie could *not* have killed her husband, so enjoy it because it gives us a unique and rare insight into the mind of a devious and twisted woman weaving together truths, half-truths, downright lies and a whole mile of crap into a narrative that exposes her for who she truly is. We will also learn a lot more about the relationship between Melanie and Bill McGuire than she would ever say out loud, and this I am obliged to tell the reader was originally reproduced in my book *Talking with Serial Killers: Dead Men Walking*:

Mr Harvey,

Your office and the media have reflected on the life and the death of William T. McGuire, and you've made it obvious that you intend to prosecute his wife. You and the media have exalted him as a decent person and a victim. He was a victim, all right. Of his greed, his big ego, and his even bigger mouth. I first met McGuire because we knew a lot of the same people. He was friendly enough at first, and loved to talk about himself along with anything and everything else he could claim to know anything about. He talked about work. He talked about AC [Atlantic City]. He talked about a house. About Virginia. About his wife. His sister. His ex-wife. You couldn't shut the guy up, which was part of his own undoing.

McGuire bragged about his position at NJIT [New Jersey Institute of Technology]. Said he had the placed [*sic*] wired and that the boss man had no idea what he was up to, which is how I imagine he got out and got away as much as he did. He talked of his connections at the local and state level, in various departments of state. How they could and would play into his consulting business. He talked of corruption at the health departments, and how it was given a pretty face by NJIT. He bragged about he once worked two full time jobs, at NJIT and at a local health office, and how even doing that he still had enough time to get in all his side action [women] and get home without the wife being any wiser. He talked about all his scams at work, the anonymity the access to some of the technologies could give him, to do almost anything he wanted at work or outside of it. He talked about blackmailing some of the higher ups at the state level who were doling out grant work to people collecting unemployment. He seemed to be unfazed by the stink his confrontations could raise in the office, stating it was their own fault for putting themselves in a compromised position to begin with. He talked of overthrowing his boss at the college, and about overthrowing the state level boss with the help of a guy named Ray. Did your office bother to note any of that during their thorough investigation? I think not.

He also loved to gamble, loved to flash card. I'd see him in AC, and at some private games to [*sic*]. The funny part is that he was a pretty good player but his ego wouldn't let him lose. He won a lot, but when he lost, he lost big and chased the money as hard as he chased some of the tail [women] that hangs around those places. He blamed everyone when he lost, the house, the dealer, even his wife, if you can imagine that. I personally find your observation that his death could have nothing to do with gambling one of the most hilarious things you've said publicly. Have you ever BEEN to AC?

Don't believe me? Ask his wife about the Stakehouse in North Jersey, and about an unfortunate accident coming home from work there late one night. What he didn't tell her was that he wasn't working, and he had lost a bundle. I heard him talking about getting pulled over on top of it that night, and how it was her [Melanie's] fault. I laughed. You can't be serious, man. She takes that from you? That and more. She likes it, is what he said and that put me off. You want to screw around on your old lady? Fine. You want to gamble away the family nut? That's fine to [*sic*]. But saying she likes it and seeing that he believed it blew me away. No wonder she ended up in bed with some doctor. Of course, you could say it was her own fault for marrying him, more her fault for staying.

More laughter from me when you leaked to the papers that this doctor friend of his wife's turned 'state's evidence'. There was nothing that man could of [*sic*] said that would hurt her for the simple reason that she didn't kill him. So that either makes you a liar, or him a coward who makes up stories to save his own sorry skin. Either way. I guess she never learned her lesson about choosing men.

Also, if you haven't figured out yet that his sister knew more of what he was up to than what she ever let on, you have had your head further in the sand than I imagined. He talked about her a lot, and I think they had a weird relationship, those two [Bill and his sister]. The guys used to joke about it a lot. She [Bill's sister], did something with real estate – he bitched about paying for her license, and he got her to give him access to one of those agent only sites. He would plug away on there for days at a time, looking up houses, looking up tax records of people he knew. She [Bill's sister] had a husband who owned some kind of pharmacy, and he talked a lot about all the scams there, and cash to be had. But in the same breath he [Bill] would complain how selfish she was not to want to put her ass on the line, whatever that meant. I tuned out a lot after I figured out how he lacked a certain amount of follow through with some ideas. He shrugged it off, saying there are all kinds of strings that get set up around stuff like that. He wanted the cash, but didn't want to get his hands dirty where anyone could see, was more of what I thought. As for the other sister, I guess the apple didn't fall far. He played us a phone message she [Melanie] left him, laughing at what a crazy she was. The message had said she would sue him and he wouldn't get his house he was buying. Christmas must have been something at their house.

We kept McGuire close because he was good for certain things – obviously things you'll never find out about. But in time he developed a drug habit. He even tried dealing. Then he decided he wanted a piece [of the action] to [*sic*]. We privately agreed against putting one in his hands. He tried Camden, Trenton, even Newark, but his problem was that he looked like a cop. No surprise the wife bought it, even if she was a damn fool for not knowing better. He always complained about how stupid she had gotten. I even asked him, wasn't she stupid when you married her? He said no way, his first wife was stupid but good in bed. The second he said was a lousy lay, but pretty. He claimed she had been smart but let herself go to hell after having kids. Which is why he felt completely justified in sticking it in anything [women] that walked. Personally, I thought he was either gay or sexually bent. He said his wife was so stupid he come home high one night, and when she asked him why his eyes were blood shot he told her he had taken viagra [*sic*]. When she asked why he got pissed and told her even that couldn't help him get it up for her. Nice guy. My point being that Billy Mac [Bill McGuire] liked an altered state of mind. I'll bet you twice your pension that the toxicology report showed

> more than a little viagra [*sic*] How about [it] H? Do you believe yet that I'm more than some random psycho writing to harass you? If not, you will.

Pausing to take a breath, and perhaps have a cup of tea, we can see Melanie's vitriolic mind working at full speed here. Not only is she giving her husband a post-mortem shit storm thrashing, she is dumping all over the State's attorney at will.

There is no doubt in my mind that she was under immense stress, her once stable life falling around her like an upscale house of cards. With nobody willing to talk to her – closest friends shocked at what had happened to Bill, her doctor lover leaving dust in his wake like Road Runner in the *Looney Tunes* cartoon series – Melanie had become persona non grata, someone to be avoided at all and *any* cost.

This 'Mafia' letter is nothing more than an hysterical, conspiratorial rant, with Melanie letting off steam while in the drink. When I compare the lengthy correspondence she sent to me with this letter, if there were invisible subtext between the lines we would see Melanie McGuire's psychopathology as clear as if it were written bold with one of Donald Trump's Sharpies. Even more fascinating are the references here in which she deliberately belittles herself in the 'second person' just as she does in her 'first-person' letters penned to me. It is her way of trying to show that she has her own weaknesses; attempts to show that she is a fair-minded individual – a cunning ploy, indeed.

But, let's move back to the letter in hand. And here Melanie's conspiracy theories are given full rein, for it seems that Bill McGuire had *her* death in mind, not the other way around if one was to believe all that this wannabe 'made man' would have us believe:

> Here's a question for you, Mr Harvey. McGuire was talking about the life insurance he was going to get. A mill [million] on the wife. Two on him. He talked about Virginia, and how that was where he was going once he made his money here [New Jersey]. How the wife hated it. When I asked him how he was planning on convincing her to move, he smiled and said he would be rid of her by then. Did [it] dawn on you that Mrs McGuire, in her 'selfish' plot to kill her husband, didn't bother to wait for him to actually purchase the insurance? Oh, she got the boyfriend with money, she didn't need it. First, I don't know anybody who would pass on two mill, money or not. Second, even if she coaxed that boyfriend away from his happy home, how much do you think it would leave for her after he paid out his old lady? I'm telling you that I don't know what he meant when he said he'd be 'rid' of her by then, but I have a couple of thoughts. And two mill on him and one on her casts a little doubt on his motivation should anything tragic happen. Did any of you in the midst of your 'dogged detective work' even ask her about it? Or are you going to sit there with a straight face and tell me McGuire meant he wanted a divorce?

Enough already, Melanie. We have all cottoned on by now that you have lost the plot. Actually, Mel, the good doctor probably never had any intention of ever leaving his wife and three children. It was all pillow talk, Mel. He was putting you in the 'Promised Land', Melanie, just so he could give you a good bonking whenever he felt the need – in between treating patients, if needs must. Moreover, and as you have a literary bent, perhaps you might have acquainted yourself with this quote from American author, John Bytheway: 'Sometimes you have to go through the wilderness before you get to the Promised Land.' Precisely, Mel, and the correctional wilderness is *exactly* where you are right now. Oh, sorry, you were saying?

> Don't get me wrong. I'm not going for sainthood myself. But what got to us about him was that he eventually turned on everyone. He talked about going to the press about a lot of money the college spent on equipment for a terrorism database that no one bothered to use. He talked about getting 'rid' of his old lady. He talked about turning in his sister's husband to the pharmacy board. Even blood wasn't thicker than water with this guy. And he wouldn't shut up. Didn't matter if he liked you or didn't or even if he owed you. He feared no payback from anyone. I don't even think he wanted the piece out of fear. Not a guy like that. He wanted to intimidate people with it. What intimidated people more was his running mouth.

Hey, Melanie, or mafiosa John aka 'Teflon Don' Gotti, or 'Cadillac Frank', or 'Ice Pick Willie' from the New Jersey outfit, or whoever you are, put down that bottle of whatever you are drinking and focus. Pray tell us what the prosecutor *should* have done. Please?

> You shouldn't care that the wife bought a gun. You shouldn't care that the suitcases were hers. You shouldn't care that the garbage bags match. I'm telling you that you shouldn't care if there's a video footage of her smiling and waving from the docks of Virginia Beach. Know why? Obviously you don't, so I'll make it simple. And it's not because she couldn't physically have done what it took two – and at one point three men to do.

To do what, Mr Joseph 'Joe Bananas' Bonanno, 'cos you're certainly not a sidekick of Joseph 'Joey Brains' Ambrosino, are you? As you 'made guys' should know, 'Mel the Moll' pumped iron in a gym as well as pumping other chappies. A petite but a strong lass.

> It's because Billy Mac brought everything that was needed to do him, and more. Not on purpose of course, but it was easier than anyone could believe. And the fight with his old lady? Probably he saved her life leaving her that morning, even if all he was doing was looking to get the hell out of Dodge for a few days. I'm guessing you didn't find any of his cell phones – the ones that weren't traceable, anyway. Point is if it was necessary, if she was with him, she would have been done the same as him. Probably worse, if you catch my drift, even if she was a lousy lay like he said. She ended up helping us, but not in any way you or your dogged detectives think. Her bad luck was our good fortune. And Billy Mac left the door wide open.
>
> So why write this? Well, I can tell you now to abandon the print analysis, and even analysis of the type [of this

letter]. This will be photocopied and handled in a manner you couldn't trace even if you did your job. So it's not hurting me any. And I've got nothing for the wife, or against her. But I read about the kids. The father they're better off without, but they don't need a Ma on death row. So now it's up to you to figure it out. She can't help you much, but did you ever even ask her? I know, you think this is a hoax. Well, allow me to part with some facts that should finally convince you otherwise:

1. I'm taking the liberty of sending this to the media, in case you want to close your eyes to this same as you have everything else in this case.
2. I'm sending it to the wife's lawyer.
3. The way the articles read last year, it made it seem like his arms were cut off. They weren't.
4. He was wearing nothing but purple briefs when you found him.
5. Ever figure out where the weights came from?

NOW DO YOU BELIEVE ME????

I *don't* believe you, Melanie. Nor, dare I say, will a single one of my readers worldwide. If only you had been as forensically aware in the killing and dismemberment of 'Billy Mac' as you were in sending out an untraceable photocopy of the aforementioned letter to the DA, you'd be down at the shore right now enjoying helpings of your favourite foie gras. So, Melanie, I guess that we can now part company with a large au revoir, along with a seasoning of bon appétit. However, I challenge anyone to find similar correspondence sent to any prosecutor in history typed out by a Mafia mobster whose bear-paw writing skills might stretch to: 'Yeah boss, ya wanna me to go feed Anthony 'Big Tuna' Accardo to the fishes?'

As I said before, Melanie was an intellectually smart woman but she was *not* streetwise. She undertook a course of action – murder – which was evil, wrong . . . and stupid. Then she proceeded to dig herself in further and further with her fantastical lies and subterfuges, flailing in her tangle of deceit.

What a Novel Idea!

It's a good binding, you see, and I thought they'd be all good books . . . But it seems one mustn't judge by the outside. This is a puzzlin' world.

GEORGE ELIOT (MARY ANN EVANS),
THE MILL ON THE FLOSS (1860)

Taking a breather here; a short break from blood, guts and murder most foul and into what amounts to some trivia, as is my wont occasionally, 'don't judge a book by its cover' is the expression warning us that one should not judge the worth or value of something by its outward appearance alone and is one that appears in many guises – 'appearances can be deceptive', the many variants of the aphorism 'all that glitters is not gold', 'beauty is but skin deep'. Often in my books, on TV, or during lectures, I use a similar analogy with regard to the outward normality of the serial killers and mass-murderers whom I have interviewed. The different masks they wear to conceal the beasts sleeping and breathing deeply within. Moreover, my *Talking with Serial Killers: Stalkers* offers some terrifying examples of how we often misjudge these 'human books' by their socially acceptable covers.

With letters typed or handwritten, or any form of electronic correspondence, be they the inane tweets spewed out by sociopathic 'influencers', or an email from a business associate, or an actual handwritten letter from an old friend, most of the time we read and believe what is intended to be conveyed. As Margaret Gullan-Whur says in her aforementioned graphology study, glancing at a person's handwriting (or even a page of their typing) is a bit like meeting someone for the first time. Not until we have read more of their correspondence, or met the person several times, do we start to see their true character, good or otherwise, and form our own opinions about them.

With individuals such as those included in this book, we already know who they are and the grim reasons why they are in prison. So, in this regard we do know something about them from the get-go. Their correspondence tells us a little more, yet it is what they don't say, or refuse to say, that hopefully tells us a great deal more about that person's psychopathology.

Donald Trump's signature tells us what sort of man he is. What is the point of slamming his Sharpie signature across a page? What is he trying to prove, who is he trying to impress? We know a great deal about this man's over-inflated self-narrative up until the present date. Being the brash, unrepentant sociopath that he is, his signature echoes his mindset perfectly, and most graphologists agree that the overall significance of large writing, is that the writer *needs* or *demands space to protect himself*. Impulse stemming from pride, vanity, enthusiasm, dynamism, strong feelings or vigorous activity may cause this need – the need to protect a basically weak ego. Indeed, every time we see 'The Donald' his face is the colour of a Valencia orange and he didn't get that from sunbathing either. However, I betcha that once he takes his clothes off his skin reverts to the colour of plaster cast from neck down to his toes.

Without wishing to be as impertinent, as others are far more qualified to discuss the subject than myself, to me it seems as a general rule of thumb that very small writing hints at a shyness in character, while large writing denotes quite the opposite.

Here's another perspective. One cannot help but be stunned by the masterful oils painted by Richard Dadd, an English artist of the Victorian era. Dadd was noted for his depictions of fairies and otherworldly folk, depicted with an extraordinary (one might say obsessive) attention to detail. We admire the beauty of his creations yet never, *ever*, do we wonder from where his ideas came. At first glance, we would never know what made this superb painter's mind tick, and so would doubtless be shocked to learn that his mind was severely unbalanced, to the extent that he knifed his father (whom he believed to be Satan) to death, then escaped to France. There, while travelling to Paris, he tried to despatch a fellow passenger with a razor, however, and was swiftly subdued and taken into custody. He suffered from paranoid schizophrenia and died on 7 January 1886, aged sixty-eight, in the Broadmoor insane asylum, where he completed his most famous works. We behold the beauty of the artwork now brushed onto a once pristine white canvas, beauty being only skin deep – *as is the oil paint.*

Dadd was a man possessed by a dreadful insanity behind the scenes, and the same applies to another long-serving

Broadmoor patient, one William Chester Minor. While heavily sedated, and often chained to a wall, he became an important contributor to the *Oxford Dictionary*. Next time you thumb through it, look for the meaning of the word 'syndrome' and think of the Canadian comic-book creator and producer Blake Leibel, co-author of the graphic novel *Syndrome*, who was convicted of first-degree murder, aggravated mayhem and torture of his fiancée, Iana Kasian, in 2016. Kasian had given birth to their daughter only weeks before her murder. It was proved that Leibel used his graphic novel as a blueprint for the gruesome slaying, something described by prosecutors as 'a case of life imitating art'. It is believed that Kasian was kept alive while she suffered at least six hours of torture. Her body was then mutilated, and pieces of it were discovered in the trash. The novel that Leibel co-wrote featured depictions of bloodletting and when Kasian was found, nearly all of the blood had been drained from her organs.

Many of us have read at least one of Anne Perry's sixty novels, all the while totally unaware that she'd committed a terrible crime aged fifteen. In 1954, when she and her parents were living in New Zealand, she went by the name of Juliet Hulme. Her parents split up, and plans were made to send her to South Africa. Her best friend, Pauline Parker, wanted to come along, but her mother wouldn't allow it. A few days after Pauline was denied the opportunity to move, the two girls went on a walk down a trail with Parker's mother and bludgeoned her to death.

And I would be remiss in failing to mention William S. Burroughs, or María Carolina Geel, Krystian Bala or James Tiptree Jr (pen name of Alice Sheldon). If you have ever watched the true-crime Netflix docuseries *The Staircase*, then look up Michael Peterson. Then there is bank robber Albert Nussbaum, and E. Richard Johnson. And there are more – writers and creators, all of whom have taken the life of another human. For those who read their books, it can be hard to reconcile the storyteller and entertainer with the killer. However, the majority of writers do not kill, and the majority of killers do not write – as we have witnessed – very well at all.

Harvey 'The Hammer' Louis Carignan, aka 'The Want-Ad Killer'

I knew that she was going to falsely accuse me of rape, and as I tried to talk sense into her she jumped out of the car and bolted. Unintentionally, I picked up a tree limb and threw it at her. It hit her one time and she fell down dead. I hate people accusing me of rape when I have never raped any woman. She should have kept her mouth shut so it was her fault, not mine.

HARVEY LOUIS CARIGNAN: TO THE AUTHOR AT INTERVIEW

Author's note: I make no apology for including material about Carignan from my 2009 study of killers I have interviewed, now republished as *Talking with Serial Killers*. This chapter draws upon my previous published writings but used here in a different context; that of his letters to me and what was written, or not written, between the lines. The research I carried out at the time, and subsequently, remains valid.

Getting to the Minnesota Correctional Facility (aka MCF-Stillwater) took some doing. Especially if one is bringing in a TV documentary crew from London, then having to road-trip in a couple of Mitsubishi Shoguns across to snow-bound Minneapolis, stay for a few days interviewing cops, filming some POVs (points of view), then drive twenty-seven miles north-east up to MCF itself, tucked right up close and personal to the Wisconsin state line.

An industrial prison, MCF is the state's largest close-security institution for adult felons, with a population hovering around 1,320. I corresponded with one of its inmates, Harvey Carignan, for several years and finally interviewed him during a full-contact visit (i.e. unshackled) in March 1995. This was the first and only interview ever granted by 'The Hammer' since his arrest for multiple rape and homicide on 24 September 1974.

> The guy's the fuckin' Devil. They should have fried him years ago, period, an' they would have queued up to pull the switch. When he was dead, they should have driven a stake through his heart and buried him, digging him up a week later to ram another stake in, just to make sure he was fuckin' dead.
>
> Detective Russell J. Krueger, Chief Investigator
> on the Carignan case, Minneapolis PD:
> to the author at interview

Top tip: beware of bears wearing a cop's uniform because Russell Krueger, of Irish descent, is built like one and he's as mean as a grizzly whose home has just been destroyed by some lumberjacks. Then Russ added: 'And you're gonna film that

ARTHUR SHAWCROSS
91-B-0193
P.O. BOX AG
FALLSBURG, N.Y. 12733-0116
U.S.A.

Dear Christopher,

I will SEE you.

Sincerely
Arthur Shawcross

INTERVIEW CONSENT FORM

N.Y.S. DEPARTMENT OF CORRECTIONAL SERVICES

I ARTHUR J. SHAWCROSS · 91-B-0193 hereby grant permission to the
Inmate Name and Number

New York State Department of Correctional Services and CHRISTOPHER BERRY-DEE
Name of newspaper,
publication, radio/TV station
to make use of my name, comments, still or motion pictures, voice recordings and/or video tape of me for any legitimate purposes including publication in news media and for professional and institutional purposes.

Signature Arthur J. Shawcross Date 1/5/93

Witness Charles Gramlich Facility Sullivan
CHARLES A. GRAMLICH
Notary Public, State of New York
Sullivan County Clerk's #2086
Commission Expires September 5, 1993

NOTICE: Inmates who are a party to any pending or anticipated legal proceeding are advised to notify their attorneys prior to conducting a media interview.

DEAR CHRISTOPHER,
THANK you FOR THE LETTER.
I would do THE 30 MINUTE INTERVIEW, but CAN you TELL ME if THERE is A CAMERA INVOLVED OR do WE TALK TOGETHER? WHICH EVER is ok.
you hAVE SPOKEN OF Funds AND THEY ARE MUCH NEEDED, MY WIFE IS IN A bad WAY RIGHT NOW. SHE IS sick with THE FLU-CHEST cold. plus hER Job is UNSTABLE FROM ALL THE Publicity THAT has GENERATED AROUND ME. EVERYONE is TRYING To gET ME To SPEAK To THEM but I WAIT. THERE is MUCH STILL going ON iN THE CITY OF ROCHESTER, NEW york. people WANT MY opinion. you CAN get iT plus wHAT MY Thoughts ARE.
WHAT ARE THE QUESTION'S you'd ASK OF ME? AS Long AS MY LAWYER understands And WHAT I CAN ANSWER.

Now THEN, PLEASE have THE Fund's SENT To MY WIFE ROSE AND SHE will disburse THEM FOR BECAUSE OF TAXES.
Do NOT SEND ANYONE To boTHER her.

ROSE M. SHAWCROSS

UNITED STATES OF AMERICA

THANK you.

P.S.
How is THE LITTLE ONE doing?.

RESPECTFULLY
Arthur J. Shawcross

The letters and other documents shown here and on the following seven pages are all from the author's extensive private archive of correspondence, over many years, between him and numerous convicted killers.

Arthur John Shawcross (1945–2008), 'the Genesee River Killer'.

2-19-08

Dear Christhopher,

Recieved your short note. your letter you wrote me On January 3, 2008. Dont so adriff. I recieve the above mention letter on January 28, 2008

Cause of the ass-hole mail-room staff who sit on there ass picking their nose or whatever.

Has I express I am more then well to write a book about my crime and express my side of the story.

you mentioned that IWC, are very Keen to work on a T.V. documentary which is rubber-stamped by me, and with a view to interview me. Only trouble is California has a law now that forbid the media from interviewing dead row inmate on Camera. Only way the prison allow interviews is in visiting room and ~~only~~ the reporter can would bring in pen and paper. No tape recorder.

I would like do the book in stages. Like a foundation of a house.

Like 1) Basic information like information about my parents, How old they were when I was born. Date of my birth to age 5.

② the age of 6-12 - covering school years, any crimes I committed

③ 13-19 How I was treated and how I treat people

④ 20-40 informing about my crimes else.

Carl Phillip Jablonski (1946–2019), ‘the Death Row Teddy’.

Dear Christopher, 26 Jan 2008

I apologize for not responding to your first letter. While I am indeed interested in telling my story eventually, and in depth, to a reputable news outlet, I am currently involved in appealing my conviction and sentence. As a result, I must defer to my appellate counsel and their advice regarding the matter. At this time we are having some difficulty with our telephone communications, and I've not been able to contact them directly. I realize that contacting me via conventional mail is less than expedient – as a result, I'd like to provide you with the contact information of one of my closest friends, [redacted], as I speak to her daily, and she might function as an intermediary. Thank you for contacting me – again, my apologies for not responding sooner.

Warm Regards,
Melanie McGuire

Melanie McGuire
#584496 / South Hall S-9
EDNA MAHAN
CORRECTIONAL FACILITY FOR WOME
PO BOX 4004
CLINTON NJ 08809

KILMER P&DC NJ 088
02 MAY 2008 PM 3 L

Chris Berry-Dee

Air Mail

00144X1000

Melanie Lyn McGuire (1972–), 'the Ice Queen'.

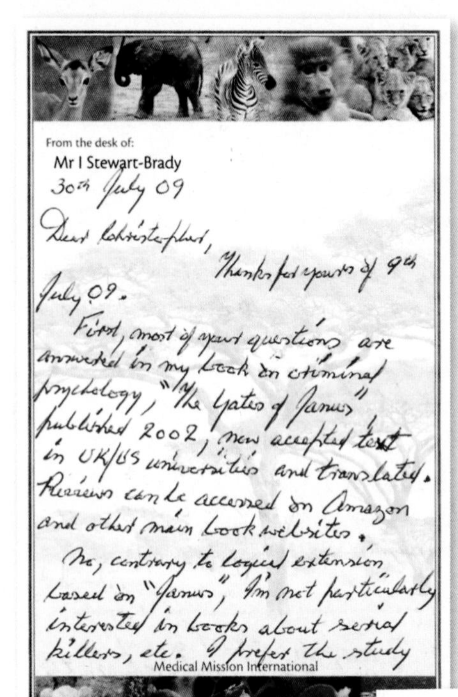

From the desk of:
Mr I Stewart-Brady
30th July 09

Dear Christopher,

Thanks for yours of 9th July 09.

First, most of your questions are answered in my book on criminal psychology, "The Gates of Janus" published 2002, now accepted text in UK/US universities and translated. Reviews can be accessed on Amazon and other main book websites.

No, contrary to logical extension based on "Janus", I'm not particularly interested in books about serial killers, etc. I prefer the study

Medical Mission International

Ian Stewart Brady (1938–2017), 'the Moors Murderer'.

2

of major criminals, such as Blair, Bush and their profiteering henchmen. As I've always stated since teenage years, you can't beat "decent, honest, respectable people" when it comes to global serial slaughter, theft, greed, treachery and hypocrisy. Which is why they exploit petty, underclass crime and criminals to distract attention from themselves and their threadbare pretensions/claims to moral superiority. Nothing new or profound in any of this, of course; just generally convenient to ignore such unpopular juxtapositions. // Please acknowledge receipt.

Best wishes,

I Brady

PS: The current satirical gall of Cherie Blair lecturing the nation on the "horrors" of "knife crime", highlights the absurdity and arrogance of the class. Greed has replaced vocation in the professions.

HAL KAREN 03-A-3087
GREEN HAVEN CORRECTIONAL FACILITY
P.O.BOX 4000
STORMVILLE, NY 12582-4000

CHRISTOPHER BERRY-DEE

14 DECEMBER 2009

Dear Chris,
I hope it's O.K. to call you Chris. It's always nice to get a letter from a former soldier. Under different circumstances I'm sure we could down some pints and exchange stories. Anyway I was kind of surprised when I got your letter because I feel that my case was not really a big deal and they put my military experience into the picture to elevate the picture inorder to get a conviction. I have never been able to tell my story before and I don't think it's anything what the T.V. shows had portrayed and if Dr. Baden would not have testified for the DA as he did, I would not be here and if I would have had money enough for a better defence I surely would have been able to prove my innocence of murder. So with all that I'll give you a quick gist of what "REALLY" happened. I meet Tammy at a topless bar outside of FT. BRAGG N.C. I had just returned from Haiti after a six month deployment and needed some winding down. I ended up getting her pregnant so we went to Las Vegas and got married. She used drugs when I meet her but during the pregnancy she did not. When Hunter was born she statred using drugs again and that's when everything went down hill. I could not get her to stop and she did not want to. One day I came home and found her dead in the bathroom. For a long time I covered her drug problem from people, it was embarrassing. So I took the body and I got rid of it and I told everyone she left because she has done this before with her first child which she left with her mother and took off. But I did not hide it good enough. I know what I did was wrong but I had my reasons and if you are still interested I will tell you them. But I feel that after you read this letter you are not going to even want to use this story. And as the investigator that you are I'll bring up just two points that you can check out for yourself. 1. How can someone go into a court room and tell a jury that this person died from strangulation when you only have some bones and not even any neck bones. 2. After almost 3 years of the body being in the woods and they still managed to find a piece of liver from her body which this alone is incredible and they test it for drugs and it comes up positive with 30 nanograms of cocaine byproduct, How can you say that that is not enough to kill someone. You would think that there had to be a awful lot to even show anything after 3 years. if you know a forensic pathologist ask him or her what they think. Anyway I don't think I'm being much help to you. Like I said before once you read this letter you'll just back away because its not the story everyone thinks it is. I tell you this and I have no idea what they said in the T.V. shows which I believe there are several That I'm not the person they made me out to be. I never hurt anyone in my life without a reason. I don't know how much help this letter is to you and your book but I do have a lot to say, its probable just does not help you. Actually I'm the one who needs help. Sometimes I wish there were more veterans with special skills that can help other veterans out with out charging a arm and a leg but that would be asking to much. Well if your still interested write me back or write me back even if your not, its nice to get a little mail, I don't have a lot of people who write me because when things go wrong people tend to turn their backs on you and just forget you. If you can I would like to read your books, I do a lot of reading. So if you can and if you want please send me copies of your books

Take care and good luck with your books.

Best Wishes

Hal

HAL (aka RAMBO) (aka HALANATOR)
(Thats the name the guys gave me)

GREEN HAVEN CORRECTIONAL FACILITY
P.O. BOX 4000
STORMVILLE, NEW YORK 12582-4000
NAME: HAL KAREN DIN: 03-A-3087

GREENHAVEN
CORRECTIONAL FACILITY

UNITED STATES POSTAGE
$ 00.98⁰
02 1A
0004623953 DEC 15 2009
MAILED FROM ZIP CODE 12582

CHRISTOPHER BERRY-DEE

AIRMAIL

00122X0001

Hal Karen (1960–).

Ronald DeFeo 75A4053
Box 338, Eastern C.F.
Napanoch, N.Y. 12458-0338

Christopher Berry Dee
The Conifer's
Botley Road
Shedfield
SO3 2HN
Hampshire
England

(June 2, 1993)

Dear Christopher,
I will get right to the point okay. After Talking to My Attorney [illegible], After Reading All Your Letter's, Promise's Deal's, etc. And seeing Now How its going on Two Year's Yes, "We" have come to the conclusion that you have been selling us a dream and trying to make money off of me and my case behind our back as Your Last Letter with the tape recording You wanted me to do said it all.

If You Cant or Won't Send Some Type of Money in Good Faith, then, We Are requesting the Immediate Return of Every thing I sent to You as Well as Letter's the [illegible] sent to you as well Because I Asked them to.
(So the Choice is Now Your's as if this is not done one way or another, then the correct Action will Be Taken with the U.S. Attorney's Office etc.

Very Truly Your's
Ronald J. DeFeo
Ronald J. DeFeo

copy to [illegible]

Ronald 'Butch' Joseph DeFeo Jr (1951–2021), 'the Amityville Horror'.

Ronnie DeFeo 75A4053
Drawer B.
Stormville, New York 12582-0010

Christopher Berry Dee, The Conifer's,
[illegible],
[illegible], England.

(March 13, 1994)

Dear Christopher,
I hope my letter finds you in the best of health and the Best Of Spirit.

To This Day Why I was Transfered To the Worse as I was in The Best Max Prison in the State NO ONE KNOW'S and Above is my New Address.

"NOW" Did You Ever Recieve the Tape's as [illegible] and Mr. [illegible] Springer who are all Witnesses in My Case and Who Know [illegible] Personally Told Her To Mail you the Tape's Five Week's Ago Yes.

I CAN TELL You There is A Problem now with [illegible] "Attorney" as She is Blaming [illegible] and I am in the Middle. Could You please let me Know whats Happening so I Know What to do As Chris its Going On three year's with "US" You and I As we have Come A long way my "Friend" As the Word Friend is Very serious as they are Very Few in My Life. Well, I will close and Await Your Reply My Friend, Thank you and Take Care;

My Best Wishes
Ronnie

9-16-09

Dear Christopher,

Hi, I hope this letter finds you doing well, and I'm sorry it has taken me so long to start to answer your letter.

It was good to hear back from you (2ND ALSO) and I want to thank you for taking the time to write back to me. I also want to thank you for taking an interest in me and my story. I'm not sure what it is you plan to do as far as the writing goes, but all I want is to tell my story and maybe it will help someone, somewhere. As Victoria, might of told you it's not about the money, and I would never ask someone to pay me. I didn't do that with her, and I won't do it with you. Besides I'm not allowed to profit from my crimes. ☺

If you wanted to help me out I would be very thankful for what ever you did or do. At the same time this is not something you have to ~~do~~. If you want to send me money for stamps and other things enclosed is some slips that show you how to do that. You can also use J-Pay and Western Union to send money right to my account. If you have any questions just let me know, or maybe Victoria, can help you.

As to what you said in your letter I will tell you what I remember and know as best as I can. This was a long time ago, and some things you just can't remember.

It all started in Rupert, West Virginia. That is where I lived, but I was born at the nearest hospital which was in Clifton Forge, Virginia.

NO LETTER
=
ONLY SLIP
+
MONEY ORDER

1. Use black or dark blue ink.
2. Print CAPITAL letters and numbers in block style.
3. PRINT all requested information.
4. Money Order, Cashiers Check, or Certified Bank Draft MUST be payable to "INMATE TRUST FUND" and include the inmate name and number. ALSO MY NAME =
5. Mail Money order, Cashiers Check, or Certified Bank Draft and completed form to the Bureau of Finance & Accounting/Inmate Trust (address below).

Florida Department of Corrections (866) 209-7250 ← IF QUESTIONS CALL
Inmate Trust Fund
Centerville Station
P.O. Box #12100 ←
Tallahassee, FL 32317-2100

CHRIS,
MAIL SLIP AND INTERNATIONAL MONEY ORDER OR CASHIERS CHECK TO THE ADDRESS SHOWN

Gary Ray Bowles (1962–2019), 'the I-95 Killer'.

Christopher Berry-Dee January 10, 2008

England

Christopher,

I received your 2 January letter. At first I was simply going to forward it to my attorney to place in the file of vultures flying overhead wanting to pick my bones for personal profit. I also often get crackpots who write claiming to be someone else, offering friendship and financial support. The last two, a woman named from Fort Lauderdale, Florida who was moving to North Tonawanda, NY to go to college. The address in Florida was a phony and the address in NY is a pizza restaurant. Shortly after that I received some kind of release agreement which was seized by the prison mailroom (prisoners are not allowed to sign contracts except through their attorneys) from someone named postmarked Colorado. when your letter arrived my first reaction was to laugh. It seems the past few month period has brought out those named "Chris." Please understand, for my protection, my attorney must first check you out.

I decided to respond, possibly wasting the precious postage, and send you one letter setting out

John 'J.R.' Edward Robinson (1943–), 'the Slavemaster'.

asshole. He's a big mother [...] built like an ape, looks like an ape. Even now, in old age, he can still do one-arm pull-ups without breaking sweat.'

'No problem,' I replied. 'I've been writing to Harvey for ages. He's good to go with me. Any chance of us guys getting hold of the Carignan files? We love the Irish, I'm into Guinness, you know. Just a glimpse of the files ... we will give them back ... honestly.'

> That Berry-Dee. He convinced me to go get the files and my supervisor gave me deep shit, but he did get to interview Harvey. God bless Chris. If it were St Patrick's Day I'd buy him a drink, but it ain't.
>
> Detective Russell J. Krueger

If there were ever a label tagged 'amoral monstrosity', it would suit 'Harv' the Hammer' extremely well. We always think of Theodore 'Ted' Robert Bundy as being the numero uno in the world's sadosexual homicide top-of-the-pops league of over-the-top murder most foul, yet by my reasoning, as far as sheer brutality goes, Carignan is on a par. I say this because Bundy never once admitted his crimes, let alone told us what terrible depravities he enacted upon his innocent victims, prior to and during his killings, nor his disgusting post-mortem degradation of so many beautiful young women. Indeed, no one knows how many murders Bundy actually committed. As for Carignan, he was responsible for *possibly* up to fifty kills – and you should take that number with a pinch of salt. After Carignan was arrested, one of America's most vicious serial killers would never use his hammer again. And here's the thing: Harvey spilled many of his beans to me, at once blaming all of his victims, telling me that it was *their* fault that he raped then bludgeoned them to death. So let's meet 'The Hammer' and try and get into the head of a man who literally destroyed the heads of so many women.

> Even now, it sometimes seems my childhood was short, only a few days long. There is nothing about it I cling to and nothing to look fondly backwards towards. From where I sat then, and sit now, it was and it is truly a pit of despair.
>
> Harvey Louis Carignan: letter to the author, 14 April 1993

Born on 18 May 1927, on the wrong side of the tracks in Fargo, North Dakota, Harvey (like Ted Bundy) was an illegitimate kid who never knew his father. His unwed twenty-year-old mother, Mary, was ill-equipped to care for her sickly boy, who failed to thrive and, in 1930, during the lowest point of the Great Depression, she started farming him out to anyone who would look after him. Thereafter, the youngster was moved from pillar to post, school to school, unable to form family roots or enjoy a solid education. He was passed around his mother's family from Fargo to Cavalier, North Dakota, back to Fargo then to Williams, North Dakota. As the FBI will confirm, this really ain't the best start to any kid's life.

Very early in his formative years, Harvey developed a facial twitch and suffered from bed-wetting until he was thirteen. He also suffered St Vitus's dance – or childhood chorea – which manifests itself in uncontrollable spasmodic jerking movements.

And, not unlike the serial killer Kenneth Bianchi, Harvey had an imaginary friend. Harvey called his invisible buddy 'Paul'.

Around the age of eleven or twelve, Harvey says he was sent to the ND Training (Reform) School at Mandan, North Dakota, where he remained for some seven years. During this time, he alleges that he was constantly bullied and sexually assaulted by a female teacher. There may be some truth in what follows, for that reform school was little more than a human warehouse where any concept of love was alien.

In a letter dated 12 June 1993, Harvey writes:

> I had a teacher who used to sit at my desk and we would write dirty notes back and forth. I was either 13 or 14 at the time – and just show me a 14-year-old boy anywhere who wouldn't willingly and happily sit in a schoolroom and exchange porno notes with his teacher. I never got to lay a hand on her without getting slapped, but she would keep me after school and make me stand before her while she masturbated and called me names and told me what she was going to make me do – some of her threats she even kept, damn it! The bitch wouldn't even let me masturbate with her! I took my penis out and she beat the living shit out of me! She had enormously large breasts. She was truly a cruel woman [...]

I have always been quite unsure why Harvey was telling me this. I suspect much of it comes from his overheated sexual imagination. Perhaps he was actually saying: 'What I would have *liked to have taken place* at Mandan – but didn't.' The flip side of this unedifying coin, of course, is that he is truthfully recounting some of the events that occurred at Mandan, where child abuse was all too common. Reading between the lines and combining what we find there with what we know as absolute facts about his killing times might give us a deeper insight into what made this depraved serial killer tick.

Am I being a tad dismissive about Harvey offering that sordid information? Maybe I am, for there is another very subtle clue here, presented right at the start of his many letters to me, and much like Melanie McGuire gave to us when she mentioned her fascination with conspiracies. This was no slip of her pen; it came from her subconscious. In other words, what flowed onto the page came from deep within her psychopathology; an unwise slip as later events would prove. With Harvey's letter above, I believe that his psychological makeup *demands* that he tells us this sordid information, in very much the same way as Phillip Jablonski did. When we read some of Harvey's letters later, we will see exactly the same thing again and again – a complete inability to stop himself from writing what one might say is homicidal pornography, although nothing close to the vile porn that dripped from the pen of Bobby Joe Long.

By the time Harvey reached eighteen, he was no longer the weedy runt who had allegedly suffered mental and sexual abuse since the age of four. The high-carb, well-balanced diet at Mandan had helped him to grow into a strapping, quite articulate, well-nourished, immensely powerful young man. With few family ties, he went straight into the US Army. He was stationed at Fort Richardson in Anchorage, Alaska, and it was here that this man exploded.

Laura Showalter

> The killer was so strong, with one punch he [Carignan] blasted a hole through her skull like a rocket slamming into a tank.
>
> Anchorage police officer: on Showalter's murder

At about nine in the evening of Sunday, 31 July 1949, a time of year when Anchorage was bathed in sunlight for most of the day, Carignan killed fifty-seven-year-old Laura Showalter during an attempted rape in a small Anchorage park. Her body was found early the following morning – he had smashed her head in with his fists. Between her forehead and her chin, her face was completely shattered. Her face was virtually destroyed from chin to forehead; bone, tissue and brain crushed to a pulp under the battering. Carignan walked away covered in blood; later he would be charged with this homicide.

Christine Norton

> He turned into something from hell. His fury came out of nowhere.
>
> Christine Norton: reliving the attempted rape by Carignan

Less than two months later, early in the morning of 14 September, Christine Norton (also known, presumably to protect her privacy, as Dorcas Callen) was accosted outside a tavern in a street in Anchorage by a tall and well-built young soldier who seemed intoxicated despite the hour. He was persistent, trying to claim acquaintanceship with her, and offered to give her a lift in his car. When she declined, he grew angrier and angrier. She thought of how a woman had recently been horribly killed in the area and was frightened, but before she could move off, he had caught hold of her and was dragging her away from the empty street. As she struggled, they fell into a deep ditch at the side of the road, the soldier on top of the young woman, tearing at her clothing, hitting her furiously, tugging at her limbs. He was heavy, extremely strong, in a rage, and intent on raping her. Yet somehow, strengthened by her terror, she managed to wriggle free and scramble up the crumbling dirt wall of the ditch (which bore her weight better than the hulking soldier's) to run back up the road to the safety of the tavern, bruised, blood-stained and in tattered clothing. From there she phoned the police, to whom she was able to give a clear description of her assailant, and it was just a matter of hours before they found and arrested Carignan.

In the meantime, it transpired that the man who on 1 August 1949 found Laura Showalter's body had seen Carignan with her the evening before his horrifying discovery but had not at the time realised anything was amiss. Both he and Christine Norton identified Harvey Carignan in a line-up on Friday, 16 September.

Carignan was charged with murder and assault with intent to commit rape. He pleaded guilty to the assault, and a written confession to the murder of Laura Showalter was obtained from him. He stood trial for the first-degree murder of Laura Showalter in early 1950 in the District Court for the Territory of Alaska, Third Division, Justice George W. Folta presiding. It should have been simple: he was pronounced guilty on both charges. He was then sentenced to hang – and this is where justice was turned on its head. Carignan had been led to believe that if he confessed he would not receive the death sentence, and while he was prepared to spend time in jail, he felt that he had been deceived and appealed. In October 1951, his sentence for the murder was overturned on a technicality – his confession, which he made of his free will, was nevertheless ruled inadmissible because it was obtained during his detention for the assault on Christine Norton, whereas he had not yet been arraigned before a magistrate for the murder.

So Harvey escaped the hangman's noose by a whisker while perhaps as many as fifty women lost their lives. Thereafter, prisoner #22072 Carignan was transferred from the Seward Jail in Alaska to the US federal penitentiary on McNeil Island in Puget Sound, Washington State. The prison would hold several notable convicts in its lifetime, including: Robert Franklin Stroud, later aka 'The Birdman of Alcatraz'; Vincent Hallinan, a presidential candidate in 1952; and Mickey Cohen, the 1930s Los Angeles gang leader. And as this book is all about writing, I am also obliged to mention fellow inmate James Fogle, published author of the autobiography *Drugstore Cowboy*. There is a brilliant movie of the same name – well worth a watch.

At this point in Carignan's narrative, and before we examine his correspondence in more depth, it is worth pausing to reflect on the deep-rooted hatred of women that resides within the psychopathologies of killers such as Carignan, Neville Heath, Bobby Joe Long, Ted Bundy and Peter Sutcliffe. Outwardly, they may present to the world as being normal people. They often are good-looking and charming to a fault, but this is merely the mask of normality that I mentioned earlier. These people have very fragile egos; they pen in their inner fury often for weeks and months on end. Then, for one reason or another – often simply because of a minor slight – they emotionally explode.

It *could* be the case that the abuse he suffered at Mandan, and which Carignan told me about, was a contributory factor. He once told me that later in his life women played mind games with his head, giving us a subliminal clue as to why he inflicted so much damage to heads, brains and bodies. Peter Sutcliffe learned early on that his allegedly devout Catholic mother was cheating on his father; he grew to despise her. Perhaps the fact that he was unable to have children was a contributory factor in the awful stabbings and mutilations to his victims' stomachs and vaginal areas after he'd rendered them unconscious with blows to their heads. Theodore Robert Bundy is much easier to understand. Ted was jilted by a beautiful young co-ed, his first true love. Her parents had seen right through Bundy's oily, shallow façade and convinced her to unceremoniously dump him which did nothing to assist his already fragile ego. Thereafter, his chosen victims were lookalikes of his first amour – he was punishing her through them.

Joanne Dennehy's motive for the three stabbing homicides and two attempted stabbing kills is documented in my book *Love of Blood*. By her teens Jo had developed a pathological hatred for men. Later, married with two little babies, which she never touched or even cared for them, she viewed her husband as merely a convenient tool to look after her children and do the housework, while sometimes she'd bring men back to their home and have rough, degrading sex in front of him.

We can apply similar criteria to Neville Heath. A narcissist to the nth degree, he despised women – witness the godawful injuries that he inflicted upon Margery Gardner and Doreen Marshall.

So many more vile killers still live among us, yet we never suspect a thing as to their deep-seated intentions. We take them at their face value – the visible ink on the page – but it is what is hidden from view – between the lines, so to speak – that is most terrifying of all. We'll see proof of that as we move on through Carignan's life, and on to the rock named 'Alcatraz'.

Alcatraz

> Laura Showalter ... Dorcas Callen? Those names mean nothin' to me. [Callen, sometimes Callan is on his rap sheet and confirmed by investigator Russell Krueger in my TV series *Serial Killers*.]
>
> Harvey Carignan: to the author at interview MCF-Stillwater

Alcatraz is the old Spanish word for 'pelican' (now it means 'gannet') and the island was named after the hordes of seabirds that made the island their home. In 1775, the Spanish explorer Juan Manuel de Ayala became the first to sail into what is now known as San Francisco Bay, and his expeditions mapped and named one of the three islands La Isla de los Alcatraces – 'The Island of Pelicans'. Over time it became the briefer 'Alcatraz'. After a century or more of use as some kind of fortified establishment, detention centre or various types of prison, it was bought by the US Department of Justice and from 1934 to 1963 was designated a federal prison. With most attempted escapes being met with either death by drowning or shooting, or by recapture, the island jail gained the reputation of being inescapable from. And that was where Carignan was transferred, on 13 September 1951, to spend the next nine years. On 2 April 1960, aged thirty-three, he was paroled. Except for his few years in the Army, he had not really been at liberty since he was a kid.

After landing at San Francisco's waterfront jetty wearing a cheap prison-issue suit, and with a bag containing his few belongings, Carignan boarded a train for Duluth, Minnesota. As Harvey explained in one of his letters to me: 'In Duluth I moved in with one of my three half-brothers but, on 4 August 1960, just four months after my release, I was arrested for third-degree burglary and assault with intent to commit rape.' No shrinking violet is Harvey, I'm sure you'll agree. The rape charge was dropped through lack of evidence, but for the burglary and parole violation, he was sentenced to 2,086 days in the US Penitentiary Leavenworth, Kansas.

Carignan was paroled in 1964, moving swiftly to Seattle where, he told me: 'On 2 March I registered as Parole Convict #C-5073.' On 22 November that year, he was arrested for second-degree burglary and, again, violating parole. On 20 April 1965 he was sentenced to fifteen years in the Washington State Penitentiary (WSP) Walla Walla, in 'The Evergreen State'.

> Don't worry, guys. My husband is the pilot. He's flying blind right now. He knows where Mount St Helens is. If he doesn't, he and I might have a problem.
>
> Air stewardess: to me and my TV documentary producer, Frazer Ashford

If you want to visit the WSP, you have to truly like flying. As the crow flies, the distance is 212 miles between SeaTac and Walla Walla. But en route, the pilot has to navigate around the 2,500-metre-high, semi-dormant volcanic Mount St Helens, which occasionally has a bad-hair day. For the record, this is higher than the plane Frazer Ashford and I flew in, made all the more exciting as the volcano was blanketed in clouds of mist – or was it steam?

Walla Walla

Walla Walla – I am reliably informed by Keith Hunter Jesperson, aka 'The Happy Face Killer' – is *not*, as I previously mentioned in one of my books, one of the tri-state cities along with Richland and Kennewick on the south-east border of Washington and Oregon. 'Walla Walla is 40 miles east of the tri-cities ... you must be totally correct 100 per cent of the time,' screams Keith in one of his letters to me, adding: 'Pascoe [*sic*] is the third of the tri-cities.' Let's give him his due, at least Keith was correct on the latter.

Now locked up in one of the oldest and most notorious prisons in the United States, Carignan applied his mind; taking a high school diploma, enrolling in many college courses including sociology and psychology; he also submitted papers on sexual psychopathy, the paranoid personality and the well-adjusted individual. He read constantly, gaining top marks; and studied journalism. All of this impressed his tutors, who stated that: 'Mr Carignan's cognitive thinking processes allow us professionals a greater understanding of the first-hand experiences that only a man like Mr Carignan can offer us,' adding possibly with tongues in cheeks: 'Presently, however, more correctional adjustment is needed before we can recommend he be paroled, *if* ever.' Yes, the italic '*if*' really does appear in Carignan's psychiatric reports. Good gracious me, there *are* psychiatrists in the US who have a dry sense of humour.

While the shrinks at Walla Walla praised Harvey for his academic achievements, they were also well aware that when talking to his fellow cons he was constantly fantasising – and at night, masturbating – about nubile young girls. We see pre-echoes of this mindset in his letter about Mandan. Harvey freely admits that he has a fixation about young flesh, which is mirrored in his victims. In a letter to me he explained: 'Young girls have to be my ultimate choice. It would be very unhealthy for me to go with a much older woman than me.' About two decades ago his pen pal was a youngish mother serving a life sentence for beating and smothering to death her baby in its cot while her partner looked on. The love letters they exchanged are enough to make one cringe.

Then in his early forties, a hulking giant of an ex-con, Harvey's chances of dating a teenager were non-existent, so he hooked up with Sheila Moran, a divorcee (some accounts say a widow) with three children. She had her own house in Ballard, the Scandinavian district of Seattle, and there he settled down with her.

As mentioned earlier, sexual psychopaths can *never* be cured, but with all those years behind bars and all of the psychiatric counselling under his belt, let's at least give Harvey some moral support here, with: 'Go for it, Harvey ... you be a good ole boy now, y'all hear. You got it made, bro. Move in. Getcha your feet under the table. Become the man of the house and let ya homemaker do the rest.' But Sheila soon got wise to her newly betrothed's character. Coming from a decent family, she was left under no illusions about the real personality of her husband, who hung around with a bunch of villains. He was always out until the late hours, tearing around in his car at breakneck speeds. He was sullen, uncommunicative, would frequently get up at night and drive long distances 'to be alone and think', he told me; sometimes he was away for days on end. After he had, without provocation, launched a vicious attack upon her aged uncle, she decided his violence and unpredictability presented too great a threat to her children and herself, and took her children and left. When Harvey found them gone, he decided to kill her. He waited in vain through the night, a hammer clutched in his hand. Sheila did not return home and they never saw each other again.

Harvey bigamously remarried on 14 April 1972. Widow Alice Johnson, a somewhat naïve soul in her thirties with two children, fell for him and thought she had met her 'Mr Right', unfortunately she'd met her 'Mr Wrong'.

Later, in his lengthy correspondence with me, Carignan avoided mentioning Sheila Moran, Alice Johnson, Laura Showalter or Christine Norton/Dorcas Callen in any meaningful way – it is as if these four women had never ever existed in his worthless life. However, and this may not come as a surprise, he did highlight this: 'Alice had been married before, had a son called, Billy, aged eleven, I think, and a very, *very* pretty young fourteen-year-old daughter called Georgia. What man wouldn't lust after that?' Of course, there was no need for him to say anything about Georgia. But he can't help himself.

At around this time, Carignan managed to lease a Sav-Mor

gas station from the Time Oil Company. He needed staff and advertised in the local papers. Soon Alice noticed that he had a string of young girls working the pumps, and that no sooner had one started than she left to be replaced by another pretty lass. This aroused Alice's suspicions, and local gossip led her to the conclusion that her husband was totally obsessed by teenage girls. He would approach any girl he saw making obscene suggestions and uttering smutty remarks. When Alice confronted him about his behaviour, he shouted and swore at her. He beat her son, and skulked about, leering at his stepdaughter Georgia, which made her feel decidedly uncomfortable – so much so that she ran away from home. Not surprisingly, the marriage collapsed soon afterwards. 'That not so innocent Georgia was begging for it. They all do at that age,' Carignan wrote to me.

On 15 October 1972, the body of nineteen-year-old hitchhiker Laura Brock was found near Mount Vernon, Washington State. She had been raped and murdered. The cause of death was found to be repeated crushing blows to the head – Carignan's favoured MO – but the killing was never pinned on him. Several witnesses apparently claimed to have seen Laura get into a silver-topped truck – like Carignan's – but nothing was ever proved.

Katherine 'Kathy' Sue Miller

> You really want the truth from me? You're dead right, Chris. Yes, I smashed their heads to a pulp. Why? Because women and young chicks always played mind games with me. Not even the psychiatrists have figured this out.
>
> Harvey Carignan: to the author at interview, MCF-Stillwater

The world owes Harvey Carignan nothing, as in zilch, but he does give us some murderous ideas on how depraved criminals go about luring young women to the most terrible of ends. So, if Carignan has any value at all, it is that he is inadvertently warning us – the amoral bigot that he is – that young girls should *always* heed the advice of their parents and never, ever get into a car with a strange man. And 'strange' Carignan most certainly was; that and a damned sight more.

Kathy Sue Miller's case offers a prime example. She was born a beautiful, healthy baby at the French Hospital in New York, on 23 May 1957. Her mother, Mary, later gave birth to her brother Kenny. Sadly, Kathy came to a dreadful end after she read a 'want-ad' in the *Seattle Times* dated 1 May 1973. Help was required at a local gas station. Fifteen-year-old Kathy wasn't looking for a job herself, but her boyfriend, Mark Walter, was.

The notice had been placed by none other than Carignan – who would subsequently be dubbed 'The Want-ad Killer' – metaphorically sitting in the shadows, trawling for young prey. At this point, I would ask the reader to recall the words of Christine Norton/Dorcas Callen: 'He turned into something from hell. His fury came out of nowhere, like he was suddenly switched on with evil.' Now imagine, if you dare, what Kathy went through soon after meeting 'The Hammer'.

The next morning, Kathy rang the number advertised. She was, remember, acting on her boyfriend's behalf at the time, but when the man who answered the phone said that he also employed girls, she excitedly thought she too would apply. Unwisely, she gave him her address and telephone number and agreed to meet him after school. They arranged that he would pick her up in his car – a maroon one, he told her – outside the

Sears Building on Utah Avenue South, and would then drive her over to his gas station to fill out a job application form.

Mary was worried, as any mother would have been. She didn't like the fact that her daughter had given her telephone number and address to a stranger. She felt uneasy about the way the interview had been arranged; in particular, the thought of Kathy getting into a car with someone she had never met before concerned her deeply. Running through her mind was a recent news article about Laura Brock, who had been raped and murdered while hitchhiking – most probably killed by Carignan, police later said.

'I mean it, Kathy,' Mary warned. 'Don't even think about meeting him!' Kathy promised not to and left for her classes, a stack of schoolbooks under her arm.

Mother and daughter rode the same bus that morning. Kathy alighted first near Roosevelt High School at 1410 NE 66th Street. Mary watched through the grimy window as her lovely daughter hurried away, turning once with a smile to wave back. The story of what followed has been compiled using police documents and details from none other than Carignan in his letters to me.

After school, Kathy flagrantly disobeyed her mother's orders and met Carignan as arranged. In his correspondence this sexual predator recalled, with unexpected lyricism that made him all the more repellent, that he had been waiting with 'growing impatience', that 'my heart skipped a beat when I saw a tall, athletic girl walking in my direction. Her blonde hair was darkened to a burnished butterscotch colour and fell to the middle of her back in thick waves. Kathy had green eyes, and just the faintest suggestion of freckles sprinkling over her fair skin. The all-American sexy lass, she was to me.'

Kathy paused opposite his car to cross the street and he looked on as the teenager, sporting a navy-blue blouse, blue-and-white jumper and blue-tinged tights, waved to him.

In a letter to me, Carignan explained that he leant across the front passenger seat and pushed the door open. However, Kathy walked to his side of the car and spoke to him through the open window. Her first sight of Harvey would have been unappealing: an unattractive man with a peculiarly domed forehead and a receding chin. Carignan looked years older than his true age of forty-five, with his skin deeply lined and wrinkled bags beneath his eyes – a deep scar running over one of them. His usual expression was a glowering frown. To smile, he had to make a concentrated effort, so he turned on all the charm at his disposal.

'Hi, you must be Kathy?' he asked, with a broad grin beaming across his face.

Kathy would have noticed the dimple on his chin, then smiled back. 'Sure, that's me.'

Motioning her to get into his car, he said, 'We need to fill in the application forms and they are back at my office ... just hop in. I'll drop you off home when we've finished.'

Carignan recalls that it was obvious to him that Kathy felt uncomfortable. 'My mom isn't too happy about this,' she explained to him, so he moved up a gear.

'Can't say that I blame her. I've got children of my own. Married, too. Nice house. Lovely woman. Yep, we can't blame your mom for being careful.'

Kathy was almost convinced by the man's reassurance. 'You sure this is OK?' she asked.

'Absolutely. Tell ya what, I'll even introduce myself to your mom when I drop you off. Everything will be fine then.'

Kathy was never seen alive again. In the wake of the crime, Harvey, whose violent record was known to police, was questioned at length, his movements watched 24/7 for weeks. But there was insufficient evidence to arrest him and charge him with abduction let alone murder.

On Sunday, 3 June of that year, two sixteen-year-old boys riding their motorcycles through Tulalip Reservation just north of Everett, found a naked body wrapped in black plastic. The corpse had decayed so badly it was initially impossible even to tell its gender. During autopsy it was found that the teeth matched Kathy's dental records. It was clear from the damage to the skull that death had resulted from a brutal battering: there were holes in it the size of a hammer head or tyre lever. Carignan writes that he also raped Kathy using his hammer handle.

Of course, we cannot know much at all about what happened after Kathy climbed into Carignan's car. Throughout his correspondence with me, although he says nothing about the actual killing of this fifteen-year-old, he recalled that his patience had been wearing thin as he'd waited by the kerbside for her to appear, if she was to appear at all. This was a man quick to anger, a man who had clearly been struggling to control his sexually driven, pent-up fury as he waited and waited. Then, when Kathy finally appeared, he switched to a 'Mr Nice Guy'; all he had to do was to persuade her to get into the car and sit beside him.

Rapid flicks of the mental switches from 'Mr Nice Guy' to something hellish is not unusual in the dread annals of criminal history. Aside from Harvey Carignan, examples include 'nice', all-American bookish Michael Bruce Ross, whom I interviewed on death row in Somers Prison, Connecticut, and smooth-talking Ted Bundy. Such men do *not* waste their time when a victim is under their control. Their perverted sexual psychopathology does not permit small talk. The moment Kathy cautiously edged up to Carignan's car, she was already a dead girl still walking. So let me repeat this: do not, under any circumstances, get close to a stranger's car if he, or she, asks for directions or uses any other pretext to lure you in.

Having studied Carignan's modus operandi, modus vivendi and modus cogitandi more than, I suggest, any other commentator on 'The Hammer', I conjecture that he would have driven Kathy some distance, then when the chance seized him, smashed her in the face to render her helpless. This was his MO – one almost identical to that of Ted Bundy – and one that would be played out again and again in Harvey's future murders; poor Kathy would never have seen it coming. Now that she was unconscious, he would have taken her out into the deep woods that night, and done what his urges told him to do. At one time in my letters to Harvey, I pressed him on Kathy's murder and he had this to say: 'Chris, those details are what I call my "string of pearls". They are secrets I share with no one not even you. These *pearls of wisdom give me intense pleasure* but as you are not a man like me, why should I waste my time revealing them to you?' [Author's italics.]

Let's consider his 'string of pearls' and this 'intense pleasure', that he shares with no one. Earlier, I mentioned 'trophy-taking', and that this can also mean a killer's sexually gratifying memories of their murders. We know from Carignan's previous prison psychiatric reports that he, like Bundy, Bianchi and Ross, masturbates constantly to these sick memories, all the while boasting to his fellow cons about his preference for young girls. Given which, Carignan's words can only mean one thing, and I am sure that I do not have to explain further.

But what of Kathy's legacy?

> I admire Mary Miller more than almost anyone I know. She has survived unbelievable tragedy, but rather than spending her life mourning her losses, she has devoted herself to helping others who have lost beloved family members to murder.
>
> Ann Rae Rule, author (1931–2015)

Kathy's mother, Mary, went on to dedicate her life to humanitarian work. In a nomination letter to the Red Cross, the well-known writer Ann Rule talked about Mary's experiences escaping war-torn Latvia as a teenager after World War II, then suffering the loss of her daughter, Kathy, and raising her developmentally disabled son as a single mother. If that is not heart-breaking, I do not know what is and, when Kathy was just four months old, her mother had a nightmare that haunted her through the following years. Mary Miller described how, 'I dreamed I had a daughter with long, dark hair. She was fourteen years old in my dream, and someone had hurt her. There was blood all over her face. I couldn't tell if she was dead, but I knew that she was terribly hurt. There was so much blood, and try as I might, I couldn't help her.'

Throughout Kathy's childhood, Mary kept a close eye on her, checking more frequently than was normal. But as her daughter retained the long hair of childhood, Mary began to relax. And when she passed the age of fourteen, Mary finally felt the danger was over. Before another year had passed, however, her nightmare came true.

Eileen Hunley

After Kathy's body was retrieved from the forested Tulalip Reservation, Seattle detectives, Billy Baughman and Duane Homan, both big men in their thirties, with each of them having a teenage daughter of about Kathy's age, and who knew of Carignan's grim criminal record, watched and hounded him with such determination that he left Seattle with the intention of going to Denver – to end up in Minnesota after first driving through California. A speeding ticket from Solano County on 20 June 1973 placed him in the vicinity where half a dozen women had been murdered in the previous two years, but there was nothing definite to connect him to these crimes. To this very day, there is still only circumstantial evidence to link Carignan to these brutal murders.

Having escaped Seattle and the clutches of the seven-man team of homicide cops assigned to the Miller case, Harvey now made his way to Minneapolis, Minnesota, and moved in with his half-brother, and here he initially bombarded his estranged wife Alice promising his eternal love. While blaming her for their separation, he continually assured her he was willing to forgive and forget. They were, Harvey announced, 'poor tormented lovers, with a love as great as Abelard and Heloise, Antony and Cleopatra, and Romeo and Juliet'. He also went to great lengths to portray himself as a peace-loving man. He described how the children had laughed to see a bird killing a snake in a television programme. He told Alice that he was horrified to see how anyone could 'so intensely enjoy the sight of killing'.

So now one can see how duplicitous 'The Hammer' was, portraying himself as being life's constant victim. He wrote how much his rent cost him; how he only made $7.60 an hour, and that was his pathology way back then, and we see it in his letters that follow as plain as day.

Further playing the victim card and that everybody was out to get him, in another letter to Alice he described how he had been set upon by a gang of five youths and beaten so severely with a claw hammer that he feared he might lose the sight of his right eye. If that attack ever happened, and of course it hadn't, Harvey never reported it to the Minneapolis police. Even if he had done so, it is almost certain that little would have happened, for the cops were far too busy investigating his own assaults.

In Minneapolis, on 28 June 1973, Marlys Townsend was standing at a bus stop on a street corner when she was suddenly knocked unconscious by a hammer blow from behind and dragged barely conscious into the perpetrator's vehicle. She came round to find herself in a pick-up truck with a huge balding man, who demanded that she touched his genitals. As Marlys scrambled for the door, her assailant grabbed her hair. Luckily she was wearing a wig, and after falling out onto the pavement she ran off down the street and managed to escape. She gave police a description of her attacker that would later match Carignan exactly.

Two months later, on 9 September 1973, came a sickening attack on a child. Thirteen-year-old runaway Jerri Billings was thumbing for a lift in north-east Minneapolis when Carignan stopped. She soon noticed, however, that Harvey – or 'Paul', as he called himself – was not heading to the address she had given, but instead was driving out into the empty spaces of Hennepin County. There, Carignan struck her on the head with a hammer and dragged her off into a cornfield where she was forced to perform oral sex on him. Jerri was convinced that the man was going to kill her but to her astonishment he let her get dressed and drove her back to Crystal, a small town just north-west of Minneapolis. 'Get out,' he said, 'and don't tell anyone, ever.' Luckily for 'The Hammer', Jerri heeded his threat. She did not report the assault until 29 October, by which time she was in reform school and it was only after seeing someone in the chapel who looked just like her assailant that she decided to speak out. The unfortunate man, Karl Olafson, bore an uncanny resemblance to Carignan and it was to take a full year to eliminate him entirely from their enquiries. In one of his letters to me, he made a passing comment about Jerri Billings: 'She was a cute kid and she reminded me of my niece.'

In the meantime, there was a lull in Harvey's attacks; the reason being that he had sidled back to Seattle in February 1974 to attempt a reconciliation with Alice and still with a leching eye on her daughter. When this failed, he struck up a relationship with Eileen Hunley who was hitchhiking and a member of 'The Way', a fundamentalist sect that Harvey soon joined too. It seems that at first Eileen felt sorry for him. He seemed like a decent, devout, hard-working man, who was trying to overcome the rough hand life had dealt him; however, he soon returned to type. By the summer she was becoming disillusioned – he was drinking hard and his violent temper began to flare up with increasing frequency so she tried to get away from him. *Murder Casebook* Vol. 80 has it that Eileen was last seen alive at her home in Minneapolis on Saturday, 4 August 1974. She did not appear at church the following day, nor did she show up on Monday at the childcare centre where she worked. Carignan turned up at the latter, claiming that she was ill and had sent him to collect her latest pay cheque, but Eileen's employers were suspicious and refused to hand it over to this big, scowling man. Instead, they notified the police of their concern. Weeks later, her body, the skull caved in, was found on 18 September, in Sherburne County. In response to my questions about Eileen's murder, Carignan had little to say, dismissively commenting: 'She was my common-law wife an' I thought she was seeing a black man so I stopped her in the street … I ran her head into a lamp pole, and I stamped her face into a drain cover until she was dead. Then I tried to feed her to some pigs.' Whether or not his account is true or not, Eileen's skull had indeed been crushed, as Detective Sonenstahl later claimed with a hammer, but it is known that a tree branch had been forced into her vagina, which, as might be expected, is denied by Carignan.

Returning to Carignan's homicidal narrative, a string of brutal sexual assaults on girls and young women throughout Colorado and Minnesota during the latter part of 1974 all bore his stamp. At least seven of the victims died; the survivors were scarred for life, mentally and physically. Those who could, mostly described their attacker as a large man, middle-aged, balding, wielding a hammer. On 8 September 1974, a pair of teenage girls, June Lynch and Lisa King, were hitchhiking, and were picked up by Carignan. On the pretext of needing some help picking up another vehicle he drove them to a rural area near Mora, Kanabec County, Minnesota. Asking one of them to wait in his car, he took the other into some woods to, they thought, give him a helping hand with this fictitious car. When the teenager left behind heard screams from her friend, she ran as fast as she could to get help. Carignan fled. His victim was alive but severely injured and traumatised. She had been beaten about the head with a hammer and sexually assaulted with its handle. The girls were able to give a description of the assailant and the vehicle he was driving: a pea-green and black Chevrolet Caprice.

The Later Victims

On 14 September 1974, Carignan picked up a nineteen-year-old Gwen Burton, a student nurse whose car would not start in a south Minneapolis car park. After he'd tinkered with the car briefly, and using his usual ploy, he told her he needed more tools and persuaded her to accompany him to fetch them. He took her instead to an area of wilderness in Carver County, sexually assaulted her several times, including forcing a claw hammer handle into her vagina. He beat her about the head with the hammer (which he was later to insist was a lug or wheel nut wrench, as though this would somehow exonerate him), and left her in a field to die. It is to be noted that to all intents and purposes Carignan was impotent, meaning he couldn't get it up unless his victims performed oral sex on him. Nonetheless, Gwen did not die and managed to crawl up an embankment on to a road where, three hours later she was found, seriously injured, and rushed to hospital. She, too, was able to give a description of her attacker and his vehicle – a four-door Chevrolet Caprice, light green with a black interior, and with Minnesota licence plates – and of some of the car's contents – down to the brand of cigarette he smoked.

Five days later, on 19 September 1974, two teenage female hitchhikers reported that they had been picked up by a man and driven in a green Chevrolet into the country where he threatened to rape and kill them. To make his point, Carignan struck one across the mouth, breaking one of her front teeth. Both were eventually able to escape by jumping out of his car when he stopped to fill his vehicle with gas. Their descriptions of the man matched those given by the previous victims.

The very next day, seventeen-year-old Katherine Jane Schultz set off for school in the morning. She never got there. The following day, 21 September, the body of a young woman was found by pheasant hunters in Isanti County, an area 40 miles north of Minneapolis. She had been sexually assaulted and had sustained horrific and fatal injuries to the head. Two days later the body was identified as that of Katherine Schultz.

Carignan had cunningly taken each of his victims into a different county in order to hinder the investigations, reasoning that law enforcement jurisdictional limits would mess the cops up. However, this latest atrocity stung law enforcement into action and, very much like Mike Malchik earlier in this book, Detective Archie Sonenstahl started to coordinate their efforts.

The attacker was described as a huge man with balding, greyish brown hair, a dimpled chin and wearing work clothes with the trousers tucked into his boots. He smoked Marlboro cigarettes, used obscene language, was incredibly strong and had driven either a green Chevrolet with a black interior or a silver-topped pick-up. This provided Sonenstahl with his first solid lead: the Isanti PD had taken a cast of brand new Atlas tyre treads found in the ground near Kathy Schultz's body, and if they could match them up a with a suitable silver-topped pick-up or green Chevrolet, they could have some hard evidence at last.

A few days later, Carignan was arrested. When I was filming in Minneapolis years later I was lucky enough to be able to interview the arresting officers who recollected for me how Harvey's arrest went down.

The idiot got too complacent.

Serial killer Keith Hunter Jesperson:
commenting on Carignan

It was 24 September 1974 and early morning in Minneapolis. The sun was up and patrolmen Robert Nelson and Robert Thompson were cruising along 1841 E 38th Street when they spotted a 1968 black-over-pea-green Chevrolet Caprice. It was parked across the road from a diner. Thompson made a slow circuit of the block, while his partner checked the police bulletin details issued the day before.

'That's it,' said Nelson. 'That looks like the car. All we gotta do is find the driver. He's a big guy and, according to this BOLO [Be On the Lookout], he's built like a gorilla.' The two cops peered through the Caprice's window to scrutinise the interior. Sure enough, there was a red plaid car rug, pornographic magazines and a Bible, all as described by several of the victims. By the gear lever were several packs of Marlboro Red cigarettes.

While Nelson telephoned his precinct requesting assistance, Thompson wandered into the diner and asked the owner if he knew who was driving the Chevy.

'Yeah, sure,' came the telling reply. 'He just saw you guys and hightailed it out back.' Minutes later, the two cops spotted

Carignan strolling casually away from them. They questioned him briefly, then arrested him and took him downtown, to be read his Miranda Rights and booked on charges of homicide and multiple rapes.

A police search of Carignan's belongings uncovered a number of maps with some 180 red circles drawn around locations, some isolated, in both the United States and Canada. Some of the circles marked places where he had gone to buy vehicles or apply for jobs; others, however, seemed to link him with a string of unsolved homicides and assaults involving women.

Suspected of up to fifty kills, one of America's most vicious serial killers would never use his hammer again. In separate trials conducted in 1975 and 1976, Carignan was convicted of just two murders, those of Eileen Hunley and Katherine Schultz, and a number of other offences. His defence was that God had told him to humiliate and kill all harlots and whores, and he was only following orders ... That did not hold water, though he was later diagnosed with antisocial personality disorder. He received prison sentences amounting to one hundred years plus life.

What follows is part of a charge relating to five counts regarding offences committed against a thirteen-year-old girl. Her name, as with those of others likely to be still alive, has been omitted to protect her identity. The document has been supplied courtesy of the Minneapolis and Hennepin County Prosecutors:

> The said –, was hitch-hiking in Minneapolis when the defendant, driving a truck-camper, stopped, picked her up, engaged her in conversation as to where she was

> going, stated that he would take her to her destination directly, forced her to commit oral sodomy upon him with the threat of hitting her with a hammer which he picked up from a compartment between the seats of his truck, compelled her to remove her clothes by threatening to 'put a hammer through your head', attempted to shove the handle of the hammer up into her vagina, struck her several times in the area of her buttocks with the hammer, when she resisted the advances of the defendant, again compelled her to commit oral sodomy on him, drove to a corn field where he compelled her to lie on her stomach where he attempted to have intercourse with her through the rectum then, for the third time, again compelled her to commit oral sodomy on him. That the defendant then permitted the victim to dress and drove her to home of a friend situated in Lakeland Avenue, Crystal, Hennepin County, where he allowed the victim to get out of the truck-camper; that, in addition to the foregoing, the defendant told the victim that his first name was 'Paul' and that his last name was 'Harvey'.

Because individuals like Harvey Carignan have traversed such sickening extremes, their souls have become like locked rooms hiding mysterious secrets. Therefore, it takes a certain sensibility to draw them out. For each case, I adopt an in-depth approach, spending an enormous amount of time getting to know the unique qualities of each killer, rather than depersonalising them with generalities based on the heinous crimes. Furthermore, while I develop a false empathy with my subject, I always take care not to sympathise to the extent that their dramas start playing in the theatre of my own mind. It is a constant balancing act between identification and analysis.

To learn anything from these evil people, you must try to put yourself in their place; follow their train of thought and feel their emotions. However, while you follow the often dysfunctional thinking processes of your subjects to some extent, you take care to remain yourself. You may draw close for a while, close enough to get a sense of these often repellent, outlandish ideas and emotions, but you must always pull back to restore the integrity of your own moral and psychological boundaries.

There have been occasions when I've interviewed serial killers that I've sensed they are seeking to shock me, make me recoil in disgust. Many do the same in correspondence, as Phillip Jablonski and Bobby Joe Long did. But if you are almost at one with their thinking, at the same time you are immunised from all they say or write. It is difficult for me to explain. I cannot really put it in any other way. And although some of the letters in this book might make you feel sick to your stomach, please try to study them as one would a blowfly preserved in amber through a microscope. Try to understand their rationale, their modus cogitandi: what makes these monsters tick. This is why it is important for those with a deep interest in criminals of this type to always read between the lines of their correspondence, which is usually where the true beast resides.

On that note, I'm reminded of words written by German philosopher, Friedrich Nietzsche. It's worth repeating them now: 'Whoever fights monsters should see to it that in the process he does not become a monster. And when you look into an abyss, the abyss also looks into you.' That's precisely what one of Harvey's psychiatrists was getting at when he told me, 'Yes, you will get to interview Mr Carignan, or something living inside his head. You'll get to interview him, and pure evil will get to interview you.'

> Most killers I talk to try to act as if they are the worse [*sic*] people I'll ever meet. In turn they tell people that I don't sound like a killer.
>
> Serial killer Keith Hunter Jesperson: letter to the author

So let's now meet this killer in the flesh and it is March 1995, and I need to make a strong point here. Even the strongest, ever-so intimidating sexual psychopath will very rarely lash out at a man. You see, they are bullies and cowards at heart, even weak-willed, and even the likes of Ted Bundy would never pick a fight with a guy for fear of having his teeth knocked out. The same applies to the hulking Keith Hunter Jesperson, Arthur Shawcross, Douglas Daniel Clark, Peter Sutcliffe, Kenneth Bianchi and Angelo Buono, or even Ronnie DeFeo Jr who bravely shot to death his entire family of six at point-blank range with a Marlin hunting rifle as they slept soundly in their Amityville, Long Island home. So, when meeting this human pondlife in the flesh, if you have done your homework, as any homicide cop will tell you that you control the game through mind control, you will win.

Harvey's personal pager summoned him for our interview at the Minnesota Correctional Facility. One's first impression will be of a lumbering hulk – when I met him, he weighed well over 240 pounds (109 kilograms) – standing over 6 feet tall, although slightly stooped because of his age, with heavy brows overhanging piercing blue eyes beneath a balding dome, huge hands attached to long arms hanging from immensely powerful, sloping shoulders. He talks in a low, husky voice. At face value, he is no beauty, yet his overall persona presents a gentle giant of a man. You could see why his 'grandfatherly' voice might easily overcome his ugliness and reassure impressionable young women and girls and lure them into his clutches. Appearances, as we know, can be deceptive.

Except for exchanging the usual pleasantries, three minutes dragged by without either of us saying very much at all, while all the time his eyes stared into my face. Harvey was summing me up. It was as if there were some alien creature, an invisible insidious force, gently probing into my mind using long, squirming tentacles of enquiring thought, exploring, touching, sensing with taste and smell. Some of the killers I've interviewed – Kenneth Bianchi, for example – radiate hatred, pure evil as hot as a kitchen stove. You can smell it. It's like foul breath. Each killer is different. Some are calm and beguiling; others are 'amusing' in a strange sort of way, as was Douglas Clark, aka 'The Sunset Slayer', whom I interviewed on death row in San Quentin State Prison (SQ). With Harvey, he was just a big dude psyching me out. He was reading me while I was reading him. But having come to know this man through several years of correspondence, and with a good knowledge of his life of crime, I knew – and *he* knew that I knew – 'The Hammer' better than anyone else, because I had been closely studying him and his letters for so long. Then, suddenly, as if a switch inside his head flicked off, a secret but twisted smile started to play around Harvey's mouth. His lips, moistened with saliva, were slightly open, but otherwise his face was without expression.

Now, try to put yourself in my shoes, because this stone-cold serial killer is insidiously fascinating to observe at such close quarters. His plate-size hands were resting just inches from mine on the table. (It is all very well writing about these beasts, or lecturing to others about them, but one never gets the true picture unless one is sitting just a touch away and able to sense their distilled evil.) For up close and personal, Harvey is the wolf in sheep's clothing; almost part-human, part-Antichrist, the stuff of our worst nightmares come true. Then he spoke his first full sentence, low, almost husky and contradictory from the get-go: 'Ya know, Chris, never did I commit a crime then commit another to keep it quiet. I committed murders to ensure that false accusations of rape would not occur.' We will see this denial attitude in some of his following letters.

The ice was broken.

My previous belief that Harvey lived in a continual state of denial – existing in a world where he admits some guilt all dressed up in mitigation while not taking total responsibility for his brutal and heinous crimes – was confirmed.

Pausing for a moment, he looked deep into my eyes. Most of the serial murderers I have interviewed are shifty and cannot maintain eye contact, but not for a single second did Harvey take his eyes away from mine. He was seeking my reaction to what he'd just said, but nothing came back from me – my blank expression telling him everything: his manipulative 'game-playing' wasn't working on this Brit. I wasn't playing by *his* rules, I was playing by *my* rules, and he was starting to realise it.

'Were you scared, Christopher?' is a question I am often asked. My reply is always the same: 'Nope! Killers like Carignan are cowards who prey on the weak and vulnerable. Did Bundy,

Bianchi, Sutcliffe, Shawcross or any of their ilk ever attack a man? Of course not! Neither did Carignan. They are gutless at heart.

As the interview progressed, it was as if this self-alleged font of all known serial killer knowledge was quietly lecturing me. Whenever Harvey admitted that he had raped and killed young women, it was always, so he claimed, as a result of 'their provocation'. He said that it was always the victim who brought up the subject of sex when he offered them a ride in his car, and the reader will see this writ large in his correspondence to me. When we think back to fifteen-year-old Kathy Sue Miller, can one imagine that innocent girl raising the subject of sex with this mega-ugly man? I can't, that's for sure. In fact, nowhere can this be better illustrated than in his written account to me of a ride he gave to a perfectly respectable nineteen-year-old nurse whose car had broken down.

The truth is, according to her police statements, that he offered to fix her car, but beforehand he explained to her that he needed to fetch his tools. This was his well-practised ruse. He then forced her into his car, drove her into the country, then brutally raped and attempted to kill her by smashing into her head with a wheel wrench. He pathetically argues in mitigation that she got into his car of her own free will; his story comprises a smattering of the truth and a bucketful of lies, something not uncommon when sexual serial killers give their accounts of their crimes. They weave fact into fiction, so that once you've checked out certain facts, which turn out to be true, you might be duped into believing that their false accounts also pass muster. All of which is proven by what follows.

This is at once disturbing and disgusting, yet the following account from 'The Hammer' offers a fascinating statement from the mind of a homicidal sexual psychopath. It does not make for pleasant reading, but let's see what you can discern between his rambling lines. As always, I quote verbatim:

> She got in and may have been somewhat nervous, but she did not seem afraid. During the ride we talked about another girl I used to see, one who had left me because I had not given her $30 I had been giving her every each and every week. It was not payment for anything, but a gift. The girl [the nurse] riding with me said she would never exchange sex for $30 – making it seem she believed the other woman had, and that herself despised her for what the first woman had done. I tried to enlighten her thinking, but she was adamant in her statement that she would not have sex for $30 because those were her words and not that she would not have sex for money, which was my thought at the time.
>
> It was then that I got the drift; that she thought I was offering her the same amount for sex and she was turning down the offer – but I am not saying she wanted money to have sex at all. The way the conversation went it could have been either, that she would not have sex for $30 or she would not have sex for any amount of money. It was no big deal to me at that time, so the conversation had no special meaning to me until much later when I tried to remember everything that was talked about and how it was said.

At this point the reader will sense that here Carignan is already starting to build some mitigation for what was to come. Let this opportunist serial killer's transference of blame begin.

When we got to my friend's place where the tools were supposed to be, I stopped the car, turned around, and immediately drove away. My friend told me if his pick-up, a 1973 ¾ ton Chevrolet, was not in the yard, to not hang around because his sons did not like me. This was a surprise because I did not know his boys. I had never met any of them [in fact, Carignan did not have any friends; he was a fantasy-driven loner]. Anyway, I drove away and stopped the car just before driving onto the main road. I put my arm around her and, although she hesitated, she did move over closer to me when I indicated with arm pressure that is what I wanted. It was not a pressure that forced her to move, not a hold that would have moved her head had she declined. Instead it was an indication of what I would like her to do, and she complied.

I can remember my thoughts as plain as it was yesterday: 'She wants it!' This in spite of the fact that I wondered why she had been so adamant in denying she would have sex for $30, which in my mind could have been any amount at the time. I slid my arm behind her head, put a slight, almost gentle pressure on her neck behind her head, and she bent down – not because of the pressure but with her own strength – unbuttoned my pants, took out my penis, and stroked it while we kissed, until I indicated with the same kind of pressure that I wanted her to suck it. She did.

When she finished, I told her, 'Spit that damned stuff out' when I saw her sitting there holding the semen in her mouth. She did – but I did hold on to her in case she wanted to jump out and run away. I was not satisfied that

> she was not going to say I had forced her to do what she had done. She looked at me, giving me a strange smile – like I was a fool for thinking she would run – closed the door, and I drove on.

One can almost hear Carignan's low voice talking there. Everything to his compensatory, warped mind, is gentle, caring, trying to understand; an effort to portray himself as a victim more than anything else. But, there is more going on here, is there not? Although unable to have actual physical sex with a woman, he resorted to oral sex; it is known that when recalling his crimes, Carignan is a compulsive masturbator even today. The late Michael Bruce Ross was too – multiple times a day, until he had sores on his penis. Kenneth Bianchi constantly masturbates to the memories of his crimes, and in Harvey's correspondence we see this sexual fantasising too; his 'pearls of wisdom' correspondence reliving, like some mental 'trophy', the terrors he put his victims through.

In her book *Discover Graphology*, Margaret Gullan-Whur talks at length about the extraordinary variety of handwriting regularly committed to paper. And it is true that 'Handwriting's genesis lies in electrical impulses originating in the brain' and 'The hand and the pen are its tools, and inky traces.' She goes on to say that reading someone's handwriting for the first time is a bit like meeting them in person for the first time; that the more you read, the better you get to know the person putting pen to paper. I'd say that this could apply also to those who type their letters, even though the appearance of each letter remains constant. Gullan-Whur says to look for breaks in a writer's 'flow', and we can see this in the sudden changes of mood in the written words that all of the killers discussed thus far have exhibited. The 'Mafia' alter ego presented by Melanie McGuire, the schizophrenic penmanship of Phillip Jablonski, and now Carignan, whose subconscious, his unconscious mental programming, compels him to retell his sex crimes and treat his perverted memories as mental trophies.

Carl Gustav Jung represented a certain kind of psychologist – three kinds, in fact: (1) he was a psychiatrist, i.e. a doctor practising psychology as a branch of medicine; (2) an analytical psychologist using the method of free analysis to draw out the contents of the unconscious mind; (3) a psychotherapist, one who helps clinically disturbed people to reach an autonomous understanding of their problem, thereby emphasising the individual's own role in his or her recovery. Of course Jung would not have been able to use (1) (2) or (3) with homicidal psychopaths, because they could never have accepted such mind-probing; they are far too streetwise to do this.

Psychologists such as Jung and Sigmund Freud believed that the feelings, fantasies and attitudes buried in the unconscious are all part of the truth about a person's real character, and could not be neatly cut off from what was observable, be it through the written word and/or physical behaviour. And as you'll know by now, in this book we are trying to fathom not only what is observable in ink but also what is invisible. Let's apply this to the facts about a few offenders' case histories.

From the crime-scene interchanges we've already explored in Locard's Exchange Principle, many serial killers deliberately take away something physical from the 'event'. It could be a lock of the victim's hair, underwear, an item of jewellery. By way of example, we need look no further than former Canadian Armed Forces Colonel Russell Williams, who not only video-recorded his crimes and took still photos but stole his victims' underwear and shoes as trophies. These he kept at his home, often dressing up in his victims' stockings, bras and panties and taking selfies. And he was the commanding officer of Canada's largest air force base; with the highest security rating. He had once ferried the Queen around. Holy shit. You could not make this up if you tried; go check him out on Google. If the circumstances were not so serious, it would be a real hoot seeing him all dressed up like that; a complete prat. But did he stalk and kill men? Of course not!

American serial killer Joel David Rifkin, now serving 203 years in prison for murdering nine women (but suspected of up to 17 kills between 1989 and 1993), took away from his crime scenes locks of his victims' hair, jewellery and other intimate items. These he kept in his cluttered bedroom. He touched them while recalling his sex crimes during his regular masturbation sessions.

Kenneth Bianchi is an arch-manipulator and who also kept many of his female victims' jewellery items to give to his common-law wife Kelli Kae Boyd, who believed his yarns that he had bought them for her to wear. When he was finally arrested in Bellingham, Washington State, police found these 'trophies' on her dressing table.

Of course, 'trophies' need not be physical items; they can be memories too. Jablonski relives his crimes in his letters. Melanie McGuire is gloating and metaphorically urinating over her husband's grave in her 'Mafia' letter to the district attorney. Graham Young relived his lethal poisonings and the agonising suffering he caused his victims by expounding to all and sundry about his knowledge of toxic substances. Michael Ross, Bianchi, and so many others, including convicted killer paedophiles such as Arthur Shawcross, Colin Pitchfork and, in extremis, Bobby Joe Long, use these 'sex memories' almost like snuff material, with no shame or repentance for their crimes. This reflects the true nature of evil. So, when we have a killer boasting about his crimes in correspondence, it effectively represents an incarcerated man's 'jack-off' material. The following passage, taken once more from Carignan's correspondence with me, illustrates the slow build-up in his mindset as he relives a crime on paper; as ever, he reveals as much by what he doesn't say as by what he does:

> While we were starting out, I told her, 'I want to fuck you. I know a place where we can go.' She asked, 'How long will we be gone? I must be back by one o'clock.' It was then about 10.30.
>
> I did have a place in mind but it was miles away. So I drove along and pulled in next to a lake. When I stopped I saw a house in the distance in the midst of some trees and a man walking our way from another direction. I turned around and drove away. During this, the girl did not make any attempt to open the car door and get out.
>
> Directly across the road from the lake a road led into a glen. It was about 500–600 feet from the main road. When we got there, I went to the trunk and took out a blue plaid blanket [subsequently recovered by police] and threw it on to the ground, and I told her, 'Get ready!' I was not happy with her for some reason, but she was

a very sexy woman, about 20 years old, and I wanted to have sex with her, especially since we already had after a manner of speaking. She took off my jeans and her panties and laid down on her back with her feet in my direction. The whole of her pudendum was pointing towards me – and it was beautiful, as was herself, a very pretty woman. Now, I do not know what other men look for or how they act, but I generally always look at the vulva, play with it. The prettier she looks in her genital area, the more I want sex.

Now, I only stopped to help the girl get her car started. When she climbed in, I only had in mind to get the tools to fix it. Sex was not on my mind, and I did not kidnap her. Everyone assumes these women and girls as innocents. They generally are not. Each and every one of them wanted something from me, either money, to drive one of my cars, or something they would not divulge. I never kidnapped them, or forced them to come with me. She is no different from the others. I am not a rapist, and the word itself is revolting to me it turns my stomach.

Yes, yes, Harvey, we get it now, but all of my readers across the world are extremely astute. It must have been terrible for you. All those girls and young women wanting something from you, 'Mr Innocent', and you accused of being a 'rapist'. Shocking, eh, Harv? But please go on. What happened next?

Despite what anyone says, we had a delightful time in that clearing until she accused me of taking money from her purse, and then I thought, 'Here we go again.' I

> became much more angry than the moment called for and acted out within the content of that anger rather than against the accusation which called for no more than an explanation that I had not taken her money. The right rear tire on my car had gone flat and I was changing it when she screamed out at me. She kept screaming that the money was not hers and almost insanely demanding that I return it. Then, in a wink, her tone changed and she told me how she wanted to trade her car for another. That I should give her $200 for the trade or she was going to say I had raped her.

Wow, Harv, this wasn't a good day, then. Flat tyre (tire). Wrongly accused of stealing money from the nurse's purse. Unwarranted demands with menaces for two hundred greenbacks. Gosh, Saint Harvey, this ain't going down too well, is it?

> Until that instant, I had gone on with the business of replacing the lug bolts on the hub; but in that instant when she made that threat, I became what I see as being uncontrollably angry and I hit her with the lug wrench – and not with the hammer as she later testified, and what is generally believed. She was fully dressed and I can see it now as plain as it was happening even now. She fell to the ground as if she had been pole-axed and she slid slowly down a 12-to-14-foot incline into a ditch, feet first, with her brown sweater rolling up under her armpits. I did not panic, but put the lug wrench in the trunk and the remaining lug bolt in my pocket, got into my car, and drove away. At about 15–20 minutes down the road,

> maybe 15–20 miles, I realized I could not leave the dear woman there to die if she was only wounded, and I had to know, so I turned around and went back to try and help her. As I drove by, there were several cars and a tractor with a wagon behind it stopped on the road, and all of the people were bending over someone that I knew was her, so I kept on driving.

Following up his letter, I reminded him that he had left the young nurse for dead in that ditch. That she had regained consciousness several hours later, lying in a pool of blood and suffering from almost fatal brain injuries. It was practically nightfall and, in dreadful pain, she crawled over a mile through ploughed fields to a road where a farmer discovered her and summoned help that morning. 'That rather shoots out your lie about returning within about forty minutes of hitting her, Harvey?' I suggested.

In his later face-to-face interview with me, he said:

> I hope that you treat me right if you write about me. I have friends in your country who look after me. They've seen your house. Long track up to it, right? You drive a silver Mercedes. Pretty young wife and two little daughters. Just treat me with respect and all will be fine for them.

In fact, Carignan saw the ambulance at the crime scene as he was returning to it not to save the nurse's life, but, concerned that she might have survived and would describe him and his vehicle to the police, to finish her off. By then, however, she had crawled to safety and been found. The only thing that kept the young woman going was that her sister had told her the previous day that she was expecting a child – and she was determined to stay alive to see the baby.

Throughout my correspondence with Harvey Carignan, he made much of what he calls his 'string of pearls'. In effect, he implied that these 'pearls of wisdom' are priceless details that he will release only when he judges the time is appropriate for him. 'The truth is my pearls of wisdom,' he bluntly stated. 'I am *not* going to release the pearls of this part of the truth at least for years,' he added, before clamming up and refusing to answer any more questions in our interview or in correspondence about the nature of his crimes, however during the early part of my interview with 'The Hammer', he devoted his 'valuable time' to presenting himself as a man of considerable knowledge. It is true that he has studied philosophy, among other subjects, during his incarceration, so one might imagine that his opinions are worth hearing. But within this beast there is a fatal flaw.

> If the truth hurts, change it.
>
> Serial killer Keith Hunter Jesperson:
> commenting on Carignan's persona

Despite having spent the better part of his worthless life behind bars, Carignan is totally unable to come to terms with his guilt. This is a trait he shares with many other serial killers. Even with the evidence being consistent and overwhelming in every case of sexual assault, rape or murder attached to him, Carignan is psychologically compelled to transfer most of the blame for his crimes onto his luckless victims. Thus, not only is he an opportunist serial murderer but a compensatory killer, for when he is exposed with all of his excuses staring him straight back in his face as complete untruths, he retreats to the trench used by so many offenders: the refuge from which he can blame the entire law-enforcement and criminal-justice system for fitting him up. Indeed, if the gravity and number of his offences were not so serious, one might be forgiven for regarding his excuses as merely laughable. Some may even say that his letters are the ramblings of a madman and, as such, should be dismissed or, at best, ignored. However, Harvey is not mad by any definition. What he refuses to say – hides between the lines of his correspondence or conveniently chooses to forget to say, or answer for when pressed – is ultimately of some interest, if we want to try and figure out how such deviant minds work.

But was this the end of what Harvey 'The Hammer' had to say for himself? It was not. It seems that my face-to-face confrontation with him had an impact; let's remember that for much of the time we were alone, with him unshackled, unpredictable, and quite able to slam me up against a wall and tear my head off in an instant. The reader will recall his veiled threat to me, about where I lived; 'The Hammer' had looked inside my mind as I had looked into his. For an instant, I recalled how his huge hands and his hammer had smashed into his prey's heads; what damage could he do to me right there and then, if he suddenly flipped? You might also recall his psychiatrist telling me: 'Yes, you will get to interview Mr Carignan, or *something* living inside his head. You'll get to interview him, and pure evil will get to interview you.'

For some reason – a reason for which I will never fully understand – my meeting with Harvey produced the most unexpected of results, which I will now share with you for the first time. Although he had promised me a tele-filmed interview, when we arrived at MCF-Stillwater he'd abruptly changed his mind, much to the chagrin of Frazer & Co. It was to be me, Harv and a tape recorder – that was it. In so many ways this was a good thing, for when they're being filmed, these monsters play to the camera. They revel in being the sole centre of attention, as did Michael Ross. Some killers want 'special treatment': a little powder on their faces; their hair groomed; candy or a cold, fizzy drink. The TV crew make them feel important, you see. The crew are stroking their feathers to inflate their egos, so that they can return to their cells and tell their fellow inmates: 'Hey, guys, I am going on the BBC.'

To be fair to Harvey, he wanted none of that malarkey. He wanted our meeting to be personal. To him, we had been penfriends for some years. He had never given any sort of interview before I met with him, and he has not done so since.

Realising that he had threatened me, by alleging he had friends in the UK that looked after his interests, he apparently felt ashamed of himself. He had, to his mind – although the veiled threat was empty and uttered in the heat of the moment – potentially cost himself the only male 'friend' he'd ever had in his life. He knew that I was a former HM Royal Marines 'Green Beret' commando; that I had always treated him with great respect; that my crew and I had travelled hundreds of miles across the US at great expense to see him, so he knew that he had let us all down big time. Yet, not once did I complain to him. I took it on the chin and I guess that he respected that.

After I had returned to the UK, the postman delivered a letter. Dated 17 March 1995, it was from 'The Hammer' and it contained all of his 'pearls of wisdom', as if this was a gift to apologise for his behaviour when I had called him out. It is a deeply personal letter, almost a 'compensatory letter' from him, and one that I have never made public before. It is typed, not a grammatical error anywhere, obviously written with deep thought and attention. So, as you are now pretty much fully aware of least a few of the bestial crimes he committed, I let you judge the following. It's one of the most remarkable letters from a homicidal maniac. However, for the sake of decency, and out of deep respect for the victims' next of kin, I will not publish here those 'pearls of wisdom' that relate to the humiliations and agonies he inflicted on them – nor, I suggest, would my readers expect me to, as they are his truthful confessions to the most awful crimes imaginable:

> Dear Christopher, your beloved family and the Cat.
>
> Greetings from the Colonies and may St Patrick's Day, which is an anathema in England this year, be good to you. Chances are you are still in The States and up to something or other [serial killer interviews]. I was too full-minded to ask when you were here; which, by the way, was great and could have only been more wonderful had I been able to see your wife and the kids as well as you, Christopher, and if only we could have had a more equitable bargain. In all truth, I did not want to do as much as I did, but I could see you were exceedingly upset and genuinely concerned, so I went as far as I thought I could without offending my attorney who, by the way, would 'eat my ass out royally', if you are familiar with the term. In English, he was as mad as a wet hen and made all

> the noises appropriate to his demeanor. The price is right for his services, but other than that he and I do not agree on much. His fee is free, which is hard to beat in this day and time, but the crap I have to take is just a little much, if you know what I mean?

At this point, I would like the reader to consider the comment I made much earlier with regard to Harvey and his typewriter, 'Clyde'. It is important to note that he used this machine to communicate with me until it broke. For a while he wrote in longhand. Almost unreadable to be sure, and I told him so. But in this letter he is, to his mind, sharing something special to him, and he is not *overtly* giving me 'intimate' details that are intended to manipulate. In that context, one might see evidence of *some integrity* here – let's say the building blocks of a sincere letter – although, I stress once again, none of which must be interpreted as any mitigation for his crimes.

> Anyway, meet Lazarus who was brain dead and I had to send to a Typewriter Savior for his Resurrection. He used to be Louis, who replaced Clyde, but I thought Lazarus more appropriate being he had actually become junk and had to be completely resuscitated. It cost me $261.15, or $185.00 more than if I had bought a new Personal Word Processor of comparable quality. I would have bought the new one except I was not allowed to. Those of us who have this style and of comparable quality can keep them, but we cannot replace them except with heaps of junk that cost no more than about $150.00, which is the [as written] equivalent to bacon and eggs for a breakfast for a family of

five. He [Lazarus] tells your Cat he is going to have to steal his mouse next time he sees him with one. There, that ought to sufficiently scare the little critter and cause him not to sit in your window with a mouse in his mouth and laugh at you. (Yah, and watch the damned cat be a she and catch me with my genders down!)

What can I say other than I wish you a safe and speedy trip home. I do not know how much of The Colonies you saw, but I am sure that in driving from Seattle to Minneapolis, which is about one-half way across the bloody place, you got some idea of just how enormous, big and wide the place really is. Also, I hope you enjoyed yourselves when you saw the country. You told me how lucky you were in evading the storms so you saw our season called Winter at its best. It can be a beautiful time of the year and there are so many wonderful and happy things to do. Have you tried skiing, sledding, snowmobile riding, cross-country skiing, wind sailing on the ice, hay rides, walking in the snow up to your butts, or throwing snowballs at each other? I have. Also, there is something special about getting in a sleigh and going to Grandmother's house for Thanksgiving Dinner, a holiday that once upon a time really meant something and was shared by all, Native Americans and we Interlopers from Europe, mostly 'Meanie Olde Englande', as I think it might have been spelled then.

Of course, Harvey did none of those 'romantic' things. Most of his time while on the 'out' he was running amok, tearing around in his cars, burning rubber, mixing with his crooked cronies, thieving, leching, raping and bludgeoning, but at least he's trying to imagine what life should have been like and not face the reality of the unfortunate fix he's in right now. Once again, here's that dissociation between reality and fact, but oh so subtle.

> Well, my friend, you have seen where I live, probably mentally measured the extent of my physical world, and I imagine you were chilled by the sight, but the size is not what bothers me: I am not fazed by it. What scares the ever-loving crap out of me is being done not to me so much as to others, especially the younger men with so much of their lives left to live, whose wishes are those of children and whose hope are being taken from them. All of them, Whites, Blacks, Latinos, and Others as the next Cro-Magnon specie [*sic*] is called, with their ethic chatterings, their pathetic makings which they hope will distinguish themselves from all others, and the steely-eyed rage they show in return for their maniacal ravings of some of the staff.

Steady now, Harvey. You were doing okay, so let's not go into a hyper-rant, please.

> It is not our persona, our outer beings, I fear for, but our futures thinking and feelings, theirs and mine, which are being taken away from us, futures we give away freely and almost innocently according to the hate and vindictiveness we feel for and perpetuate against each other. [Here, Carignan is back-handedly referring to his hatred towards women in general because, as he has stated many times, 'They played mind games with my head.']

If only we could redirect this wasted energy in a common direction, toward some common goal, there would not be anything we could not achieve. We would be men and seen as human beings instead of as names society so conveniently foisted upon us to set us apart and to place us at the lowest part of the human junk heap. If only we would not wear our deficits like badges and our social scars like medals of honor, we would no longer be White Trash, Niggers, I-ties, and Slant-Eyed Motherfuckers, but fallible human beings fulfilling our human aspirations, a contributing forces [*sic*] to be reckoned with, pulling together instead of apart, and a group united together instead of a mob pulling every way and having to form gangs and to seek protection from behind the lines of their limited parameters.

. . . Just once, if only for a Limited [*sic*] while, we might inhale the scent of freedom instead of breathing in the odors of each other's sweaty bodies and the lingering nausea of human excrement that prevails over even the pine smell of industrial-strength deodorizing disinfectant used liberally and to no avail, and be more than the ignorant animals we are thought to be, treated like, and people think we might have become due to the smell of our stinking thoughts that are inwardly boiling away our self-esteem, our caring for ourselves as individuals and as a whole, and the dreadful odor or our dead Loves we suffer over through the darkest hours of the night instead of sleeping and steeling ourselves for our tomorrows. Dear God! What do we teach each other?' [Spelling and punctuation as written.]

'The Hammer' went on and on for another eight double-sided pages, and I simply cannot put you, dear reader, through any more of his literary purgatory. I mean, I would love to, of course I would, but you might either need to seek psychiatric counselling (not recommended, for the reasons mentioned earlier) or turn to the drink then throw yourself off a cliff (certainly not recommended either). Yet after his rant into his world where elephants fly, lead balls bounce and fairies reign supreme, his 'words of wisdom' were signed off with:

> I hope you had a magnificent trip on the way back and splendid times away from home and a safe and satisfactory trip on the way back. My heart is with you, each and every one. Take care of yourselves. I cannot afford to lose even one of you, I need all of you to care for and to love.
>
> Your friend, Harvey.

Phew, I wonder what you make of that lot? It seems very much as though there are two characters living inside Harvey's head – one good, the other deadly evil. Both totally inconsistent with each other. As my late friend, the former Lord Chief Justice Geoffrey Lane, Baron Lane, AFC, PC once wrote to me: 'There is good in the worst of us. Oddly enough, prison sometimes serves for that fact to be proved', but in Carignan's case he can never learn nor will he be able to: aged ninety-five, he died of natural causes within the walls of MCF Oak Park Heights, 5329 N. Osgood Avenue, Minnesota, on 6 March 2023.

Ian Stewart Brady, aka 'The Moors Murderer'

We do whatever we enjoy doing. Whether it happens to be judged good or evil is a matter for others to decide.

IAN BRADY, *THE GATES OF JANUS: SERIAL KILLING AND ITS ANALYSIS* (2001)

Along with tag-team accomplice Myra Hindley, Ian Brady ranks among the worst serial killers in British criminal history. Little further introduction is required here because all that you will ever want to know about this murderous couple is extremely well documented elsewhere.

Two sadistic killers of the utmost depravity.

Mr Justice Fenton Atkinson: on Brady and Hindley

The span of their crimes, which became the subject of extensive worldwide coverage, ran from 12 July 1963 until 7 October

1965, when Brady and Hindley were arrested. Their victims were: Pauline Reade; John Kilbride; Keith Bennett; Lesley Ann Downey and Edward Evans – aged between ten and seventeen. At least four of the children were sexually assaulted. Two bodies were discovered in 1965, in shallow graves dug on the bleak, grey Saddleworth Moor, an area of the Peak District National Park, in north-west England, that bears the suitably ominous name of the 'Dark Peak'. In 1987, police uncovered a third grave on the moors, that of Pauline Reade. Keith Bennett's body is also believed to lie there, although the whereabouts of his final resting place remain unknown, despite several searches over the years. Both killers were given a full life tariff. Hindley died of bronchial pneumonia on 15 November 2002. Brady died by natural causes, his sell-by date expiring on 15 May 2017.

I have not read Brady's book *The Gates of Janus: Serial Killing and its Analysis*, for what I believe is a sensible reason: this diagnosed sexual psychopath's opinions and analysis on serial homicide are, quite frankly, neither here nor there. More of interest to me is the never-before-published correspondence that Brady sent to me while he was incarcerated at the high-security psychiatric hospital Park Lane, now named Ashworth, in Maghull, ten miles to the north-east of Liverpool.

Before we begin, let's remind ourselves of Mr Justice Fenton Atkinson's description of Brady and Hindley, while also bearing in mind that neither of these two monsters ever exhibited a shred of remorse. Myra Hindley tried to curry some mitigating favour with a bunch of left-wing do-gooders – including Long Longford, famed for championing social outcasts and unpopular causes and especially notable for his lifelong advocacy of penal reform. Whether Lord Longford had it in mind to try to reform

Brady and Hindley is something else, but the Lord Chief Justice Geoffrey Lane does not seem to have been in agreement when he wrote: 'This is the case if ever there is to be one when a man should stay in prison till he dies.'

Brady's biro-written letters to me were upon 'Medical Mission International' 11 x 12-cm cream notepaper, featuring coloured photos – one each of an antelope, elephant, zebra, baboon, white cuddly bear cub, monkey, giraffe and some people pushing a rubber boat through some water. These were, of course, very small postage-stamp photos, as you will have gathered. His notepaper had been designed for him bespoke: atop the front page had been personally printed for him: 'From the desk of: Mr I Stewart-Brady'.

If that is not obsequious from a man of his ilk, I don't know what is.

Mr I. Stewart-Brady's first letter to me from his 'desk' is dated 30 July 2009, kicking off with 'Dear Christopher, Thanks for yours on 9th July 2009'. As he had a lot to say within so small a page, written on both sides, his handwriting was neat and readable.

> First, most of your questions are answered in my book on criminal psychology, 'The Gates of Janus' published 2002, now accepted text in UK/US universities and translated. Reviews can be accessed on Amazon and other main book websites.
>
> No, contrary to logical extension, based on 'Janus', I'm not particularly interested in books about serial killers, etc. I prefer the study of <u>major</u> criminals, such as Blair, Bush and their profiteering henchmen. As I've always

stated since teenage years, you can't 'beat decent, honest, respectable people' when it comes down to global serial slaughter, theft, greed, treachery and hypocrisy, which is why they exploit petty, underclass crime and criminals to distract attention from themselves and their threadbare pretensions/claims to moral superiority. Nothing new or profound in any of this, of course; just generally convenient to ignore such unpopular juxtapositions. Please acknowledge receipt.

Best wishes,

Ian Brady.

PS: The current satirical gall of Cherie Blair lecturing the nation on the 'horrors of knife crime', highlights the absurdity and arrogance of the class. Greed has replaced vocation in the professions.

Which strikes me as a lot of 'Speakers' Corner' set-the-world-straight, top-of-a-ladder blathering. And what's more, did you know that Brady, who was pathologically obsessed with the Nazis, actually received German language lessons from a senior university professor while in the nuthouse? He was tipped to land a job as a translator if ever he were to be released. When future prime minister James Callaghan – then the Home Secretary – popped in to visit Brady at his desk, this paedophile praised the Nazis for their 'efficiency'. Actually, that last point stuck with me, and I started wondering if I had missed something.

My editors are always informing me that I have missed many, *many* things. Some of my readers and critics say the same thing. And my publisher's lawyers are always telling me not to write certain things. So I asked myself: Was Brady really being groomed for a job as an ambassador in Berlin within some future Callaghan government? Because not-so-long-ago-released prison records now reveal how prison governors, and a welfare officer, praised Brady's intelligence and excellent use of Hitler's oratories 'with a cracked grin', stating that they hoped that the German classes would end with him leading a 'healthy normal life in society'.

Then I woke up in a cold sweat: German language classes for Brady? C'mon, are these leftie clowns kidding us, or what?

> My crimes were no different to massacres being carried out by US troops in Vietnam.
>
> Ian Brady: to a prison chaplain

After which came this utter fantasy-driven drivel from the chief education officer at Durham Prison: 'If Brady continues to come along well in his German I see no reason why he should not make a living one day as an interpreter or translator,' adding: 'The tuition given to Brady has given a new interest to him in life, begin [*sic*] to pull him out of himself on the long hard road to *a healthy normal life in society*.' [Author's italics.]

By now the reader will be thinking, 'What the fuck are these fools going on about? This is taxpayers' hard-earned money being thrown at a sexual psychopath who still refused to reveal the locations of his victims?' It may be of some interest – although to whom, I simply don't know – that Brady also passed courses in English literature, maths, psychology and was encouraged to pursue a university degree – at the taxpayers' expense, once again, of course. Then comes the juicy stuff. Brady, who strangled some of his victims with string or a shoelace and buried them on Saddleworth Moor, was given lessons – wait for it, wait for it – in knot-tying while in jail, by a young female therapist who became infatuated with him. A prison spokesperson commented: 'Reluctantly, we had to separate them because of our fears their bond was becoming unprofessional.' You really couldn't make this up if you tried.

So back to I. Stewart-Brady's desk and the contents of his letter to me. It occurred to me to look up some online reviews of *The Gates of Janus*, and they are a mixed bunch. Whether or not his claims that the book is 'accepted text in UK/US universities', especially those with large Jewish campuses, seems at best debatable. It all comes across as a lot of over-egging-it, if you ask me. As for any knot-tying – may I be so blatantly crass in suggesting that the best knot of all would have been in the form of a hempen noose tied around his scrawny neck?

Poisoned Nibs

My fellow-prisoners […] seemed to me in no way morally inferior to the rest of the population, though they were on the whole slightly below the usual level of intelligence, as was shown by their having been caught.

THE AUTOBIOGRAPHY OF BERTRAND RUSSELL, 1951–69

A dry wit, had Bertrand.

NOTE: what follows was not, I stress *not* penned by a serial murderer but it does earn its place in this book because it was written at the behest of one of the most evil men in US homicidal history, and although one short note from a pretty much nondescript prisoner might not amount to a hill of beans, the following account has more twists and turns than fiddling with a Rubik's cube. It proves that corresponding with dangerous criminals can be a risky business indeed – as authors far better than me will agree, even more so when a letter that at first blush seems innocuous enough, harbours cunning most foul between the lines.

Miguel Langebeck was not a criminal big-hitter by any stretch of the imagination, but he did earn himself a fifteen-year stretch as inmate #192103 J2S3 at Florida State Prison (Main Unit) in Starke. In August 1995, I received an unsolicited letter from Langebeck, which started: 'Dear Christopher. Receive my greetings and best wishes. We haven't been formally introduced, but a mutual friend asked me to write to you. Gerard Schaeffer [*sic*], as you know a fellow litigant for prison reform and prisoners' rights, is the mutual friend I speak of.' Now that other name I knew. He was one of America's most heinous serial killers: Florida ex-cop, Gerard John Schaefer Jr.

One can instantly sense 'flowery' prose, perhaps along the lines of Graham Young's letter quoted earlier, or one from Mr I. Stewart-Brady. I soon got a sniff of a jailhouse lawyer here too – (another Ian). Miguel's penmanship was okay, grammar reasonably good, yet for the life of me I was certainly *no* mutual friend of Schaefer, nor Langebeck for that matter. The former I had no interest in at all, the latter I had never even heard of, so this letter came right out of the blue.

Curious to a fault, I looked up Langebeck's details on the Florida Department of Corrections website, to learn that he had been arrested in Miami-Dade County on 1 February 1990 for cocaine trafficking. He was released on 1 October 1998 – his present status 'unknown'. Small fry when it comes down to it, most certainly not in Schaefer's bestial league, yet why would Langebeck write on Schaefer's behalf. I sensed some naughtiness going on here.

Let's deal with the remainder of Miguel's letter first:

> He has informed me of your interest in his plight and being somewhat of a litigator myself, I was drawn by our mutual views on prisons today.
>
> I hope you overlook my boldness in writing you, but it's also to offer my time and services if needed since Mr. Shaeffer [*sic*] has closed a book deal which he'll be working on, withdrawing himself from any further legal work until his completion of his project.
>
> I'm currently undergoing some research for some Virginia prisoners, for them to attack Virginia's Parole Board's new stringent guidelines. I'm trying to demonstrate an Ex Post Facto clause violation. Hopefully when completed it'll be entertained by the courts with merit [...]

Straight off the bat, I knew that at the time of Langebeck's letter, Schaefer had grievously annoyed several authors who were now treating him like a literary plague. And the first thing the reader will notice will be the utter hypocrisy of the letter. Langebeck could not even spell Schaefer's name correctly, moreover; plus, I didn't give a jot about Schaefer's plight either. Here we have Mr Langebeck, a convicted cocaine trafficker by profession – a trade costing tens of thousands of lives a year – using typical jailhouse shyster legalese while banging on about a number of subjects: Schaefer, a sadosexual serial murderer who didn't give a damn about his many victims' rights; something about a book deal; fellow prisoners' rights; and something to do with an 'Ex Post Facto clause violation'. To be honest with the reader, I hadn't a clue about this 'Ex Post Facto' stuff; you probably don't either, then, straight out of Brady's and Carignan's playbook. Langebeck rails on:

> I've been amazed, at how the prisons in this country, abuse and outright disrespect the rights of the inmate body. They're the first to criticize other nations in human rights issues, yet they are probably the biggest culprit of human rights violations. I believe, that the major problem has been the media portrayal of crime offenders, that have the general public appalled of being victimized, causing a general disconcern for prisoners only enhancing the public's views toward harsher sentences, focusing more on punishment rather than rehabilitation and education.

And, Miguel, the point of your letter is ... what? Please get on with it.

> Like all typical capitalist nations, their expertise in maintaining a façade impression on the world, always point a finger, instead of deal with reality, keeps its people blind of the facts. Yet, there's always hope, as long as a few care and bring it to light.
>
> Yours Truly,
>
> Miguel Langebeck

I am not sure if Miguel had studied at the 'Professor Ian Stewart-Brady Berlin University of Schwachsinn', so I haven't a clue if he had received a Doctorate in Flannel. I can't even confirm what the Virginia Parole Board made of Langebeck's *ex post facto* submissions. However, I am 100 per cent sure that the Virginia Supreme Court justices would *not* have messed their pants if they'd ever got as far as flicking through it all. Moreover, I am 200 per cent positive that if convict shyster

Langebeck's 'inmate clients' chose him to represent them, their sentences would have been quadrupled for wasting everyone's time, with any of them serving six months for shoplifting ending up in the electric chair. I was starting to think that 'Miggie' was yet another member of 'The Complicated Surreal Club' – a jerk-off who rode around the prison on a pink, three-wheeled Toy Town bike with a shiny ding-a-ling bell – and turned the last fragments of my dwindling attention to Mr Schaefer. I will trouble the reader little with this serial killer's narrative – Wikipedia is pretty thorough in this regard and there are several TV documentaries and interviews available on YouTube. Nonetheless, what follows *did* interest me.

There are plenty of narcissistic jailhouse attorney wannabes (think Ted Bundy and Kenneth Bianchi, for instance) – a litigious bunch of halfwits who get a perverse thrill out of wasting millions of dollars of taxpayers' money firing off lawsuits to all and sundry. Most of the time they use lined, yellow prison-issue stationery, although I once received a short note written on toilet paper from one prisoner. Sadly the text was all unreadable, so I replied thanking the chap for his ingenuity and enclosed several sheets of one of our better-known, softer, perfumed brands featuring a puppy should he feel the need to write again or have a sudden need to do something else.

Despite the fact that all of Schaefer's appeals had been rejected, off he went filing meritless lawsuits. First in his firing line was true-crime writer Patrick Kendrick, who described Schaefer as: 'an overweight, doughy, middle-aged man who preyed on victims who were psychologically and physiologically weaker than him'.

Patrick, congratulations. That portrayal is right on the nail.

Further down range came litigation aimed at other authors: Sondra London; Colin Wilson; Michael Newton; and former FBI Special Agent Robert Ressler (whom Schaefer targeted for describing him as a serial killer). Indeed, Schaefer sued Ressler all costing the former cop a fortune to defend, because at that time Schaefer had only been convicted of two homicides – although more charges were being loaded into the DA's magazine. The FBI's *own* criminal lexicon defines a serial killer as having murdered three or more victims with a cooling-off period in between events, so Schaefer had a moot point.

Sondra London, an old girlfriend from high school, collaborated with Schaefer in writing and publishing crime fiction but soon learned that his 'fiction' was rather closer to fact than was comfortable, and ended her association with Schaefer, repudiating his story that he was merely a 'framed ex-cop' who wrote lurid fiction. When she stated that he was indeed every bit the serial killer he simultaneously boasted of being, he repeatedly threatened her life and filed suit against her for calling him a serial killer in print.

In support of her defence against the lawsuit – which was costing her time and money to defend, of course – Sondra London compiled an exhibit of photocopies of 500 incriminating pages of Schaefer's handwritten correspondence; the judge dismissed his case without further ado. In a further turn of the screw, she generously provided Newton and Wilson with the same 500-page exhibit too, so his lawsuits against them were also kicked out.

Up until his death, Schaefer continued to threaten Sondra London. He also wrote letters to Kendrick, suggesting that he had willing agents who would do his bidding and that he 'would hate to see something happen to your family'. Unfazed, Kendrick went on to write novels often describing brutal murders that he relates to his experience with this former police officer turned *really* bad. So Schaefer got himself screwed once again. These psychopaths never learn, do they?

It was at this point that I twigged on to the fact that Langebeck's letter was even more full of garbage than I'd first imagined. Why? Before 1995, all of Schaefer's efforts to have his *own* book published had been blown away. Since then, he'd been fishing for authors to write his story and, being the obnoxious control freak that he was, he blew them out every time. Then, I recalled that Sondra had edited a 1993 book called *Knockin' on Joe: Voices from Death Row*, and I vaguely recalled that she and I had spoken a couple of times on the phone. Somehow Schaefer had gotten wind of this, so *via* slippery Langebeck, he was trying to draw me into his web of deceit.

Gerard Schaefer was one of those up-his-own-backside prison idiots who never learn to shut up so, not unsurprisingly, he was making enemies fast and furious. Not only was this litigious, pseudo-religiously bigoted loudmouth a former cop who had abducted, tortured, raped and hung up to strangle to death at least two (although probably around thirty) of Florida's precious little darlings, he'd pissed all over the law-enforcement agencies who had hired him in all good faith to 'Protect and Serve'. He had used his uniform and his shield as a means of luring these trusting girls to their deaths. Now this smug, filthy little man was courting TV interviews and litigating against anyone who said a word against him. He had become a snitch in an attempt to curry favour with the guards, and using his status as a 'death-row law clerk' to get confidential information from prisoners that found their way to the prosecutor's office, only to be used against his fellow inmates. It is no wonder that in the year before his own murder he had human excrement thrown over him several times and his cell was twice set on fire. Now almost under siege, he made another fatal mistake by grassing on an inmate who was well respected in the prison. Bad move, Gerard.

At this point, please look up some of the TV-taped interviews of this fat bespectacled creep on YouTube. See for yourself what sort of man he was. Look at his eyes. His sickening grin, the obsequious piece of work only a sexual serial killer can be. I also strongly recommend the book *Knockin' on Joe*, edited by Sondra London, and published by Nemesis Publications. Strong stuff. Highly recommended, no-punches-pulled accounts. Not intended for a bedtime read.

US penitentiaries are not nice places in which to set up home. 'Newbies' chain-shuffling through the gates are entering 'The Belly of the Beast', especially the younger lads. Pretty boys are soon exploited – if you catch my drift – with the older cons being streetwise enough to keep their mouths superglued tight and snitches summarily dealt with; the correctional officers usually turn a blind eye. So Mr Schaefer really should have known better, but his psychopathological mindset was so ingrained, that he, like so many other psychopaths, never learned the error of their ways.

The pen is mightier than the sword.

Edward Bulwer-Lytton, Lord Lytton,
Richelieu; or The Conspiracy, 1839

On 3 December 1995, less than a month after I had received Langebeck's letter, Schaefer was found stabbed to death and trampled upon in his cell. One eye had been gouged out by a pen – prison punishment for snitches, or grasses – giving a new meaning to the above famous metonymic adage created by Bulwer-Lytton. All of which made for a most fitting end to a monster who was pathologically addicted to making everyone's lives a misery by using pen and ink to cause a stink. His writings to Sondra London were homicidal porn, he was reliving his crimes in ink, but in making his so-called 'book' a novel, and hoping to make a fast buck, he was gloatingly memorialising in the third person, and using Sondra London as the one to catch the heat.

Official sources put out the story that inmate Vincent Rivera killed Schaefer over an argument about a hot cup of water – it might have been coffee – but after attending the murder trial and debriefing Rivera, the admirable Sondra London, I believe, exposed what amounted to a cover-up, saying that the hot water story was implausible, noting several little-known facts:

- A full palm print in blood was found on the wall of Schaefer's cell, which in lab tests failed to match those of either Schaefer or Rivera – unconfirmed evidence that was thrown out instead of being presented to the jury.
- Expert testimony at Rivera's trial also established that the patterns of the footprints on Schaefer's corpse matched those of prison service issue, worn by prison officers but not by inmates.

Already serving a life sentence for two previous homicides and robberies, Vincent Faustino Rivera was sentenced to an additional 53 years and ten months for killing Schaefer. He never confessed to the crime, or to having had a motive to kill Schaefer. But he *did* write to Sondra London and tell her of a similar incident in that prison, claiming that he'd been an 'ear-witness' to the prison murder of death-row inmate Frank Valdes by prison officers. Valdes was on death row for his part in the fatal shooting in 1987 of a prison officer during an attempt to help an inmate escape. (A fellow inmate also involved in the shooting was executed in 2013.)

In his letter to London, Rivera alleged that he'd written a complaint to the prison authorities about an earlier assault by prison staff on Valdes, who occupied the cell next to him. Rivera's claim was ignored and he was still being held in a cell next to Valdes's when the second, fatal beating took place. Rivera knew what was happening – he had heard it before.

In the trial that followed Valdes's death, prosecutors stated that the attack on him was to prevent him discussing 'mistreatment of prisoners and writing letters' to the press. The defence's story was that Valdes had threatened one of the officers, leading to an extraction team being called to his cell. He had then, they alleged, killed himself – by the unlikely means of taking a nose-dive off his bunk into the bars of his cell. The autopsy showed that a number of Valdes's ribs had been broken and there were 'prints of correctional officers' boots' on his skin, therefore the Florida Department of Law Enforcement (FDLE) ruled that Valdes died as the result of a beating, and nine officers were arrested. The officers, who were fired from their jobs, refused to talk; four were acquitted and three years later all charges against the remaining defendants were dropped.

And here I return to the title of this chapter: 'Poisoned Nibs'. There is a common thread running throughout all of the aforementioned characters: an almost overwhelming, pathological desire to write countless letters, protesting about their communal welfare and prison rights while ignoring their victims' rights, attempting to sue all and sundry, at once poking their criminal noses into the business of others when they would have been better advised not to have put pen to paper at all. Have we not seen so much of this with the other killers featured within these pages thus far?

Endnote: before we move on, I'd like to address a point often claimed in articles, that Ted Bundy admired Gerard Schaefer: 'We often spoke together about our crimes, and Ted thought of me as his equal,' Schaefer boasts. 'We are both attorneys at heart fighting against the downtrodden.' All of which conveniently ignores the fact that Bundy was housed on death row while Schaefer was in the general prison population with no access to 'The Green Mile' remotely possible – apart from in Schaefer's wildest wet dreams.

As for Miguel's letter to me, guess what? I didn't reply.

Hal Karen and Ronald 'Butch' Joseph DeFeo Jr, aka 'The Amityville Horror'

There is no fire like passion, there is no shark like hatred, there is no snare like folly, there is no torrent like greed.

SIDDHARTA GAUTAMA

As regards the following case, the epigraph above defines the subject of this chapter to a T.

One more pertinent quote before we get going, this one relating to egotism. It's from Publilius Syrus's *Moral Sayings*, *c*.50 BC:

A cock has great influence on his own dunghill.

All of which seems most fitting for the subject of this chapter. I'll open with a bit of trivial travelogue.

A hamlet in the town of East Fishkill in Dutchess County, New York State, 'Stormville' is named after the siblings Jacob and Rupert Storm, a pair of settlers. According to the town's own website, the area is located at the intersections of 'Dutchess County Route 216, Old Route 52 and Seaman Road', and 'was begun as early as 1739'; Derick Storm is noted as the earliest individual to 'take up land' here. The website adds that the Storm family were slave owners and that a 'slave cemetery' can be found on Phillips Road. And this will excite my readers even more: Stormville's flea market is reportedly well worth a visit although, alas, 'pets are not allowed' to the event.

As you will have gathered by now, I love my etymology. The term 'flea market' may well have originated with the French 'marché aux puces' ('market of the fleas'), a reference to the sales of used merchandise, quite possibly flea-infested. And the reason that pets aren't permitted? Apparently because if an animal hasn't got fleas when it goes into such a market, it will most certainly have some when it leaves. For more information about the Stormville Airport Antique and Flea Market, including the dates, hours and rules, check out their website.

As this book is all about writing, you'll be delighted to know that East Fishkill was the birthplace of one Mr Platt Rogers Spencer – the inventor of the leading US business-handwriting style of the nineteenth century – in 1800. For those of my readers more inquisitive than me, one can take it as gospel that Platt was the originator of the Spencerian script – a popular system of cursive handwriting. To add to his bona fides, he was a teacher and active in the business school movement. So, if you care to ask me, it's a damned shame that there is *no* pigeon-shat-upon statue of him *anywhere* in Dutchess County, although there is the Platt Rogers Spencer Monument in Geneva, Ohio, where he lived and died.

Spencer's elegantly flowing copperplate-style script was adopted Stateside from the mid-nineteenth century to the mid-1920s for business correspondence. Think Coca-Cola's logo, still bearing a strong resemblance to its 1880s manifestation, or Ford's logo, dating from 1911, and you will get the idea.

But we are not in Stormville to discuss its history, or, indeed, calligraphy in general. Nope, we are going to visit a place called Green Haven, which is not – as one might at first imagine – an exclusive retirement home with lush gardens, or an exclusive private hospital or expensive health-and-fitness spa. Green Haven, on Route 216, is in fact a maximum-security facility near the town of Beekman. Behind its grim walls are warehoused circa up to two thousand highly dangerous offenders. It opened in 1949.

This prison, one of the last 'big houses', contained New York's execution chamber during the time the Empire State briefly had the death penalty. Indeed, New York's notorious 'Old Sparky' was moved here from Sing Sing (the former Ossining) Correctional Facility in the early 1970s.

I mention this glittering, highly embroidered criminological trivia because no fewer than 614 men and women were fried in Sing Sing's 'Old Sparky'; and believe this or not, I have sat in it. It's antiquated, sure enough. Some traces of the cables still exist, but it was the head piece I found morbidly fascinating. It was falling apart and going rusty. While I was sitting comfortably in 'Old Sparky' and examining the 'Hot Hat', my TV producer Frazer said to the warden: 'There is something wrong with that chair.' A look of confusion crossed the warden's face and he replied, confused, 'Oh, sir, and what is that?' With a smug smile, Frazer replied: 'It ain't switched on!'

With a TV producer like that, who needs enemies? But did you know that the first design for an electric chair was drawn up by a dentist, with an electrician adding the wires shortly thereafter? Well now you do, so give this some thought when you next open your mouth to *your* dentist. Or maybe not.

Hal Karen

In late December 2009, a letter dated the 14th of that month, from Hal Karen – DIN #03-A3087 – of Green Haven Correctional Facility, dropped through my letter box. It was typewritten and Hal was replying to my initial interest in his case. There was nothing spectacular about him. He was not a serial killer or anything like that, but I wanted him to tell me his side of the story of why he was convicted of killing his wife. And then, without him knowing, to compare his written 'story' with the official file.

The reader might be asking: 'Christopher, why did you select Hal?' To be straight with you, I really don't know the answer to that very sensible question. I get a lot of very sensible questions from my very sensible readers for which I have no sensible answers, but somewhere sleeping at the back of my mind was the vague memory that testifying for the state in Karen's case was none other than the world-renowned Michael M. Baden, MD, an American physician and forensic pathologist who was at the time director of the NYS Police medicolegal investigations unit. An impressive if at times contentious figure, Dr Baden has been involved in the investigation of a number of high-profile deaths and cases, including the assassination of John F. Kennedy; the O.J. Simpson trial; Phil Spector and his role in the death of Lana

Clarkson; the shooting of Michael Brown; and, more recently, the deaths of George Floyd and of Jeffrey Epstein (he does not share the accepted view that Epstein committed suicide). Although highly controversial, Dr Baden knows his stuff and his books are a fascinating read. A Dr James Gill testified for the defence. I've digressed. In a nutshell, Hal Karen wrote to inform me that, to his mind, the medical examiner, Dr Baden, made a mistake. I quote verbatim:

> Dear Chris,
> I hope it's O.K. to call your [*sic*] Chris. It's always nice to get a letter from a former soldier. Under different circumstances I'm sure we could down some pints and exchange stories. Anyway I was kind of surprised when I got your letter because I feel that me [*sic*] case was not really a big deal and they put my military experience into the picture to elevate the picture in order to get a conviction. I have been able to tell my story before and I don't think it's anything what the T.V. shows had portrayed and if Dr. Baden would not have testified for the D.A. as he did, I would not be here and if I would have enough money for a better defence I surely would have been able to prove my innocence of murder. So, with all of that I'll give you a quick gist of what "REALLY" happened.
>
> I meet Tammy at a topless bar outside of FT. BRAGG N.C. I had just returned from Haiti after a six-month deployment and needed some winding down. I ended up getting her pregnant so we went to Las Vegas and got married. She used drugs when I meet [*sic*] her but during the pregnancy she did not. When Hunter was born she

started using drugs again and that's when everything went downhill. I could not get her to stop and she did not want to. One day I came home and found her dead in the bathroom. For a long time I covered the drug problem from people, it was embarrassing. So I took the body and I got rid of it and I told everyone she left because she has done this before with her first child which she left with her mother and took off. But I did not hide it good enough. I know what I did was wrong but I had my reasons and if you are still interest [*sic*] I will tell you them. But I feel better that after you read this letter you are not going to even use this story. And as the investigator that you are I'll bring up just two points that you can check out for yourself.

1. How can someone go into a court room and tell a jury that this person died from strangulation when you only have some bones and not even any neck bones?
2. After almost 3 years of the body being in the woods and they still managed to find a piece of liver from her body which this alone is incredible and they test it for drugs and it comes up positive with 30 nanograms of cocaine by-product. How can you say that that is not enough to kill someone? You would think that there had to be an awful lot to even show anything after 3 years.

If you know a forensic pathologist ask him or her what they think. Anyway I don't think I'm being much help to you. Like I said before once you read this letter you'll just back away because it's not the story everyone thinks it is. I tell you this and I have no idea what they said in the T.V. shows which I believe there are several. That I'm not the person they made me out to be. I never hurt anyone in my life without a reason. I don't know how much help this letter is to you and your book but I do have a lot to say, its probable just not help you. Actually I'm the one who needs help. Sometimes I wish there were more veterans with special skills that can help other veterans out there without charging and arm and a leg but that would asking too much.

Well if your [*sic*] still interested write me back or write me back even if your [*sic*] not, its [*sic*] nice to get a little mail. I don't have a lot of people write me because when things go wrong people tend to turn their backs on you and just forget you. If you can I would like to read one of your books, I do a lot of reading. So if you can and if you want please send me copies of your books.

Take care and good luck with your books.

Best Wishes

HAL (aka RAMBO) (aka HALANATOR)

(That's the name the guys gave me).

I don't know what you make of that letter, full of [*sics*]. On its face it is polite, respectful, fairly well written, almost self-effacing. My only gripe would be that he only referred to his wife's name, 'Tammy', the one time; elsewhere it is 'it', or 'the body'. Regarding the post-mortem issues, however, he may have raised something of interest. The downside it seems to me is that there is some transference of blame, with Tammy being at fault because she, according to him, was a drug addict. He was a serving soldier, yet had any man arrived back home to find his wife dead on the floor, I suggest that he would have dialled 911, got paramedics to the scene asap, then gone searching for her will or any existing paid-up life insurance policies and a list of local undertakers. But Hal didn't.

As has been my wont throughout this book, I'll try to consider the subtext of this letter. One cannot fail to note that although the couple had a baby, Hal had no respect for the mother; he simply took her corpse out some place isolated and dumped it. 'But I did not hide it good enough,' he says – *'it'* meaning the mother of his child. That he signs off with 'HAL aka RAMBO' aka 'HALANATOR' – the name the guys gave me', I suggest, is a figment of his imagination.

Green Haven is one of the toughest penitentiaries and it still houses some of the worst of the worst, and I know this because I have been in there – not as a convict it goes without saying. That these extremely hard Yardies, Crips, Bloods, American Front (white supremacists), Tongs, Triads, Mafiosi of pick 'n' mix all-sorts including the Gulf Cartel, along with outlaw motorcycle clubs from the 'Bandinos' through to the 'Warlocks', serial killers beyond counting, would have nicknamed Hal 'Rambo' would be side-splittingly funny if it were not so serious a matter.

The long and the short of it is that, in 2003, Hal Karen was, in legalese, 'convicted of murder in the second degree, offering a false instrument for filing in the first degree and perjury in the second degree in connection with the death of his wife in June 1999 and his subsequent efforts to conceal her death'. His sentence was an aggregate term of 26⅓ years to life.

Tammy was last seen on 27 June 1999. According to Hal Karen, a former Special Forces paratrooper, his wife had said goodbye to their child, taken some of their belongings from their home and taken off in a stranger's car not to be seen again. A month later her sister reported her missing to the police; for his part, Hal had filed for divorce and sought a protection order against his wife in the Family Court. That all smelt a bit fishy but the stench got even worse when, almost three years later, in March 2002, decomposed human remains were discovered in a garbage bin tied into two rubbish bags at the bottom of a steep 80-foot embankment in a wooded area a few minutes' drive from the couple's home.

Forensic investigators examining the find were able to establish through a DNA test that the body was Tammy's. In such cases a spouse is frequently the first suspect, and what clinched the killer's identity for the police were the military appearance of the cord used to tie the bags onto the bin, and, specifically, the knots used, which were used by Special Forces paratroopers. When Hal was confronted by police and shown the evidence he changed his story about Tammy's departure. He told police that he found her dead of a cocaine overdose in the bathroom of their home and admitted that he had placed her body in the bin and rolled it over the embankment. At his trial he maintained that he had disposed of his wife's body and concealed her death because he feared that her use of cocaine would result in his loss of the custody of his child. The thought that he would lose his child if he ended up in prison apparently never crossed his mind, as it didn't with Melanie McGuire.

Hal's defence was that his wife died as a result of a cocaine overdose. A second medical examiner testified that while *some* evidence of cocaine was found in the victim's remains, the amount would have been 'insufficient' to cause Tammy's death. And it is here that Hal raises his moot point. So: how long does cocaine stay in one's system, bearing in mind that Tammy's remains had been found some three years after she had gone missing? Well at no charge to the reader, it goes like this:

How long cocaine remains in the system

- Blood: two days
- Saliva: two days
- Urine: four days
- Hair: ninety days

If one is a long-term and/or heavy drug user, traces of the drug can be found many months or even years after complete cessation, and this is how the second pathologist formed his opinion – while forming no conclusion either way as to whether Hal Karen was right or wrong. Hal's beef is that the pathologist gave the impression to the jury that on this issue alone he, the defendant, was lying. Yet the medical examiner at the same time inadvertently confirmed what Hal Karen had claimed from the outset – that his wife was a hardened drug addict.

So, was Hal Karen's defence team fast asleep?

I'd argue that the defence team *was* asleep, if not in a coma. In hot and humid conditions, or under water, a body will completely decompose within weeks or less, especially if insects and other forms of life are about; in the frozen Arctic, it can take years; in temperate conditions, it can take from a few weeks to several years for a body to decompose into a skeleton, depending on factors such as ambient temperature (it would decompose faster in hot summer than in winter), humidity, the presence of insects, and so on. By now, after rotting for some three years after her tragic death, Tammy would have become all but bones and a liquefied mass; that she died of traumatic asphyxia would have been a matter of some highly speculative guesswork, yet somehow the defence team didn't pick up on this. Supporting evidence offered to the jury by the State's attorney's investigating officer established that, according to the official case notes from the trial *People* v. *Hal Karen* from July 2005, 'given the position of the toilet and sink, it would have been impossible for the victim to have been in the position as described by the defendant when he allegedly found her body in the bathroom.' Well, guys and gals, we all know how allegedly bent some cops can be, do we not – 'a light touch can hang a man', 'tis true.

According to the same source, another piece of hearsay evidence produced by the prosecutors was that, according to her sister, Tammy was planning to leave her husband, and that Hal told police that 'his wife had ruined his life he had been angry with her for stealing cash from his wallet'. But does this prove motive for murder most foul? Of course not.

I'm no Lieutenant Columbo, but retrospectively I believe that Hal Karen truly messed up from the get-go. Did he deserve an aggregate term of 26⅓ years to life in prison? I'll let you decide, but as the New York Department of Corrections website confirms, he is no longer behind the grim grey walls of the Green Haven Correctional Facility in Stormville. Indeed, where he is these days no one seems to know – not even him, I'd hazard a speculative guess.

Ronald 'Butch' Joseph DeFeo Jr

DeFeo, on the other hand, is definitely dead. He was found guilty of the 1974 killings of his father, mother, two brothers, and two sisters in Amityville, Long Island, New York. Condemned to six sentences of 25 years to life at the Sullivan Correctional Facility, the previously mentioned maximum-security prison for men at Stormville, Fallsburg, New York – making a minimum sentence of 150 years. Given the notoriety of the case, his whereabouts were not always easy to discover, but when Ronald DeFeo and I finally started corresponding he was incarcerated, according to the address he gave, at the Eastern Correctional Facility in Napanoch, Ulster County, New York, another maximum-security men's prison, and one of the oldest such institutions in the Empire State. Then, in about March 1994 – if another of his letters is anything to go by – DeFeo was, to his extreme annoyance, transferred to Green Haven Correctional Facility, Stormville, New York.

My aim was to make a television documentary about 'The Amityville Horror' and interview him on camera. My homework informed me that DeFeo was a litigious mass-murderer; a money-greedy little guttersnipe who bathed in his notoriety. Knowing this, I cast my hook well baited with goodies that would appeal to him: some of my CV; copies of my previous book covers; promises of money, international TV fame and a book deal – all false – and waited for him to respond.

Butch jumped at it. I mean he *leapt* from his bunk and started writing letters, sending documents, giving me just about everything he had access to. Initially, therefore, everything was all rosy in the garden. In reality, however, he had fallen foul of several of the deadly sins, namely 'greed' and 'lust' (for money), 'wrath' (to get some revenge for being, as he saw it, wrongly convicted), misaligned egotistical 'pride', and I will add 'sloth' because he was, until his death from natural causes on 12 March 2021, an amoral gluttonous weasel. He was also a pathological liar and, in my humble opinion, one of the worst letter writers in American criminal history.

It soon became obvious that 'Ronald the Impatient' thought that Rome actually was built in a day, for on 2 June 1993, using a biro, he frantically wrote the following letter on lined, yellow prison-issue stationery. I include it verbatim in this book because: (1) it has never been released before; and (2) it shows what an obnoxious, narcissistic piece of work he was. As always, I quote verbatim, grammatical warts and all.

> Dear Christopher,
> I will get right to the point okay. After talking to My Attonrey FRANCEL TROTTER BELLINGER, After Reading All Your Letters, promise's Deals, etc ANd seeing Now How its going on Two Year's Yes, "WE" have come to the conclusion That you have been selling us a dream ANd trying to make money off of me and my case behind our back as Your Last Letter with the tape according You wanted me to do said it all.
>
> If You Can't or Won't send some Type of Money in Good Faith then We Are Requesting the Immediate Return of Every thing I sent to You as Well as Letter's the Nonnewitze's, Springer, Davidge sent to you as well Because I asked them to. So the choice is Now Yours as if this is not done one way or another then the correct action will be Taken with the U.S. Attorney's Office etc.

Very Truly Your's
Ronald DeFeo BOX 338, Eastern C.F.
Napanoch, N.Y. 12458-0338.
Copy to Francel Trotter Bellinger/7442 9th, Street, NW.

The reader should understand that throughout his several court proceedings, indeed, right up until the day of his departure to hell, DeFeo had been trying to profit from the godawful point-blank shootings of his parents and four siblings. He'd despatched all of them via the trigger of his .35-calibre Marlin rifle as they slept warmly in their beds.

Aside from his nothing-to-read-between-the-lines scrawl, the attorney he mentions – Francel Trotter Bellinger – was apparently so concerned about her client's complaint that *not once* did she contact me. There was a very good reason for it, too: DeFeo 'pro-bono lawyer-shopped' as fast as a Monday morning quarterback vainly scrambles for a touchdown, enjoying a very singular lack of success, as each lawyer dumped him until one shyster called William Weber saw a pot of gold at the end of the rainbow and milked the murders for all he could back-pocket. So, now fully aware of this man's psychopathology, I replied with:

Dear Ronnie.
Thank you for your letter, 2 June. Noted. My film crew and I will be on Long Island circa September 1994. Lt Robert Dunn and Det. Dennis Rafferty, Homicide, Yaphank Police HQ (who gained your confession for multiple murder with the assistance of a Long Island telephone book smacked around your head), His Honor

Mr Justice Stark, Chief of Amity PD, Greg Greguski, two of your former attorneys plus the State's attorney, and your best friends Mr Nonnewitz and a Barry Springer, along with others have already agreed to appear on camera for our documentary programme.

I have been to your former home, 112 Ocean Avenue, LI. I have examined and handled all of the exhibits inc: the murder firearm a .35-cal Remington lever-action rifle, victims' clothing, ballistics – bullets and cartridge casings – CSI photos.

We respect your desire not to work with us. We all wish you well in your endeavours.

One day, when it is convenient to me, and I am a very busy man, I will return all you have requested. Please advise whomever attorney you are now instructing. Thank you.

Christopher.

Job done and dusted. However, if the truth be known I was still trying to entice 'Butch' to appear on camera; to become one of the killers Frazer Ashford & Co. and I were making in the aforementioned TV documentary series, hence the two-year back-and-forth correspondence and my stalling tactics as we hoovered up all Frazer needed to make the programmes. The book idea didn't come along till much later; the chapter on DeFeo originally appearing in my 2003 book *Talking with Serial Killers,* and the reason I selected 'Ronald the Impatient' was that, much like all of the other killers within my brief, he had never been interviewed for a TV programme before. I was intent on becoming the first to meet-and-greet the man who had spawned more 'based-upon-a-true-story' horror movies, books (factual, fictional and floating between the two), over-heated magazine and hyped-up press articles than one can count – with William Weber's assistance that is.

Getting 'The Amityville Horror' on camera would be a scoop.

I have included that letter from 'Butch' in this book because it sums him up in a nutshell. There is nothing concealed between the lines of his letter that should concern us; it is all writ large. Ronnie was too dumb to try to covertly manipulate anyone. Thick as a plank was our Ron, making it ever so easy for me to get him to conform to my wishes, while allowing his ego to think that he was the shot-caller, with all of his imaginary legal advisors behind him. We will see the same fondness for legalese when we meet John 'J.R.' Robinson later. An evil man J.R. certainly is, but there are moments in his letters when even he becomes a real hoot.

Just a few weeks before we were due to fly to America, I received a letter from Ronnie dated 13 March 1994. It had all come about as me having previously dismissed him out of hand; I had told him that we had enough interviewees, as well as Ronnie himself, on audio tape anyway so we were going to make the programme without him. He had got wind of this through one of his pals on the outside and, not wanting to lose out, he penned this:

Dear Christopher,

I hope my letter finds you in the best of health and the Best of Spirit.

To this Day Why I was Transfered To the Worse as

I was in The Best Max Prison in the state NO ONE KNOWS and here is my New Address.

"NOW" Did You Ever Recieve the Tapes as Lin and Roger Nonnewitz and Mr BARRY Springer who are all Witnesses in My Case and who know Bellinger Personally Told Her to Mail you the Tapes Five Weeks Ago Yes.

I CAN TELL You There is A Problem now with Francel Bellinger "Attorney" As she is Blaming Paul Woods and I am in the Middle. Could you please let me know whats Happening so I know what to do as Chris its Going On three years with "US" You and I as we have come A long way my "friend" As the Word Friend is very serious As they are very few in my life. Well I will close and await You Reply My Friend, Thank you and Take Care.

Ronnie DeFeo 75A4053
Drawer B.
Stormville, New York, 12582-0010.

I've been fuckin' waiting for two hours for you. Who ya think I am? I got better things to do.

Ronald DeFeo's less-than-welcoming greeting
prior to his TV interview with the author
at the Green Haven Correctional Facility,
Stormville, New York

Ronnie's ego was mega big, as big as the entire Empire State, I think, but therein lay another of his flaws. He kept boasting to fellow inmates, correctional officers and any lawyer whose ear he could catch that none other than the BBC were coming all the way from the UK to interview him. He was confident that the world-famous broadcasting station believed that he was innocent and that he would be paid a handsome fee for his time, for which any attorney acting in his interests would receive a fat bung. When I started contacting the authorities, stating categorically that we were *not* from the BBC, DeFeo still kept fishing. By then, however, the more enlightened of his lawyers had dropped him flat having realised that their client, nor they, would receive not a dime.

As it is, there are many TV documentaries on DeFeo and the Amityville murders freely available on Google (a search for either 'Ronald DeFeo' or 'Amityville Horror' will suffice). Gruesome crime-scene photos can be found elsewhere if you have the stomach to view them. And of course the many books and articles I mentioned above – including my own *Talking with Serial Killers*, my colleague Ric Osuna's *The Night the DeFeos Died: Reinvestigating the Amityville Murders,* Jay Anson's book *The Amityville Horror*, which inspired shelf loads of books, many having nothing to do with the actual case, but much to do with supernatural horror. Similarly with films: a single act of mass-murder led to a web of money-spinners for everyone except Ronnie.

I will leave you with this. The weapon used in the DeFeo slayings – a .35-calibre Marlin 336C lever-action rifle – is one of the choice firearms for taking down deer, bear, elk, even moose. Most .35-calibre rounds travel at around 2,100 feet per second and this load generates circa 1,900 pounds of energy. To get a sense of the power of this firearm and the noise it makes, look up 'Marlin 35 Remington Range 2' online, or something along those lines, then imagine these shots being discharged at point-blank range into two sleeping adults and four kids inside a relatively small house in the dead of night. Yet despite all of this, DeFeo was twice married while behind bars, to women who wanted to have children with him, who provided him with funds, built a website to which thousands of his sicko fans could contribute and inanely chitter-chatter among themselves like monkeys in a zoo.

Ronald Joseph DeFeo Sr (forty-four), Louise Marie Brigante DeFeo (forty-three), Dawn DeFeo (eighteen), Allison Louise DeFeo (thirteen), Marc Gregory DeFeo (twelve) and John Matthew DeFeo (nine) are buried in the Saint Charles Cemetery, East Farmingdale, Suffolk County, New York.

Ronald 'Butch' Joseph DeFeo Jr died aged sixty-nine and was cremated. I think that he is still dead to this very day.

Gary Ray Bowles aka 'The I-95 Killer'

I hope my death eases your pain. I want to tell my mother that I am sorry for my actions. Having to deal with your son being called a monster is terrible. I'm so very sorry. I never wanted this to be my life. You don't wake up and decide to become a serial killer. I'm sorry for all the pain and suffering I have caused.

GARY RAY BOWLES: LAST WORDS BEFORE HIS EXECUTION

Azure peepers earned Frank Sinatra the popular nickname 'Ol' Blue Eyes'. He led a colourful personal life, often becoming involved in turbulent affairs. Of course that useless titbit of information has nothing at all to do with the now deceased #086158-P-3226-S Gary Ray Bowles, formerly of Florida State Prison (FSP) in Raiford, except that the letters I received from him always bore two Frank

> Sinatra postage stamps and this serial killer had brown eyes anyway.

Executed on Thursday, 22 August 2019 by lethal injection, Bowles had been nicknamed the 'I-95 Killer'; he'd murdered six gay men, the majority of whom had lived within the vicinity of the East Coast's Interstate 95 highway, between March and November 1994. He encountered most of his victims in gay bars, offering them sex in return for money and a place to stay, then strangled or bludgeoned them and made off with their cash and credit cards. Police found Bowles's fingerprints and probation records at the scene of his first victim's death in Daytona Beach. CCTV footage also caught him using the man's ATM card. So desperate were cops to catch Bowles, he appeared on *America's Most Wanted* programme multiple times and made the FBI's 'Most Wanted List' just three days before he was brought in for questioning in connection with the murder of his final victim, Walter Hinton, whose head was bashed in with a 40-pound concrete block. Another victim was found with a dildo jammed down his throat.

> Each of the murders was brutal. It was not an instant death, like somebody getting shot and dying from that gunshot … It was a life-and-death struggle.
>
> Bernie de la Rionda, Jacksonville prosecutor: to the *Daytona Beach News-Journal*

In mitigation before sentencing, Bowles's attorney brought up his client's troubled childhood. Gary's father had died of black lung disease before he was born, and he and his older brother were raised by their mother and a series of stepfathers – some of whom were abusive. After fighting back against the last stepdad, Bowles left home aged fourteen, making money as a male prostitute. Despite several appeals, and spending twenty years in a 6-foot by 9-foot cell, Bowles was never reprieved. Florida Governor Ron DeSantis, probably doing the only sensible thing in his entire GOP career, signed the death warrant on 11 June 2019. His last meal consisted of three cheeseburgers and a side of French fries.

I wanted Gary's story in his own words, and here it is, never published before, scant though it may be. In the original letter his handwriting is neat and he used small capital letters throughout. Moreover, each letter contained two Inmate Trust Fund Deposit Forms – one which he filled out as an 'example', just so that I didn't make any mistakes. Let's call it a letter from a 'Dead Man Walking, Talking and Writing and On the Hunt for Cash'.

> DEAR CHRISTOPHER.
> ... I'M SORRY IT HAS TAKEN SO LONG FOR ME TO GET BACK TO YOU TO ANSWER YOUR LETTER. IT WAS GOOD TO HEAR FROM YOU AND I WANTED TO THANK YOU FOR TAKING THE TIME TO WRITE TO ME. I ALSO WANT TO THANK YOU FOR TAKING AN INTEREST IN ME AND MY STORY. I'M NOT SURE WHAT IT IS YOU PLAN TO DO AS FAR AS WRITING GOES, BUT ALL I WANT IS TO TELL MY STORY AND MAYBE IT WILL HELP SOMEONE, SOMEWHERE. AS VICTORIA [Redstall, a British-born American actress and true-crime writer who has interviewed such killers as Gary Ray Bowles and Keith Hunter Jesperson]

MIGHT HAVE TOLD YOU, ITS NOT ABOUT THE MONEY, AND I WOULD NEVER ASK SOMEONE TO PAY ME. I DIDN'T DO THAT WITH HER, AND I WON'T DO THAT WITH YOU. BESIDES I'M NOT ALLOWED TO PROFIT FROM MY CRIMES ☺.

IF YOU WANTED TO HELP ME OUT I WOULD BE VERY THANKFUL FOR WHATEVER YOU DID, OR DO. AT THE SAME TIME THIS IS NOT SOMETHING YOU HAVE TO DO, IF YOU WANT TO SEND ME MONEY FOR STAMPS AND OTHER THINGS ENCLOSED IS SOME SLIPS THAT SHOW YOU GOW TO DO THAT. YOU CAN ALSO USE J-PAY AND WESTERN UNION TO SEND MONEY TO MY ACCOUNT. IF YOU HAVE ENY QUESTIONS JUST LET ME KNOW, OR MAYBE VICTORIA CAN HELP YOU.

What a nice man one might think, yet does one not sense at least some impertinence in him enclosing two inmate trust fund deposit forms from the get-go? Anyway, being a 'Mr Penny-Wise', I had accidentally misplaced these forms until I started writing this chapter some time ago. (God moves in a mysterious way, His wonders to perform.) Gary ditched the capitals and henceforth used script:

AS TO WHAT YOU SAID IN YOUR LETTER I WILL TELL YOU WHAT I REMEMBER AND KNOW AS BEST AS I CAN.

IT ALL STARTED IN RUPERT, WEST VIRGINIA. THAT IS WHERE I LIVED, BUT I WAS

BORN AT THE NEAREST HOSPITAL WHICH WAS IN CLIFTON FORGE, VIRGINIA. [Here Gary ditched the capitals and henceforth used script.] I had one older brother, William Franklin Bowles, Jr. who was born Feb 2, 1960, and my mother was 6 months pregnant with me when my father passed from black lung disease. He was a coalminer. I don't know, not from my first few years, but my mom moved us to Kankakee, Illinois. When we were young there was a few stops along the way to there but I don't know the name of the towns. I was raised by my first stepfather, William Otto Fields, who had two kids later with my mom (Pam & David). I thought he was my dad till of was 6 or 7 yrs old. We took a trip to West Virginia to visit my grandmother just before she passed away. I found out then who my dad was. After our return home things got bad. My mom worked nights at Ford Motor Company, and my dad worked days. After work my dad would drink and the kids got no help from him. When I got into trouble he would beat me with a belt, leather strap, fists, and we had a willow tree and he would use a whip like branch from that. It was bad and my brother also got beat a lot. His kids were younger then.

When I was 8 yrs old I played a lot of sports. In little league baseball I was a catcher, pitcher, shortstop. I was really good, and I wanted to be a baseball player. I was, and I am still a big clubs fan. I also played football with all of the kids from my neighborhood. We lived in a small 3 bedroom house, and most of the houses in my neighborhood were all the same. It was three streets with a total of about 400 to 500 homes altogether in the whole area.

We had a high school and a baseball field as part of the neighbourhood. It was a nice place to grow up. I just have a normal family life. We never ate together, and no-one helped with homework. I was not very good in school, and my highest grade completed was 6th Grade and I was in my 7th Grade when I left home. I went to school called Martin Luther Kids Jr. High.

When I was 9 yrs old I was smoking pot, not a lot, but some. When I was 10 yrs old my mom left my dad, and we moved to Joliet, Illinois. We moved a few times before she met Chester 'Chet' Hodges, and they got married when I was 12 yrs old. I was not even allowed to go to the wedding. He drank a lot and so did my mom. I was forced to live in the basement, and by 13 yrs old I was kicked out of the house and was living in the garage. There was no heat, and I had had enough. I didn't know if Chet was home and I went in the house. He was drunk and started beating me. We ended up in the driveway, and I grabbed a brick and I started hitting him in the face and head. Looking back I think I really wanted to kill him but my mom came home and she pulled me off saying just that, that if I didn't stop I would kill him.

That was the breaking point for me and I told her we did not have to live this way. She took her share of beatings as well with a broken arm and other things. I told her it was either him or me. I will never forget her words: "Don't make me choose". I put what few things I had in a bag, and I left. I didn't say anything to her. That first night I stayed in the back of a U-Haul moving truck.

I find myself reading a well-written letter from a death row inmate who has committed six of the most brutal and sickening crimes imaginable, yet nothing jumps from these pages that even hints at psychopathy. No bullshit – à la Melanie 'Ice Queen' McGuire, Harvey 'The Hammer' Carignan or Kenneth Bianchi – from Gary Ray Bowles at all. Or is there? For although he appears to be telling it as it is, quite obviously he is leaving a heck of a lot out, as will soon become apparent.

> The next day I went to one of my friend's house and he hid me in his garage. It had heat, and a bed ☺. A week later the two of us took a bus to Buras, Louisiana, to go and stay with his dad. His dad worked off shore on an oil rig. I was 14 yrs old now, just turned, and his dad got us a job working with him. We had to say we were 16 yrs old, the legal age to work then. It was a really small town, and everyone worked off shore. We would work for two weeks and then be off for two weeks. My first pay check was over $700. I wrote my mom and sent her a copy of the check. She never wrote back and I didn't see her again until after I was 18yrs old. We ended up getting busted for being under age and I was only able to work for 6 months or so. My friend stayed, and I was off on my own. I hitched to New Orleans, and on the way my first ride is how I got started in the gay hustling business. The guy offered me $20 to suck me off. He was surprised by how big I was and if I want, he told me I could make a lot of money doing this kind of thing and that is how I became a hustler. I did this in New Orleans, and I even met a woman who took me in for

the same thing. I had sex with her, and her friends, and boy did I learn a lot.

All for now. I'll write again next week to tell you more. Take care ... let me know what you think.

Gary Ray.

This litany of non-useful info was almost unbearable to read and certainly not as exciting as watching grass grow, but I did write back to never hear from Gary Ray Bowles again – most probably because I didn't send him any cash. Or perhaps because he had some explaining to do about his arrest in 1982 for beating and sexually assaulting his twenty-year-old girlfriend, for which he was previously sentenced to six years in prison, because, you see, it's often what is not written on the page which matters the most.

Even more explaining for him to do in 1991 when, after his release from prison, he was convicted of unarmed robbery during the theft of an elderly woman's purse, a crime for which he was sentenced to four more years behind bars, which was signally another omission in his correspondence. He was released after serving two years. But we should primarily concern ourselves with Bowles's first confirmed kill. At the time of the discovery of the body, he became a suspect but was nowhere to be found – as a result of which five more men are known to have been murdered in the most godawful ways.

On 15 March 1994, Florida police found the body of fifty-nine-year-old John Hardy Roberts at his Daytona Beach, Volusia County home. He had been beaten about the head and strangled. His car and wallet were gone – his credit card was later used in Georgia and Tennessee. Bowles had been staying at Roberts's home, and had left fingerprints and even some documents in his own name. He was immediately and unsurprisingly a suspect – but there was still no sign of him. The missing car was later found in Georgia.

On 14 April 1994, the body of thirty-nine-year-old David Alan Jarman was found at his home in Wheaton, Maryland: he too had been beaten and strangled; his credit cards, keys and vehicle were gone (the vehicle was found a week later in Baltimore). On 4 May, Milton Bradley, seventy-two years old, was found dead behind a shed on a golf course in Savannah, Georgia. He had sustained a blow to the head and been strangled. On 13 May, forty-seven-year-old Alverson Carter's body was found at his residence in Atlanta: the MO was the same as in the previous killings. And on 18 May, Albert Morris, who was thirty-eight, was found dead in his trailer in Hilliard, Nassau County, Florida. He had been hit on the head, shot and strangled. It later transpired that Bowles had lived with him for about two weeks.

Then came the murder of forty-seven-year-old Walter Jamelle 'Jay' Hinton, whose body was found on 18 November 1994. By now Bowles was already a suspect in five other, similar murders, and on a wanted list; it was only a matter of time before he would be found. He was arrested on 22 November. Under questioning, he eventually confessed to the six murders, but was arraigned on that of Hinton. He was indicted before a grand jury in December 1994.

Documents available from the Supreme Court of Florida (Gary Ray BOWLES, *Appellant* v. *STATE* of Florida, Appellee. No. SC96732. Decided: October 11, 2001), quoted below) give details of the trials (first and subsequent hearings).

Summarising the case as presented at Bowles's indictment, the appeal courts stated:

> Appellant [Bowles] met Walter Hinton, the victim in this case, at Jacksonville Beach in late October or early November 1994. Appellant agreed to help Hinton move some personal items from Georgia to Hinton's mobile home in Jacksonville. In return, Hinton allowed appellant to live with him in his mobile home.
>
> On November 22, 1994, police arrested appellant for the murder of Walter Hinton. During subsequent interrogation, appellant gave both oral and written confessions regarding Hinton's murder. Appellant stated that upon returning home from going with Hinton to take a friend [Richard Smith] to the train station, Hinton went to sleep and appellant kept drinking. Appellant, Hinton, and the friend had drunk beer and smoked marijuana earlier. At some point in the evening, appellant stated that something inside 'snapped'. He went outside and picked up a concrete block, brought it inside the mobile home, and set it on a table. After thinking for a few minutes, appellant picked up the block, went into Hinton's room, and dropped the block on Hinton's head. The force of the blow caused a facial fracture that extended from Hinton's right cheek to his jaw. Hinton, now conscious, fell from the bed and appellant began to manually strangle him. Appellant then stuffed toilet paper into Hinton's throat and placed a rag into his mouth. The medical examiner testified that the cause of death was asphyxia.

The pathologist later 'observed on Mr. Hinton's body five (5) broken ribs, abrasions to the front and back of his right forearm, and more abrasions on the outside of his left knee'. His findings tied in with Bowles's own confession that Hinton had struggled desperately with him, despite the injuries to his face. The court found that 'The victim was strangled while conscious for a time sufficient to suffer a physically and mentally cruel and torturous death'.

The account continues:

> Mr. Hinton was found inside his locked home on 22 November. His sister and her then fiancé became concerned when he failed to respond to telephone calls and knocks on his door. After several days went by without word from Mr. Hinton, the fiancé broke into his mobile home and found his dead body wrapped in sheets and bedspreads.
>
> Mr. Hinton's watch, car keys, automobile and stereo equipment were missing from the home. His wallet was found on the floor next to the bed. The Defendant was seen after the murder driving Mr. Hinton's car.

At his appeal hearing, Bowles weakly explained that his theft of Hinton's property was an 'afterthought' and not 'the motivation for the murder'. This directly contradicts his earlier claim during the FBI interrogation, when he said that he had expected to find money in the victim's trailer home or on Hinton. There seems no reasonable doubt that the murder was committed in the course of an attempted robbery.

In imposing the death penalty, the trial court identified five aggravating circumstances. Whether the reader is an anti-death-penalty advocate or pro-death-penalty supporter, they make for sombre reading. I quote verbatim:

> (1) Bowles was convicted of two other capital felonies and two other violent felonies; (2) Bowles was on felony probation in 1994 when he committed the murder as a result of a July, 18, 1991 conviction and sentence to four years in prison followed by six years' probation for a robbery in Volusia county; (3) the murder was committed during a robbery or an attempted robbery, and the murder was committed for pecuniary gain (merged into one factor); (4) the murder was heinous, atrocious, or cruel (HAC); and (5) the murder was cold, calculated, and premeditated (CCP).

Perhaps now we are beginning to see Gary's letter to me in a different light. Getting into the nitty-gritty of this man's criminal past, we learn that on 27 September 1982, in Hillsborough County, he was convicted of sexual battery and aggravated sexual battery. He had subjected his girlfriend to a brutal sexual assault of such violence that, as reported in the case notes, she suffered 'contusions to her head, face, neck, chest, as well as bites to her breasts. She also suffered internal injuries including lacerations to her vagina and rectum'. For this he was jailed for six years. A couple of years after his release, Bowles pushed an elderly woman to the ground and stole her purse. He was apprehended and, on 18 July 1991, a Volusia County court convicted him of unarmed robbery.

During his incarceration for the murder of Hinton, Bowles was convicted, on 10 October 1996 in Nassau County, of first-degree murder for the slaying in May 1994 of Albert Morris; and on 6 August 1997 he was convicted in Volusia County of first-degree murder and armed robbery. This was for the March 1994 killing of John Hardy Roberts. Bowles pleaded guilty to both.

What I found particularly interesting were the two mitigating factors put forward by Gary Ray Bowles following his death sentence for the Hinton murder – and this provides yet another bullshit example of a defence attorney trying to get a client if not completely off the hook, then at least to blow some smoke into the jury's yard to cause doubt that the well-deserved death sentence would be inappropriate. The suggestion was that at the time of the crime Mr Bowles was suffering 'extreme emotional disturbance', thus he was of 'substantially diminished capacity to appreciate the criminality of his acts at the time of the murder'. In a nutshell, he was claiming temporary insanity. I would argue that's all very well if it had been applied to the Hinton murder *alone* – an isolated case of temporary insanity without any of the mitigating factors present. But for Bowles to use this defence in the context of *six* homicide cases is too ludicrous to even think about – it cuts no ice at all, would my reader agree?

To put a legal slant on this issue, and to keep it brief, an 'aggravated murder' is a killing made more serious by its violent circumstances. Unfortunately, in the UK although these offences carry a natural life term, many monsters who commit such acts are later released back into society, such as homegrown Brits Graham Young and Colin Pitchfork. Our American cousins see it differently, however: over there, murdering someone in furtherance of another serious felony – say a robbery, rape or killing a cop or a public official such as a prison officer or while trying to evade arrest – carries a mandatory natural-life term with zilch chance of release. Better still, in my opinion, in multiple/serial killings, as with Bowles, a damned good execution.

The mitigating factors kick in when defence attorneys (mostly in the US) attempt to reduce their client's sentence by bringing up something trivial – let's say bad potty-training, or the defendant having been denied breast milk and forced to wean off green-top instead of full-cream up until the age of fifteen.

Before we move on with Mr Bowles, as a side note – and to make this issue of bullshit psychiatric mitigation more interactive for the reader – look up the 2008 YouTube documentary *Interview with a Serial Killer* about Arthur Shawcross, who featured earlier in this book. It's a damned good programme featuring Captain Lynde B. Johnston, the prosecutor Charles J. Siragusa and others whom I met during the making of my own TV documentary. In particular, I would ask you to listen to the defence's psychiatric mitigation put forth by forensic psychiatrists Dorothy Otnow Lewis and a colleague, and how their evaluations of Shawcross were basically shit-canned – not only by common-sense police officers and FBI criminal profiler Gregg McCrary, but none other than prosecution psychiatrist Dr Park Dietz, whom I admire greatly. And, have we not seen examples of this psychiatric mitigation smoke-blowing before with the examples of Messrs Colin Pitchfork, Graham Young, Phillip Jablonski et al? Yes, we have; indeed, even with Harvey Carignan and Peter Sutcliffe, psychiatrists for the defence vehemently argued that their clients truly believed that they were following the Word of God.

As well as his alleged state of 'extreme emotional disturbance', another suggested mitigating factor was that Gary Bowles was a 'gay-hater'. This is based on his remarks to some of his pen friends, to whom he wrote: 'A gay raped my mother.' He also tried to claim that his girlfriend, who was allegedly expecting his child, had an abortion when she learned he was a sex worker whose clients were gay men – a tenuous bit of logic. No mention of this came up at his initial trial; when the judge was subsequently told that he was a hater of gay men, the death sentence was reversed, and another hearing called. Indeed, Bowles was to appeal several times. The claim that he hated gay men was, sensibly, not accepted as a mitigating factor. The fact that he targeted such men – those men to whom he willingly prostituted himself – must surely be because he saw that he could weasel himself into their homes and benefit from their hospitality.

So, let's cut to the chase here. A controversial subject it is indeed, but having read his letter, we cannot say that this man was so mentally upside-down that he did not realise that his offences could well earn him the death sentence, if caught. Yet he sailed on regardless. As his Honour Mr Justice Thomas M. Stark once told me during a 1994 filmed interview at his Riverhead, Long Island courthouse:

> Society makes the rules. People have to live by them or anarchy breaks loose. Most know what punishment might await them if they step over the red line. It is their decision. In states where the death penalty applies, society merely supplies the rope, the electricity or the drugs to execute them. Christopher, if it were one of your own children who had been raped, butchered, then killed, tell me that forgiveness would be in your heart?
>
> And there would be no chance of that!

So, I might well ask all of my readers Judge Stark's open question, but what I will say is this: didn't Gary Bowles live a well-fed, well-watered life behind bars at the US taxpayers' expense? He enjoyed free accommodation; food, Medicare and he racked up several million dollars of public money with his pathetic appeals to save his own worthless life. Meanwhile, Mr Hinton's agonising appeals to Bowles – and those from his other murder victims, including his former girlfriend, whose womb he destroyed – all fell on deaf ears.

For a stone-cold serial killer, his signature being shoving leaves, toilet paper, even dirt, socks and sex toys into the mouths of his victims, and unlike serial killer John Wayne Gacy, whose last words were reportedly 'Kiss my ass', Bowles did have something to say after he was strapped down onto the execution gurney:

> I'm sorry for all the pain and suffering I have caused. I hope my death eases your pain. I want to tell my mother that I am also sorry for my actions. Having to deal with your son being called a monster is terrible. I'm so very sorry. I never wanted this to be my life. You don't wake up one day and decide to become a serial killer.

After his death warrant had been signed by the state's governor, Bowles was moved to a 'Death Watch' cell that measures 6 x 9 feet wide and 9.5 feet high, and he was able to order a last meal, the cost 'not to exceed $40'. He opted for three burgers, fries and bacon. As the lethal drugs were administered, he went white, coughed once and died.

John 'J.R.' Edward Robinson, aka 'The Slavemaster'

In seeking truth you have to get both sides of a story.

WALTER LELAND CRONKITE JR,
AMERICAN BROADCAST JOURNALIST

Although what I am about to say might offend some of my readers, let me be blunt: if anyone deserves a painful lethal injection it has to be 'The Slavemaster'; nevertheless, what if there are three or four sides to a story, or even more? What if there were a person who has so many sides to his personality that, like a chameleon, he could change his outer persona – his social camouflage – at will, and had multiple personalities hidden beneath that could change in a heartbeat too?

Meet 'J.R.' Robinson, without doubt the most psychopathologically complicated serial killer I've ever dealt with.

The first question you'll ask is doubtless: 'Where is Robinson right now?' Actually, he is on death row at the El Dorado

Correctional Facility in 'The Wheat State', aka Kansas. He is on the 'Green Mile' for killing eight females, leaving five of their bodies to decompose in their own juices in barrels on his property and in a lockup he'd rented.

Dumb move, J.R., especially considering that at one time you were telling the world that you were hyper-intelligent. May we remind you that you are residing on 'the row' because you first pleaded 'not guilty', then flipped, changing your tune to 'guilty' to avoid the death sentence out of state, then back to 'not guilty' as soon as you were extradited to Kansas?

While hoping not to be accused of plagiarising my own writings about J.R. (I covered him in my book *Dead Men Talking*), I will summarise his story as briefly as I can, as we are more concerned here with the letters he wrote to me. Letters in which he categorically denied being a sadosexual pervert. 'BDSM?' he wrote, incredulously. 'What does that mean [...] what does Slavemaster mean [...] and NEVER EVER tell me that I said that golf balls can give a girl sexual excitement. I have NEVER played golf in my life.'

This Mr Robinson is someone to behold. To be fair to J.R., it isn't particularly unusual for a tenant of death row to spend years protesting his innocence of the crimes for which he stands condemned. After all, when faced with the prospect of execution, who wouldn't make some effort towards self-preservation? And, wow, J.R. once, way, way back when he was a thirteen-year-old Eagle Scout, stood before Queen Elizabeth II, and later was on a charities board and received a bogus award of 'Man of the Year', as reported by the *Kansas City Star* (to their subsequent extreme embarrassment). He became quite adept at forging letters and documents to help him along, did J.R.

Despite having no qualifications whatsoever, J.R., you were once employed as an X-ray technician by none other than retired Brigadier General Dr Wallace Harry Graham, who for many years was the personal White House physician to President Harry S Truman and his wife, Elizabeth. You fleeced Dr Graham and bankrupted his medical practice, did you not?

J.R., my readers are now well impressed and anxious to know more.

'Manager of a TV rental company' appears on your richly embroidered CV. But no mention of you tuning into the firm's funds and stealing thousands of dollars. And you were a contemporary Saint Albertus Magnus OP: scholar philosopher, patron saint of the natural sciences thrown in too. Goodness me, J.R., my readers would never have guessed that it was you who first invented hydroponics. In this regard, your glossy, sixty-four-page brochure promoting your (bogus) hydroponics modestly claims it was you who trail-blazed and pioneered this mouth-watering subject; that would come as a *big* surprise to the ancients, who somewhat thought that this had been their idea – witness the Hanging Gardens of Babylon and the Aztec nation's *chinampas* ('floating gardens') of Mexico, to take just two examples. So, it should not surprise my readers to hear that your company, Hydro-Gro Inc., consulted NASA on growing plants in outer space. If you say so, we believe you, John. And I sympathise with you that Richard Branson has *still* not replied to your proposal that he offer you a $2-million cash-up-front book deal for you to 'tell all'. Not so long ago, Richard was a tad busy launching his mega-sized cruise ship, *Scarlet Lady*. When it leaves my city's port, I watch it go by. Long it is, bro: the bow goes by on Monday, the stern a month later. The height is 66 metres. That's tall, J.R., as tall as your phantasmagorical stories.

So, John, this sadosexual stuff. Are you sure that you never trawled the World Wide Web's BDSM chat rooms to entice young women and their kids into your own homicidal web? Because you see, I have all of the perverted letters you wrote to a former female FBI special agent. Pretty lass, wasn't she? As cute as Agent Clarice Starling in the movie *The Silence of the Lambs*, yes? Ever heard of the compound noun 'honeytrap'? No, I didn't think so.

At this point in J.R.'s narrative, I should remark that he signally fails in his CV to flag up that he thieved from everyone he came into contact with, including in 1985 conning his brother into adopting a baby – for a hefty fee, of course – from a young woman he 'rescued' from a battered mothers' home and then beat her to death. In short, with John Robinson we have one of history's most complicated serial killers, but when we read between his lines, perhaps he isn't too complicated at all. Yet cruelly he didn't give a damn about the disgrace he heaped upon his devoted wife and children. He did not blink an eyelid when he persuaded an acquaintance to invest in one of his crooked businesses on the promise of a swift, high return, so the guy could get his wife, who had cancer, the palliative care she needed during her final days. J.R. fleeced him too.

For the record, Robinson had spent several previous stints in prison for fraud. Once while behind bars, he seduced a governor's wife. Upon his release she moved in with him; he killed her, drawing upon her funds until they were exhausted. In the main, bespectacled J.R.'s murderous MO was simple. Especially once he had discovered the internet, which in those early days, and more so today, presented so many possibilities of committing nefarious deeds. Posing as a very successful businessman and using the best type of calm, reassuring patter known only to shady used-car salesmen, he trawled the internet's BDSM websites searching for easy prey. Places where lonely young women swam in shoals, seeking either a 'Slavemaster' or a better way of life, using the prospect of 'hope' as bait, a lure to catch prey.

Mr Robinson promised everything, with assurances of financial rewards too. In one instance, he offered a mother with a mentally retarded daughter a well-paid position as a carer on his non-existent millionaire grandmother's non-existent yacht. As soon as they were in his clutches, he battered both mother and daughter to death, then carried on drawing upon their state and disability allowances using forged signatures. They ended up rotting in barrels.

It came as no surprise to your author when J.R. penned a letter to me, dated 20 February 2008, making unreasonable demands straight off the starting blocks:

> I was represented by court-appointed attorneys who did NO INVESTIGATION, hired no experts, tested nothing and admitted in court a day prior to my trial that they had not read any discovery documents.
>
> Before I enter into any form of correspondence with you, I want $400,000, although that amount may be adjusted depending on need. My attorney will control all information and distribution of funds. Don't blow smoke! I don't have time for meaningless delays. I will await word from you.

For unadulterated arrogance that takes the biscuit, wouldn't you agree? And, John, it's no wonder your attorneys did nothing, because you pleaded guilty from the get-go, and is it not so that most of the bodies were soon found on your property and in a secure lockup rented in your name? And scores of documents police found in your house linked you to all the dead women. What about all the internet searches you made for the girls, who wound up dead in the barrels you bought – along with the receipts the police have – and mountains of paperwork showing how you enticed victims into the world of BDSM?

At this very early stage in our correspondence John was totally unaware that I knew all about his criminal antecedents. And he had plenty. Between 1969 and 1991 he was convicted four times for embezzlement and theft. While some of his thefts could be considered trivial – he once appropriated $300-worth of postage stamps from the company he worked for – mostly he went for more significant hauls. In 1980, doubtless with the help of forged credentials, he was appointed director of personnel at a firm. Very soon he zeroed in on the company's cheque book and funds, using the former to direct quite a lot of the latter into his own bank account. More often than not he seems to have earned nothing worse than a fine and probation (which he was not averse to violating) and when he was sent to jail – for instance, when he laundered $40,000 into one of his fraudulent paper companies – it didn't slow him down. He did, however, get barred for life by the Securities and Exchange Commission from engaging in any kind of future investment business. Excellent credentials I'm sure you will not agree?

Between the mid-1980s and 2000, Robinson was incarcerated several times for embezzlement; he also spent time online, usually in BDSM chat rooms. And he devised a new and thoroughly unpleasant way of gaining money. A number of women, mostly young, vanished, but their families did receive the occasional letter from them, with, at least, authentic signatures, and their bank accounts continued to be drawn on, and cheques sent to them cashed. The bodies of five of them were found in barrels near or on Robinson's land. Once detectives had cause to obtain search warrants (following separate complaints of theft and assault from two women), they found the bodies in the barrels and arrested Robinson.

One of the women who had come to him had had a young baby with her: she was never seen again, but, as touched on earlier, J.R.'s childless brother and sister-in-law, in exchange for hefty 'legal fees', found they had adopted an orphan baby through him, Robinson having beaten the mother to death.

Robinson is known to have killed at a minimum eight women, three of whose remains have not been found, and it is thought he is guilty of further murders of women who mysteriously vanished. He stood trial for theft, fraud, kidnapping and murder in both Kansas and Missouri, and was convicted of capital murder on two counts in Kansas, for which he received the death penalty, and convicted of first-degree murder on five counts in Missouri, for which he received life without parole.

> He had no real employment, unless you consider figuring out ways of scamming people out of their money to be real employment.
>
> District Attorney Paul Morrison:
> at J.R. Robinson's murder trial

Returning to my correspondence with Robinson, my carefully baited hook to entice him into my world of criminal literature was now in his mouth. The phoney deal I offered was that he could write what he wanted to say, for reproduction, verbatim, in a single chapter for a book. In fact, I then generously went further: he could even have his *own* book if he most graciously agreed.

The reverse psychology I was using with this particular piece of over-the-top, low-life narcissist is not rocket science. Your author was playing upon John's over-inflated ego, because the easiest people to lead up the garden path are the ones who have been doing pretty much the same thing to themselves from the day they could walk. If you can convince them that a fast buck is to be made, then you can lead these pathologically greedy people almost anywhere, as with Ronnie DeFeo in an earlier chapter.

J.R. had become so ensconced within his narcissistic mindset that this would become his downfall. The prospect of his having the platform of a complete book on the cards was an offer he could never have refused.

With tongue in cheek, I also offered him the opportunity to be interviewed by one of the UK's leading top-end television producers, ostensibly giving him the chance to say what he had to say to prove his innocence, all of which embedded my hook even deeper into his gullet.

Note: to put it mildly, J.R.'s letters are exhaustive. For the most part, they might seem to be the inane ramblings of someone who should be chained to a padded cell wall and only allowed to walk, wide-eyed and dribbling, through some nuthouse garden escorted by some very large men wearing whites. But John is not like someone who lies down on the grass and starts having an in-depth discussion with a daisy about Darwin's theory of evolution. Actually, he is very intelligent in a totally cooked upside-down sort of way.

By reverse engineering J.R.'s MO, I made him an offer he could not refuse. He replied:

> Yes, I will agree to your offer so *I will allow you* to go to the next phase, the expert phase, photos and testing. Then to complete the necessary testing that has never been done. Each step of the way, *we* will evaluate and adjust *our* investigation or approach as required. [All author's italics]:

Can you see this podgy-faced, short-sighted, sweaty, overweight lump of lard right now? He added this:

> The proposed budget is fairly simple at this point but may have to be adjusted depending on need:
>
> - Database: $100,000.
> - Investigator: $150,000.
> - Travel: $20,000.
> - Experts: $60,000.
> - Attorneys: $50,000.
> - Communications, copies, supplies: $10,000.
> - Equipment: $8,000.
> - Misc: $2,000.
>
> TOTAL: $400,000.

He continues seemingly quite oblivious to the fact that no inmate, condemned or otherwise, can receive bags stuffed with money, or have it sent to another party; it's against the rules, you see:

> My first letter to you was perfectly clear about the possibilities available to you. Yet you responded with a request for information about my formative years, assuming it would be no threat to my future legal status. Unfortunately, that is not the case. When I win a new trial, it will be necessary to prepare a 'mitigation case' containing the VERY information you now seek. My attorneys did NOT investigate or provide any mitigation at my first trial.
>
> I did offer you a smidgen of palpable researchable material right there in England. It is very, very valuable information. In November of 1957, I was a 13-year-old Boy Scout who travelled to London to appear in the Command Performance for the Queen. No one has yet recovered the newspaper articles of that trip. As you see, everything is tied together [...]

Correction, J.R.: just a minute's search on the internet brings up a press cutting of you and your fellow scouts in London talking to our late queen. In any case, who, or what, is 'tied together'?

For a convicted serial murderer who rarely comes up for air, I struggled to not start hyperventilating and collapse on the floor in carpet-rolling hysterical laughter as J.R. continues:

> I offered you the opportunity to do a real-life true crime book and documentary. One that would expose blatant police and prosecutorial misconduct, fairly present the

real evidence including complete details of the lives of the victims, and perhaps unveil the real killer. You could of course simply go for the titillating, sensationalized products based on the fiction story already out there. That decision, of course, is yours.

The 'titillating products' J.R. refers to are the official trial and appellate court documents, which I already had in abundance. You can get these documents too. Many are available online; if not, the Americans are very agreeable to send you most of what you will need under The Freedom of Information Act, courtesy of the US Treasury.

In many respects, John 'J.R.' Edward Robinson is much like John David Guise Cannan and John Wayne Gacy – sadosexual serial killers who pose as businessmen with all the apparent trappings of integrity and unlimited wealth. They use a hunter's skills to trawl and entrap their prey. However, whereas bisexual Gacy tortured then murdered young lads for sexual perversity, J.R. searched the internet for his victims, motivated both by BDSM urges and financial gain.

If I may, I'd like to draw an analogy between J.R. and the legendary wreckers who were said to have used lanterns to lure sailing ships onto the rocks. In a modified form, this is precisely what he was doing in his correspondence – it's an opportunity of a lifetime for you, grab the opportunity while you can, he is suggesting. Thus, this predator, this human parasite sent out attractive signals that were intended to entice the vulnerable towards him, rather like a female firefly that fools males from another species into approaching her by using a flashing code. Once the intended prey does so, it is summarily eaten.

We all want the good life, do we not? Each of J.R.'s victims was searching for something – some kind of dream perhaps – and along comes a knight in shining armour. It might be that friend who was tempted into investing in one of J.R.'s businesses so that he could soon pay for his dying wife's medical care, or offering to adopt a baby for his own brother because the couple could not have a child of their own. But underneath this façade is a monster – rather than a gateway to your dream, he turns out to be your worst nightmare come true.

J.R. was, and still is, a salesman – a purveyor of faulty goods and piles of bullshit. When you read his letters he comes across as almost a cartoon character (if the context were not so horrific). Yet one can clearly perceive his warped psychopathology shouting out as he puts pen to paper.

I am a fair man, and if any credit is to be given to J.R., it is that he is determined. He says that for the past years he had been 'tireless [in his attempts] to locate individuals, companies or organisations willing to assist in the completion of the necessary investigation, testing, etc. To fully disclose the real story.' I pressed him often about his use of internet BDSM chat rooms, but he always responded vehemently that he was fitted up by the police; that never once in his whole life had he ever been into bondage or been a 'Slavemaster'. Let's return to his correspondence with me:

> Determined to prove my innocence or die trying I began writing letters to anyone I could think of for both the UK portion of my case as well as those who might possibly help on this side of the pond. I wrote to Alan Hayling – head of documentaries at the BBC, in March 2007, and

received not even a courtesy reply. I recently wrote to Mr Felix Dennis, owner of *Maxim* magazine who lives in Stratford-upon-Avon, and have no word yet.

My basic offer has been very simple. If they would provide the initial funding [the $400,000] for the investigation and testing, along with the equipment necessary, I would give them access to the results no matter the outcome as long as everyone agreed that nothing would be made public until my attorney, acting upon my instructions, authorized release.

Quite what J.R. means when he mentions 'the UK portion' of his case, God only knows because all of his murders and scams came under American jurisdiction. The reader will have now come to the correct conclusion that J.R. is a fucking idiot, and if the matter were not so deadly serious, one would be forgiven for sticking up two fingers to be followed by F★★k off. No doubt that the BBC and *Maxim* were likewise bowled over by the generosity and once-in-a-lifetime opportunity offered them by J.R Undeterred, and indeed moving up a gear, J.R. wrote on:

The cost of putting all discovery information onto a searchable interactive data base, investigating, testing, travel and equipment will be about $400K and will require at least twelve months to complete. The investigator will need some specialized equipment, video and digital recorders capable of two concurrent recordings. All funds would be disbursed by an attorney. I would receive nothing but an allocation to cover supplies and postage.

But J.R., you don't have an attorney because anyone with half a legal mind has washed their hands of you, so my readers do not really need to read between the lines here, do they? By now, this homicidal clown who resides in La-La-Land with his already distended ego is inflating faster by the minute, for J.R.'s verbosity all but bursts into song:

> We are starting from scratch with a thorough methodical investigation of everything. Every document, every photo, every video, every witness, testing every item and utilizing acknowledge experts to evaluate to calculate every person or object.
>
> To facilitate this investigation we [the royal 'we', I guess] have obtained every page of material connected to my case, some 300,000 more or less. Here is how we anticipate proceedings:
>
> a) data base will be designed with unlimited search capabilities. All documents will be scanned, cross-referenced with new documents as developed.
>
> b) full time investigator will be hired under the supervision of my attorney. He/she will complete the legwork required to secure records and documents previously ignored, and conduct video interviews with all witnesses.

Perhaps J.R. felt that he needed a little extra incentive to lure me in, for he continued:

> I may be able to up the ante for you. For several years I have been in contact with a person who befriended Denis

> Rader, the confessed BTK serial killer of 10. This person visited him in jail and corresponded with him regularly. This individual claims to have details and information never before revealed and has been working on a book. The person who has the information, wants to do a book, but has no industry name. The two of you should be able to do a great 'insider' true crime book and a documentary about BTK. You and your publisher could end up getting two for the price of one. I will await word from you.

Yes, J.R., I am sure that my publisher would literally leap at your suggestion of me co-writing a book about BTK with a fucking halfwit. My editors are already at their wit's end with me sorting out this chapter, you homicidal clown. Nevertheless, J.R. then returned to a well-trodden path – the plaintive theme of the wrongs he'd endured:

> I was embezzled out of over two hundred thousand pounds over a three-year period. To that end I have received preliminary word that a non-profit organization – Reprieve – operated by an attorney Clive Stafford-Smith [*sic*] OBE has agreed to help. My attorney has replied to a letter I received from them, by email, and we are still awaiting a reply [...] Finally I must tell you that I am working with a group of college students to publish a book of my poetry and short stories. An attempt to raise money for the required investigation. No credit would be given – no author named. The book will, if published. Simply be written by 'A CONDEMNED ON KANSAS DEATH ROW'.

Great idea that, J.R. A knockout title, to be sure ...

> ... for the record, I will explain exactly how the Kansas Department of Corrections mail system works. When a letter is received it is automatically date stamped on the outside of the envelope. Then the letter is opened by the censors, date and time-stamped, read and all the letters to the inmates in segregation copied.

And so he goes wittering on and on and on for another ten pages of excruciating drivel. It was at this point in our 'business relationship' that I demanded that J.R. give me, at the very least, his attorney's name so that I could check out some of his claims, at which J.R. lost the plot.

Point of fact: no pro-bono attorney would touch J.R. with the proverbial barge pole. He snapped back with: 'YOU, BERRY-DEE, have wasted my valuable time.' Backtracking, he then ranted on:

> I have never asked you for $400,000. I have never asked anyone for $400,000. I didn't say I was going to use students, and if you print this I might sue you. I fucking told you that I never used the internet, and I was never into BDSM and I was never into kinky sex. I was a happily married business man with many awards. FUCK OFF!

Psychopaths, such as J.R., never learn from the errors of their ways. Even as I write he is, when he can afford some postage stamps, trawling for gullible folk and enticing them to send him 'donations' so that he can start up another nefarious scam. He is still asking people to send in their own poetry so he can claim it as his own work, get the crap printed and sold through a friend to raise funds for his prison commissary to buy a few luxuries, such as extra chocolate cookies, candy and the like.

We should be mindful, however, that this scumbag still hasn't revealed the locations of several more of his victims' bodies, thereby denying closure to their grieving next of kin, and this is why your author cooked up the idea of a 'honeytrap' by introducing a woman who has had hands-on, blue-chip experience of dealing with serial killers for years. If anyone could get inside the head of John Robinson it would be the woman we'll call 'Annabel Leigh'. This ex-FBI agent had a degree in criminal justice and I asked her if she would study J.R.'s life and crimes. Thereafter, we set him up. We turned the tables on this evil man who has, for decades, been turning the tables on just about everyone he came into contact with. The results were both disturbing and electrifying. And when J.R. twigged on that he had been conned, I am sure that he was not best happy.

So, let's meet 'Annabel Leigh'. As the reader will see, this extremely clever lady taught me more than a lesson or two about approaching and writing to serial killers. She put me in my place from the get-go, although we both agreed that we each brought our own skill sets to bear. So enjoy.

Annabel Leigh, aka 'The Honeytrap'

'A sprat to catch a mackerel.' We all know that this means something along the lines of 'a small investment of some form or other in the hope of a larger gain'; the idiom goes as far back as the mid-nineteenth century. Enter Annabel Leigh, who subtly worked her way into John 'J.R' Edward Robinson's sensibilities while I was feeding him my own bait. I think we were a great double act. We'll proceed to J.R.'s letters to Annabel (all previously unpublished) but first, this slap to me from her:

> In trying to get inside the heads of serial killers, any attempt to appeal to the better side of a psychopath's better nature will be judged by these master manipulators as a sign of weakness, for conscience is something they do not possess, and one's efforts will fail.
>
> Christopher, you should be using their own 'victimology' against them. It is the strongest weapon of all. You would have achieved much greater success with John Wayne Gacy had you presented yourself as an attractive young man when you wrote to him – falsify a 'pretty' photo if needed be – so that Gacy could have sexually identified with you; in his subconscious you becoming a possible victim, and a photographic image that he could masturbate over while locked up in his prison cell.
>
> You, like so many criminologists and psychologists, miss the obvious. With respect, you guys fail to think outside of the box. If you're writing to a female killer, you should use a multi-sensory approach: the written word which has to appeal to the inmate's way of thinking; photographic stimuli that will conform to their victim type or previous lifestyle and, finally smell – the latter being the most important. A spray of expensive cologne will linger in her cell long after the written word has been absorbed, making your letter stand out, and bring back memories of her better days long past [it was this same

TOP TIP that helped me hook Melanie McGuire, the reader will recall]. The same approach works even better with men. If it fits with his MO, a sexy photo, a splash of perfume, and they have to reply, and this is why I adopted this approach with J.R. Robinson.

While this may seem very unprofessional from me, I think that your thousands of dedicated readers will appreciate my no-nonsense approach, being: Mr Robinson's thought-processing system seems, for the better part of his life, to have been hung between his legs at the same time folded up in dollars in his wallet. For my part, I see no reason why nothing much would have changed today. Therefore, I hope that you, and your readers, will find the results of my correspondence with J.R. of some interest.

Annabel Leigh.

Sadly, Annabel's own correspondence with J.R., is not for publication, and for professional reasons I understand why. However, although it might now seem an obvious plan, its very simplicity was its beauty. Annabel was setting a honeytrap and he walked right into it. In a neat and educated hand, she wrote to him posing as someone interested in him as 'a person'. Insisting that she was not interested in his criminal offences, she enclosed, with her first letter, a photograph – not of her, of course, but someone she thought he might find appealing. She told him that she was fascinated by BDSM; she liked controlling, mature, strong, businesslike men. Considering that J.R. had recently blown me out, one would have thought that he would have been very careful about whom he wrote to next. He wasn't. True to form, he replied with this:

> Annabel,
>
> I received your letter. First of all let me explain that I have some simple rules for anyone that I write. You must realize that all kinds of people write me. It usually happens when some story is run on TV. All claim to want to 'be my friend' when actually all they want is to receive a letter from a death row inmate. My attorney located a blog that tells people how to write to me to receive a response. If that was your goal, here you are.

In truth, at this time Robinson had no attorney; moreover, no such blog existed. What he's claiming in his own overblown way is that he has a lawyer who at no charge trawls the internet on his behalf. In fact, anyone can look up Robinson's full details and address by visiting the Kansas Department of Corrections website, then clicking 'Inmate Locator'.

That notwithstanding, off he went again:

> I laughed when you said you were into true crime, if you have read either of the books written about me, you just read a media created fairy tale. 85% of the material is false, but people like to read crap so that's what they write. The DA who prosecuted me had his wife, who runs a media company, create quite an evil persona of me.
>
> OK, the rules Annabel – first, if you really want to communicate with me you MUST send me a copy of your driver's license and a photo ID that shows who

> you are, your birth date, address. Second, don't ask me about my case. I have maintained my innocence from the beginning. My case is on appeal and I don't need to discuss it. Third, if I detect any phoney BS I won't respond again. Fourth, you must guarantee me that anything we write remain completely confidential.

The reader will observe Robinson's psychopathology working flat out once more. Denigrating the DA and Mrs DA, pouring scorn on well-known, highly respected authors, laying down his ground rules from the get-go, and about to leak a whole shed-load of perverted BDSM garbage, which – had he actually been appealing his sentence – would have had his imaginary attorneys in seizures. As for maintaining his innocence from the beginning – oh, no. He had admitted all of his crimes to escape the death sentence in one state only to be extradited to Kansas where he now sits a short, stumbling walk to the death chamber.

He continued:

> Annabel, if you write me here is a way to do it. On the front of each page write a very normal letter. If you want to write other information about your BDSM experiences, fantasies, etc, write them on the back of the pages like a separate letter. The censors only read the front of each page.
>
> Your list of lifestyle interests like you copied it from [as written] the alt.com website questionnaire [the website where he found one of his victims, Suzette Trouten]. If you are seeking, tell me but understand I am very demanding.

I am enclosing information that tells you what can and cannot be sent in ... actually it's a list of don'ts. Look good at the information about photos, "sexually obscene material or nudity". Yes, I want you to send pictures but they have to get past the censors so use your head.

I'm enclosing you information about how you can help out financially. I live in solitary confinement, I don't work (they won't allow it) and I have very limited funds. If you want to help out with postage and supplies you need to follow the directions.

You say you have two degrees, in what, from where and when?

How involved do you want to get? Are you interested in helping if I need typing complete, computer searches, light investigation? Tell me about your computer literacy, etc. I will give you the opportunity to tell me all about yourself and I want you to be very frank about what you're looking for! I need someone who will be committed to help me. If I'm ever going to prove my innocence I need a person on the outside I can really trust.

Goodness gracious me, J.R.; Annabel isn't applying for a job, bro ...

So, there you have it. The beginning, where we go from here is up to you ... I mean everything!!!

What type of animals do you have? Are you willing to take this to whatever level?'

There may come a time when I need to ask a favor, are you willing to help?

> Thanks for the letter and the picture. I hope it's just the first of many. You are very pretty. I will be not only a Master to you but a father too ... Oh, last rule – if we're going to do that you have to commit to write at least once a week.
>
> JR
>
> P.S. If you have experience in setting up websites or blogs, let me know.

From here on, the completely off-the-wall Robinson didn't waste any time in returning to his over-controlling ways. He said that he was in a 'foul' mood because someone was 'attempting to sell an envelope' supposedly written by him on the internet for $40. 'I hate that kind of exploitation and crap,' he told Annabel, adding, 'and that's why I'm careful about writing to people. They use me and I hate it!! Your first assignment is to go online and see if you can find out who it is for me.'

Despite being told by Annabel that she wasn't interested in his criminal case history, J.R. volunteered that his 'conviction was more than a miscarriage':

> I was framed, and that's what I have to prove. My appeal when filed, will result in a new trial. But, when that happens I have to do everything necessary to prove my innocence. Your degree might come in handy if you are to work with me ... help me investigate what needs to be done, etc. In time I will reveal what has to be done ... I do have attorney's [*sic*] provided by the state for my appeal. One is a young woman who I trust. She tells me I will get some relief either a new trial or convictions reversed. If

> not, there are more appeals and whatever the case it will require heavy investigative efforts. This is not a game!!! We believe we know who set me up, why it was done and how. Now we have to prove it.

Isn't J.R. Robinson morbidly fascinating? Here he is totally embedded with an imaginary frame-up scenario, writing about an attorney who does not exist, while previously he mentions 'light investigative work' but now it's 'heavy investigative efforts', that are required. So by means of the written word and the concealed subtext of his letters, he is allowing us to venture deep inside his mind. Ever the authority on BDSM – although of course he categorically denied to me he'd ever heard of the subject – J.R. goes on to tell Annabel, 'Submission has to be a total commitment without reservation.' Then, completely contradicting himself, he adds: 'Obedience is voluntary and must be given, accepting the Dom as her Master, following his instructions. Tell me about any fantasies you have, how, why, what. I also need to know what you think I can offer you.'

Jumping from one subject to another, he returns rapido to funding and empire-building:

> Annabel, check out how difficult it is to set up a web site. I've had an idea ... for a long time now to set up a non-profit organization specifically to help death row inmates with $s for investigators, lawyers, etc. Yes, there are a lot of anti-death groups out there, but none actually help the inmates. They protect, hold vigils and raise funds to pay big salaries. Hell, with your smarts we might just do ... Of course you would probably have to move here [to

> Kansas from her supposed home in California] when it really got going. So the web site would have to be very professional, able to accept donations, tax free, etc. I've been working up the idea for a while. Interested ...?

Reading between J.R.'s lines we find echoes of the murderous hunting techniques he used on his many victims and how he managed to fleece pretty much everyone he came across. I mean a lot of these folk were blessed with high intelligence, but perhaps not. However, then, this monster's mind now switches back again to perverted sex as if he cannot resist the subject with this unhealthy missive, so close your eyes if needs be:

> I like my submissive shaved and able to complete simple tasks ... like masturbation. I want her to be able to begin, just to get to the point of release and stop. Wait a moment, begin just until she is ready and stop again, repeating this four times, it takes practice, then on the fifth time feeling the massive release ... Do it. Write about it. How did it make you feel ...?

I have no idea what Annabel's husband may have thought about J.R.'s sex lessons, but having continual back-channel access to his letters to Annabel made me wonder what the prison censors were making of it all. One gets the impression that he's almost all but out of control when he writes: 'You say you like poetry. Do you write it? What kind?' And: 'Send me something you have written. I too like poetry and would you like to do a book of it but not identify the author of a book and short stories from an anonymous death row inmate. Hell, with self-publishing it should be easy! Just need someone to type up my poems, locate pictures on the internet to go with them and go. You MUST type it out for me.'

Bear with me, dear reader. I guess that by now you'll be thinking that voluble J.R. is stark raving bonkers. But no, J.R. is sane; not perhaps completely sane as he reminds us that:

> I just finished a two-year project and wrote a disertation [*sic*] on the history of the death penalty in Kansas. From territorial days to today. A reference librarian at the Kansas Historical Society got me the research information. It's pretty good ... needs to be typed out also, so you can do this as well! Can't send it out, no money ...!

To check out J.R.'s claim, I contacted the Kansas Historical Society. Surprise, surprise, they can't find a trace of his 'disertation' enquiries anywhere, although the history of the death penalty in Kansas can be found on their website. Then, without drawing breath, he suggests to Annabel:

> One letter a week, photos that will please me. Now, in your next letter at the end of it under your name, I want you to put something make-up color on your erect left nipple and make a print of it. A nice, small, round print, and you will enjoy 'it'...

John also generously educates Annabel about his leisure activities by explaining that he loved to play golf, although it would be fair to say that he would not know the difference between a putter and a driver. However, he does tell her that he likes golf balls (again please close your eyes now, ladies):

> Also next time you're out shopping, pick up a package of golf balls. 3 balls in a package, and locate some really small tiny rubber bands. Insert them into your vagina when you next go dancing. You will find that I am demanding, but reasonable. I want you to be all you can be and still commit. You'll understand more about that later ...

If I had been Annabel I would have asked J.R. what specific brand of golf ball he is promoting, maybe with his proposal that this brand sponsors him and helps him get off death row. Hey, John, now that's a damn good business idea if there ever was one.

I have to stress with a wry smile that I am not making light of this man's terrible crimes. I am, however, suggesting that the Kansas Department of Corrections are, to say the least, somewhat lax by letting him write then post garbage like this out. And he's still raking in cash. I imagine myself as the parent of one of J.R. Robinson's victims who were enticed into his web, bludgeoned to death and ended up as a stinking black mucky mess in one of his barrels. The quicker he's strapped to a gurney and executed the better it will be for the still grieving next of kin and society too.

Meanwhile, still he rants on to Annabel, boasting that he draws 'sarcastic cartoons about politics, my case and prison', adding:

> My attorney keeps the originals but I have sent some signed copies to certain individuals. One [copy] was sold

> with my permission by a local battered women's shelter for $750. When I found out that a guard's wife bought it I had a great laugh. I do hate it when people write to me and con me and then sell envelopes, etc, for personal gain.

When I asked the Kansas Department of Corrections to confirm whether Mr Robinson was indeed such a popular and accomplished cartoonist, a spokesperson *eventually* replied: 'It is the policy of the KDOC not to comment on an inmate's custodial details, so I am afraid I cannot answer your question. I can tell you that this inmate does not attend any art-related activity because of his security status combined with his inability to draw a straight line.'

That was, perhaps, the best letter I have *ever* received from *any* department of corrections. It shows that Kansas has a dry sense of humour after all.

After all of our work in drawing him out, Annabel and I eventually agreed to pull the plug on J.R. In his last letter to her, he finished off with:

> I AM expecting one letter a week from you. I want to know everything about you. And you must sign the Slave Contract and send it back to me instantly. I want to know your body measurements. How it reacts to my directions to what turns you on, how intense your reactions and release. What kind of experiences have you had, your most memorable that left you completely quaking and exhausted. Do you enjoy doing it and why. How complete do you envision your submission to be. Where did you grow up? What kind of brothers and sisters ... what was

> your first experience with sex? Were you abused? Do you really understand what total commitment means and are you ready? Now that I guess that you're a bit moist you may have some works to do! You might look for some padded tapestry hangers ... PS: Perhaps the nipple imprints should be in something light ... now do the right one ... Lemon juice?

J.R., you have come unstuck. The tapestry hangers, what the hell is that all about? Perhaps we will never know. As John Steinbeck wrote: 'There are some among us who live in rooms of experience we can never enter.' I suggest that the room inside John Edward 'J.R.' Robinson's head is one of them. His appeal was flat-out denied. At the time of writing, sadly – for me, at least – no execution date has been set. If the reader wishes to become more interactive with J.R., one can easily find his DOC number and location on the internet – although I'd leave aside the BDSM stuff, and do not mention my name or he won't be a happy bunny.

Go on, make his day.

Summary

To bring this book to a conclusion, I must stress that everything I have written here represents my own thoughts and conclusions. If I have made any grammatical errors, technical mistakes, or if any reader takes issue with what I've written or even if my syntax is a bit up the creek, I will take it on the chin in good spirit.

As I've explained, I have files of letters from serial killers, mass murderers and other homicidal killers in my possession. Deciding which of these to include in this book has been a very difficult task. On that note, I'd like to add that a sequel has been commissioned in which I'll include some of the extraordinary material I've been obliged, because of word-count restrictions, to leave out of this title. On the menu will be:

Viva LeRoy Nash

Until his death from natural causes (he was ninety-four) in 2010, LeRoy (one of the longest-serving inmates in the US, and the oldest on death row) penned hundreds of letters to me. Riddled with arthritis down to his fingertips and using just the plastic infill tube of a biro, he struggled valiantly with every single word, and without complaint, to document his life's narrative. LeRoy was one of the original 'Angels with Dirty Faces' throughout the Great Depression. His story would make a great movie.

Michael Benneman Sams

This individual is easily one of the most devious, sick and twisted kidnappers, extortionists and one-off killers in British criminal history. No one of his ilk had ever been seen before and no other offender has yet matched Sams's guile and cunning. His correspondence with me, my visits with him in prison and his taunting letters to police all illustrate 100 per cent exactly why this sequel came into being: my fascination with the written page versus the subtext; the subjective mindset of the killer versus the objective facts.

David Mulcahy

This convicted serial rapist and killer preyed on women in tandem with the notorious British 'railway rapist' John Duffy. Mulcahy's exclusive letters to me are a real mind-bending whatdunnit, whodunnit, whereabouts-dunnit. And he raises some questions about the integrity of his conviction, so is what he writes all phoney-fake or is he telling the truth … that is for my readers to decide?

Douglas Daniel Clark

Doing himself no favours, if anyone could find a man who looks like a crazed, foul-mouthed serial killer, Doug fits the bill, yet he is quite a funny guy in a strange kind of way. Also known as 'The Sunset Slayer', Clark is probably innocent of most of which he's been sent to death row for, yet he sits there today as a condemned man, while efforts are afoot to overturn his conviction. I found that he was a fascinating man to interview on death row at San Quentin State Prison; probably a patsy, who was fitted up by the cops and a devious woman, he most certainly was.

Bobby Joe Long

This serial killer dubbed 'The Classified Ad Rapist' reeled off multiple pages of the most sickening material I've ever had to stomach. This chapter could easily ruin your appetite so be warned.

Charles Lannis Moses Jr

Dubbed by the media 'The Lonely Fugitive' and 'Outlaw Mosey Wales' – the latter after a well-known Clint Eastwood Western – Charles was a fugitive drug dealer who did anything to avoid capture. He barrelled along from Nebraska to Wyoming, with the authorities in hot pursuit, in a desperate flight fuelled by drugs and punctuated by gunfire. As with LeRoy Nash, Charles spent hundreds of hours carefully, and I might even say beautifully, writing his fascinating life's story.

And in truth, I have not even touched the tip of the literary iceberg when it comes to the countless monsters who have written to your author to date.

There's a saying that 'truth is stranger than fiction'. By presenting in this, the first of two books, a selection of correspondence from some of the most dangerous criminals convicted in recent years, I hope I've offered you the chance to appreciate the disparity between the fiction of what they've written and the true facts. To gain a little more understanding of the nature of psychopaths and sociopaths who believe that your property, your life and the lives of your children are theirs to do with as they please. And as for any remorse from them – forget it.

I'll end as I usually do. Happy days. No nightmares, please and God bless ☺.

christopherberrydee.com